GLORY, PASSION, AND PRINCIPLE

The Story of Eight Remarkable Women at the Core of the American Revolution

Melissa Lukeman Bohrer

We know the men of 1776. Now it's time to meet the women. From First Lady Abigail Adams to the trailblazing poet Phillis Wheatley, this inspired volume illuminates the lives and contributions of eight quintessential American women.

G*lory, Passion, and Principle* is an elegant, authoritative work that soars on the strength of its author's infectious passion for her subjects, her painstaking scholarship, and her knack for compelling storytelling. Much has been written of the brave deeds and prowess of the men who drafted the Declaration of Independence. But not nearly enough has been written about the vital women of the era—women whose contributions to the struggle for freedom rival those of any of their male counterparts.

Melissa Lukeman Bohrer reveals women who flourished against the odds, most without benefit of formal education or world travel. In eight revealing chapters, Bohrer investigates the lives of:

- Abigail Adams, the wife and primary confidante of John Adams
- Sybil Ludington, the sixteen-year-old who rode twice as far as Paul Revere to alert patriots
- Deborah Sampson, who posed as a man and fought as a Continental Army soldier
- Mercy Otis Warren, the influential political playwright who roused anti-British sentiment
- Phillis Wheatley, the slave, poet, and first published African American
- Nancy Ward, the leader of the Cherokee tribe and key architect of the Treaty of Hopewell

Melissa Lukeman Bohrer traces her own lineage back to the Mayflower. A former columnist for *The Brooklyn Heights Press*, she is a graduate of Columbia University and Brooklyn Law School. She lives in New York City.

History
Atria Books • April 2003
0-7434-5330-1 • $24.00 U.S./$38.00 CAN
320 pages • 6 x 9

GLORY, PASSION, *and* PRINCIPLE

The Story of Eight Remarkable Women at the Core of the American Revolution

MELISSA LUKEMAN BOHRER

ATRIA BOOKS

NEW YORK • LONDON • TORONTO • SYDNEY • SINGAPORE

ATRIA BOOKS

1230 Avenue of the Americas
New York, NY 10020

Designed and composed by Kevin Hanek
Set in Adobe Caslon

ISBN: 0-7434-5330-1

First Atria Books hardcover printing April 2003

10   9   8   7   6   5   4   3   2   1

ATRIA BOOKS is a trademark of Simon & Schuster, Inc.

For information about special discounts for bulk purchases, please contact Simon & Schuster Special Sales: 1-800-456-6798 or business@simonandschuster.com

Printed in the U.S.A.

I dedicate this book, with love,
to my three children, Zoe, Remy, and Jake,
and to my incredible husband, Abram.

Contents

~

Acknowledgements

THIS BOOK IS AN OUTCOME of the work of many hands other than my own, and I would like to express my thanks to those who helped it into being. First and foremost, I would like to thank my dedicated, brilliant brother and agent, Noah Lukeman, without whom this book would never have come about. His fantastic advice, his unwavering support, and his expertise in writing truly are evident in every page of the book. Thank you from the bottom of my heart. To my wonderful editor, Tracy Behar, whose belief in this book was clear from the start, and whose guidance, wisdom, and keen eye shaped much of the writing—working with her was an honor, and I am deeply grateful for the opportunity to have done so. At Atria, I would also like to thank Judith Curr, for her support of the book; Wendy Walker, for her razor-sharp editing; and Brenda Copeland, for her steadfast support and help. I would like to thank Daniel Meyerson, for his unconditional support and guidance in the writing of this book, and in all that I do. Thanks to Lewis Kaufman—his expertise in stamps, and his willingness to help, proved invaluable. I would like to thank John Fabiano from the Allentown—Upper Freehold Historical Society, who so generously spent an entire afternoon educating me on the Battle of Monmouth and the history of Molly Pitcher: his knowledge proved unbelievably helpful. I would like to thank Cathy Lawrence Scharlou for her help in researching Phillis Wheatley, and for her support and friendship throughout the years. I would also like to thank Robbie Redmond in Tennessee for her support in my research on Nancy Ward.

A main resource in researching the lives of these women was historical societies—places, I discovered, staffed with incredibly dedicated, helpful people, mostly history lovers themselves. Out of fear I will miss someone, I will thank the entire staffs at the following societies: the Putnam County Historical Society; the Tennessee Historical Society; the Monmouth County Historical Association; the Cumberland County Historical Society; the American Antiquarian Society Library; the New York Public Library Research Room; the Schomberg Library; and Kathryn M. Neal, curator of the Givens Collection of African American Literature at the University of Minnesota.

On a personal note, I have been blessed with the closest of families, and it is to them that I wish to say thanks for all the love, encouragement, laughter, and perspective I receive: To my mother, Brenda Shoshanna, who gave me a true example of what it means to live a life of love; to my father, Gerry Lukeman, for his ceaseless support, in so many ways, and for the unconditional love and belief in me he has had since I was young; to my three beloved brothers— Josh, Adam, and Noah—whose place in my life has always been and always will be central in my heart; to my new sister-in-law, Yana, a true sister; to my uncle Danny, the person who brought the power of books into my life; to my wonderful mother-in-law, Esther Bohrer, who spent two entire summers helping me with my children so I could write, for all that she does for me, which is too much to mention here; to my late father-in-law, Benjamin Bernard Bohrer, whose memory stays with me each and every day; to the entire Panes family—Cheryl, Eddie, Jessica, David, Howie, Kim, Nicholas, Natalie, and Nancy—for their support and love; to my brother and sister-in-law, Barry and Chris Bohrer, and my nieces, Carly and

Sylvie, for continuing love and support; to my two daughters, Zoe, and Remy, who inspired me with the idea for this book, and continue to inspire me every day; and lastly, but most importantly, to my wonderful husband, Abram, who has always encouraged me to follow my heart, you are my soul mate, my best friend, and the love of my life. Thank you for all that you do.

Preface

The heroism of the females of the American Revolution has gone from memory with the generation that witnessed it and nothing, absolutely nothing, remains upon the ear of the young of the present day.

—CHARLES FRANCIS ADAMS

A s I sat with my daughters in traffic one day, we played a game. They would ask me about any topic at all, and I would have to try to answer it. After we had played for a while, "America" was suggested, and we were off. They asked about presidents, they asked about soldiers, they asked about the children and their schools (which of course meant boys only). Suddenly my older daughter asked, "Didn't the women do anything?"

I thought about it and realized I had described the story of the founding of America without having once mentioned any women. Immediately, I offered Betsy Ross as the woman who sewed our flag, but after that my mind drew a blank. Was it that I didn't remember any of the women from that time, or was it that I had never been taught?

As a mother of two young girls, this observation bothered me, both for my sake and theirs. Too often, when one speaks of the American Revolution, well-known names such as John Adams, Thomas Jefferson, and Paul Revere come to mind, as they should; but the committed and brave women who also incited revolutionary fervor are forgotten. I hope to help us remember them by telling the story of eight women, truly remarkable for their courage and passion, for the way in which they transcended the myriad of obstacles before them, embracing a cause that was larger than all of them.

The crucial role women played during this time in history has been brought to light recently by the work of a handful of historians focused on what has been popularly called "herstory"; much work remains to be done. There have been great women throughout history, but the women of America, of this period in particular, seem especially forgotten, as the Revolution is continually attributed to the founding "fathers." This one-sided version of history needs to be amended, as history is not just passive, dead knowledge—we proceed in our future based on our past. When we learn of the cumulative human experience of a people and how they lived, but are not told of the contributions of half that population, we lose precious examples of human potential that existed before us. The power of history, and the power of myth, can hold one of the greatest gifts of all: inspiration. Thucydides, a great historian, quoted Pericles when he said, "We serve as examples to others." But for women of this day, to whom are we to look for inspiration and examples of wisdom, bravery, and strength?

There are plenty of women in the history of America, it turns out, to admire; and there are deep-rooted female mythic figures as well. But what happens when history is blurred by myth? Some of the women in this book, like Abigail Adams and Phillis Wheatley, have been chronicled beyond measure, and leave little doubt as to the veracity of their existence. Others, though, like Molly Pitcher or Lydia Darragh, are more nebulous in the record books: many insist they existed, and will produce records to prove it; others insist they did not, and will produce their own records to prove otherwise.

As I sat one morning on the actual Monmouth battlefield on a sweltering June day—the very date in history the battle took place—I sat for several hours with two leading authorities on Molly Pitcher.

Each of these scholars arrived with bundles of original papers, and each had devoted many years to studying her. I expected concrete facts, an authoritative history—at the very least a unanimous account. I was shocked to listen to them disagree on nearly everything about her. I began to realize that history, even in the most devoted, meticulous hands, is at least part myth.

As I looked out on the battlefield, I watched thousands of reenacters assume battlefield positions. They had come from all parts of the country; not especially wealthy, they had nonetheless spent thousands of dollars on authentic revolutionary wardrobe, regalia, and props. Devoted to their reenactment, they wore several layers of wool uniforms in the June heat and carried thirty pounds of equipment. For many of these men, a pivotal part of this day, of this battle, was Molly Pitcher. If Molly is a myth, she is a myth that has transcended fact, a myth that has, 200 years later, become a symbol for the revolution.

Is a myth a lie, or a shorthand way of recording the experience of a culture? Often a myth inspires, offers a way of looking at the world we may not have seen before. The Greeks understood this intimately as they handed down an entire history through the use of myth. Sir Thomas Browne once called us "man, that great amphibian, living in divided and distinguished worlds."

It is necessary for our daughters to know of women who lived their lives with power and influence—and it is also necessary for us as women today. We inherit the history we are given, and somehow it gets accepted as true; but history is, in its truest sense, interpretation, and the eyes of the interpreter make all the difference. We have seen history through male eyes for long enough; let us survey the landscape once again, this time through the eyes of the woman.

GLORY, PASSION, *and* PRINCIPLE

Sybil Ludington

Caption TK

With the Wind in Her Hair

SYBIL LUDINGTON

But she was too tired when she got home,
to realize the worth of the deed she had done.

—MARJORIE BARSTOW GREENBIE

Putnam County, New York 1777

ON A COLD and cloudless winter night, Sybil Ludington blew out the candle in her brother's bedroom and fearfully tightened her grip on her rifle's stock. She leaned forward and peered out the large window; a deep darkness had enveloped the whole of her father's grounds. There was no moon that night, nothing at all to see by. She strained anyway, looking south, out past the house and into the extended lot. Nothing but craggy black shapes, which she knew—prayed—to be trees. She pulled back, leaving the window ajar so as to hear any ominous sound. She tiptoed out of the room, the floorboards creaking, trying not to wake her six younger siblings or her mother, who was sleeping with the newest baby, two-month-old Abigail; and with a solemn nod she joined her waiting sister in the hall.

The news had at first come as a shock, but the longer she dwelled on it, the more she realized the inevitability of British soldiers coming after her father. Not only was he a colonel, not only was he protector of crucial Patriot supplies, not only was he the key to conquering the strategic Hudson Highlands, but above all, he used to be one of them. A Loyalist. The utmost vengeance, Sybil had come to learn in her short, hard life, was always reserved for one of your own. Indeed, General Howe himself had placed the bounty on her father's head: 300 guineas. A shocking sum. Enough to buy their whole town.

It all started the summer before. General Howe had landed on Staten Island with 9,000 troops; with him, under his brother's command, came a British fleet from Halifax and an armada of 130 warships and transports. By mid-August 1776, 32,000 fully equipped, highly trained British and German soldiers had taken Staten Island and proceeded to invade Long Island.

General George Washington immediately saw the danger. He knew that saving Long Island was hopeless at this point, but he also knew that supplies were in as much demand as men, and if he could save their critical stash of food and ammunition in White Plains—which surely the British were aiming for—then he could at least have a partial victory, and would be able to rally for a comeback at a later date. Without it, the entire Northeast could be in jeopardy. He called upon the Patriots' most skilled defender of supplies—Colonel Ludington—to defend this most critical stash. Ludington obliged. Despite a terrible and bloody defeat at White Plains, the supplies remained virtually untouched. Immediately following the battle, General Howe put a price on Ludington's head, dead or alive.

⚜

Sybil and her sister strained their eyes in the darkness. Though their property was a sprawling 230 acres, much of it was wooded. The clearing in the back stretched to about half an acre, gently sloping, leading to a stream, on the other side of which stood thick woods. From her vantage point at the window, she could see her father's gristmill and the corral, the only other structures on the property. It was possible the enemy could be hiding behind these, but unlikely: should anyone approach due east, the horses were sure to make noise. No, they would come from here—from the south.

Sybil was fighting sleep when she heard the sound of breaking twigs and cracking ice; she snapped to attention and listened. Hurried footsteps followed, scurrying over the frozen winter earth. The sounds came from the gristmill. She leaned forward, heart pounding, and saw silhouettes of dark armed figures emerging slowly from behind its walls. Muffled, urgent voices followed. A never-ending supply of men seemed to creep out from behind the building. They were heading for the house.

She could feel the muscles in her body tighten. Bounding up the stairs, she ran for Rebecca, but saw Rebecca running for her. Her heart sank even more. This could only mean they were approaching from the back, too. Noise suddenly rose up all around them, confirming what she already knew: she and her family were surrounded.

Quickly lighting candles in every room, Sybil and Rebecca ran noisily throughout the house, waking their ten younger brothers and sisters. They shoved weapons and candles into their hands, yanking them out of their beds. They dropped the younger ones in front of windows and bid the older ones to pace, guns held high, as they had rehearsed. Sybil ran to her post. As she watched, the men seemed to slow and then stop, looking at the windows. Their noises died down. They now seemed unsure.

Sybil raised her musket with a shaking hand and leaned it against her shoulder as her father had taught her. She squatted, aimed the rifle to the sky, and held her breath. She squeezed the trigger. The shot crackled with a deafening noise, and the kick knocked her back to the floor. She scrambled to her knees and looked out the window. The men were running.

Records indicate that Sybil had in fact spotted Ichobod Prosser, a notorious Tory who had come after her father in hopes of the reward, and his men. Prosser's band of armed Tories, estimated at some fifty men strong, had planned to abduct the colonel, torture him, bring him back, collect the reward, and watch as he was put to death. After seeing the many windows light up in the colonel's home and the figures marching in almost every window, they had second thoughts. Years later, when they learned that it was in fact Sybil and her siblings, they confessed to be "ignorant of how they had been foiled by clever girls."[1]

Sybil's ruse had worked; it was the beginning of a "constant care and thoughtfulness towards her father that prevented the fruition of many an intrigue against his life and capture."[2]

Arriving in 1761 as a staunch Loyalist, Henry Ludington served in the French and Indian war as part of the Second Regiment of Connecticut, troops in the service of the king. He also fought in the Battle of Lake George. But by the mid-1770s, Ludington's loyalty to the king was shaken, as was many of his neighbors' and friends'. This was not particularly unusual, as many colonists were becomingly increasingly angered and dismayed by the continual taxation heaped upon them by the British. Voices were starting to be heard decrying the notion of "taxation without representation." Newspapers printed many stories of abuse by British soldiers toward Americans. Many Loyalists began to question their commitment to a king who was so heavy-handed, so petrified of his subjects yearning for a small degree of self-determination. Many, including Henry Ludington, began to embrace the idea of independence. In 1775 Henry Ludington officially broke from the king, renouncing his position in the royal army. His reputation preceding him, he was immediately embraced by General George Washington, who needed men exactly like him.

It was 1776 when Henry Ludington was named colonel and given a regiment in Dutchess County, along what was then the most direct route between Connecticut and the Long Island Sound. It was a strategic site and one of the most crucial for the Patriots. The Hudson Highlands were the key to defending a huge territory. If they fell, the entire Northeast could be divided. It was also the most dangerous area to defend: sandwiched on both sides by deep and dense woods, the small province of Fredericksburg was easy prey to gangs of Tories and Royalists on the one side and small bands of rogues on the other. The townsfolk were increasingly harassed, threatened, and robbed by these outlaws, sometimes even kidnapped and killed.

Ludington's regiment consisted of 400 men, all farmers whose homes were scattered about the sparsely settled area of the nearby towns. He was forced to bring them into active and constant service, although none were professional soldiers, and some resented the duty. The system of communication was poor, and weapons and supplies rudimentary.

Colonel Ludington's importance in the small precinct of Fredericksburg grew gradually over the years. He and his wife went on to have twelve children, the oldest daughter, Sybil, born in 1761. By all accounts, Sybil was a feisty, independent girl who spent her childhood tending to her many younger siblings. From the time she was old enough for chores, Sybil worked in her home, sewing, weaving, cleaning, cooking—embracing all the domesticity required of her sex. Never given a formal education as were her brothers, Sybil did learn to read and write, though not exceptionally. Education was apparent in the Ludington home, for the children were literate; but its value and importance was measured with the boys and almost nonexistent with Sybil and her sisters. Sybil's brothers were sent to school and practiced their lessons at home; Sybil and her sisters, on the other hand, were educated in domesticity, reared for their expected roles as mothers and wives. Besides, a house filled with twelve children could only spare so much time for reading and writing, and this usually took place around the hearth, with the whole family assembled together at night.

Sybil was impatient with education anyway; her real love was the outdoors, horses, and her father's activities. In fact, her mother commented more than once that her oldest was quite a tomboy. In what little spare time she had, Sybil rode horseback, becoming quite expert at it, riding both straight and astride, surprising those who knew her with her speed, agility, and love for it. She would ride her father's big bay, a husky thoroughbred gelding, traveling the many fields and paths through the woods and on into neighboring towns. At age fifteen she was given her own horse, a one-year-old colt she named Star for the white patch on his nose. Watching his daughter ride horseback, with her hearty laughter and seeming abandon, her long auburn hair flying away in the wind, her father more than once marveled at Sybil's independence.

When her father was given his own regiment, Sybil would spend hours watching him train his militia on the farm. Observing throughout the entire summer, fall, and winter of 1776, she developed a deeper understanding of what was at stake for all of them. With a keen and interested eye, she learned about her father's men, frequently journeying with them to their homes or on some errand, and found herself increasingly emboldened by their patriotism. Sybil yearned to take part in the events surrounding her. On the night of April 26, 1777, she found a way to do just that.

April 1777

The night of the twenty-sixth began like most others. Though a frighteningly strong thunderstorm had been raging all day, the Ludington children had occupied themselves inside with a variety of household chores and games. Colonel Ludington had been away for three days with his militia in an effort to shore up Patriot supplies; he was expected home that evening. Sybil and Rebecca had helped their mother with supper and with washing up the little ones, and after a hearty meal of beef and potatoes, the family had settled before the hearth. Little Archibald, ten years old, prided himself on lighting the fire, and the fire he made that night was big enough to warm them all.

As her family sat listening to little Derrick practice his reading, Sybil peered out, searching the night sky for any sign of her father's return. In the distance she could see a vague red glow in the sky, and she turned away, overcome by a feeling of foreboding. She rested her head against the pane, and before she knew it was fast asleep.

The front door swung open, waking Sybil with a start. She reached for her rifle, but before she could find it, she saw it was her father. She relaxed and ran over to him with the others. He walked in dripping wet as the family gathered around, the older ones helping him with his hat, boots, and jacket and the younger ones, happy to be part of the commotion, clamoring for his attention. Sybil's mother put a kettle on the fire. Eager for news of their father's adventures, the family listened attentively while Colonel Ludington settled before the fire and shared news of his latest exploits.

Before her father could bring his cup to his lips, there was suddenly a loud pounding on the door. Jumping up, Colonel Ludington, still wet, grabbed his musket and motioned Sybil's mother to take the children out of sight. They huddled behind the parlor door, although Sybil went with her father, grabbing her rifle and standing by his side. He gave her a reprimanding look, but the pounding came again.

"Ludington!" a voice called out. The colonel moved to the side of the door and peered through a small window. With a sudden look of recognition, he quickly moved from the window, lay down his musket, and opened the door.

A rain-soaked man practically fell into the foyer, water dripping from hat to boots, a look of terror Sybil had never seen before in his eyes. He gasped for breath.

"Good God, man, what is it?" Ludington cried as he grabbed the man's arms, helping to steady him.

"Danbury has been sacked, sir. It is burning! The whole town is burning! The British have taken over!"

The colonel's face dropped in horror as he stared, glassy-eyed, into the distance. The Patriots had recently transferred massive supplies from Peekskill to Danbury, near the border. Meat, flour, rice, sugar, molasses, rum, powder, shoes, clothes, utensils, uniforms . . . critical supplies. Their destruction meant disaster. And if the British were already at Danbury, that meant they could overtake the Highlands in a matter of hours.

"The British are headed this way, sir, right now. We need your men."

"Who else has been sent for?" Ludington asked.

"You are the only one, sir."

It was a moment Sybil would always remember. The look of gravity on her father's face was unlike anything she had seen before. He stared at this messenger, this farmer of small frame, and slowly his look of shock turned to one of command.

"I cannot alert my men," Ludington said. "I must remain here to organize them when they arrive. You will go. I will give you the routes—"

"I cannot sir, I cannot," the messenger interrupted. "I cannot ride one moment longer," he cried.

The colonel's face flushed with rage. He grabbed the man by the shoulders, and shook him with an anger that frightened even Sybil.

"You *will*, damn it! You will!"

But the messenger only cried and, as if in deep resignation, slumped down against the wall onto the floor, head in hands. The colonel stared at the man, and slowly his rage lifted, replaced with a blank desperation.

"Good God, man, do you realize what will happen if we do not stop them?" he said, more to himself than to the messenger. No answer came forth from the man, his head low as if browbeaten.

A look of fear mingled with horror filled Ludington's eyes. As the rest of the family froze in terror, a bolt of lightning cracked overhead, momentarily filling the night sky. No one spoke.

A wave of feeling suddenly rushed up in Sybil like she had never felt; a sense of purpose, of destiny. She knew then what she must do.

"I will go, Father," it is believed she said, as if someone else had spoken the words.

A low, muffled wail escaped her mother's lips. Her mother knew what that meant. It was a ride that had brought men in their prime to their knees. It was not a ride—it was a sentence to death. Those woods were treacherous, even in the daylight, filled with thieves, outlaws, hostile Indians, Royalists, Tories, wolves, and bears. If somehow she didn't get killed, she would get captured, which would mean death. If somehow she didn't get killed or captured, she would certainly get lost, which would mean a later, slower death.

Sybil caught her brothers and sisters staring in astonishment. The look on her father's face deepened to one of greater horror; he half turned away, but she rushed up and grabbed his arm.

"Father, you have to let me go," she pleaded. "I know the routes. There is no one else."

Her father turned and looked deeply into her eyes, and slowly she could see his look change to one of admiration, then of respect, a respect she had only seen him give to other men. When he finally spoke, it was the voice of command.

"Get ready."

Not five minutes later Sybil appeared downstairs, dressed and ready to go. She had pulled on long wool stockings under an old pair of her father's pants, and tied them tightly with a worn piece of cloth. She wore Archibald's long-underwear shirt, and had thrown her mother's thick cotton shawl over her shoulders. She tucked her pants into her riding boots and pulled her long auburn hair back with a string. Her big green eyes looked more innocent and beautiful than ever.

Star neighed outside the door, prancing impatiently in the rain. Her father had saddled him up and stood beside him, waiting.

Sybil quickly and quietly embraced each one of her siblings, then her mother, in whose eyes she found the fear she herself was trying so hard to defeat. Embracing for what then might have been a last time, she felt a clenching sadness well up inside her. Rebecca and Mary had started to cry, and she quickly turned and walked out, shutting the heavy oak door behind her.

Her father grasped Star's mane too tightly, trying to keep him still. He thrust his musket into Sybil's hand as she approached and gave her a quick once-over. She sensed a change in his manner: gone was friendly compassion; he now surveyed her as a soldier. He adjusted her stance, squaring her shoulders to face him, and shouted over the rain.

"You'll ride south toward the lake. Go through Carmel and Mahopac, but stay to the west on the path. Tryon has men in the woods, on the southeastern border, and cowboys and skinners have been spotted as well—try to steer clear of the lake if you can. Circle up and head northwest after you have reached Mahopac. Ride until Stonewall and then turn back southward home. Along the way, bang at every possible house. Wake the men no matter what. Tell them to be at my house by daybreak, if they want to spare their lives. Bid them spread the word."

"What do you mean, father, 'cowboys and skinners'?" Sybil asked, trying not to sound afraid.

The colonel had forgotten that this young girl had never entered the woods at night, and had only heard vague talk of armed men living there.

"It is a word we use for pro-British marauders who roam the county plundering farmhouses. Skinners are more dangerous. They are separate bands of mounted brigands who claim attachment to us or to the British, whatever suits their mood. They are a mean lot. They rob and kill and hide in the woods southeast of the lake. That is why I warn you not to wander too far over into their area."

Sybil felt as though she might run back into the warmth and safety of her home at that very moment, but the thought of disappointing her father and not being brave enough to help him and his men was too strong. Stonewall and back. That was over forty miles.

"Keep your wits up. Should you encounter anyone hostile, ride away with all your might. You are as good a rider as any of my men. You can do this. God be with you, my child," he said, and lifted her onto her horse.

Records indicate that Sybil mounted Star astride, and her father handed her the gun. She felt a wet chill run up her spine as she turned one last time to look at her house. Her mother had joined her father in the doorway, the warm glow of light behind them.

Sybil kicked Star, as she had done a thousand times before, and in a matter of seconds they had blended into the darkness and were gone.

⚘

Well-known paths and familiar markers during daylight had always made these woods inviting to Sybil; but now, in the deep darkness of a stormy night, she felt herself in foreign territory, enemy territory, and she did not like it at all. The trees before her loomed dangerously overhead, arched and twisted forms of blackness, their branches reaching toward her, their sprawling height swaying with the storm. The paths she knew so well now seemed to mock her. Noises seemed to confront her from all sides, impossible to decipher; she couldn't tell if it was the cracking of fallen sticks and branches underfoot, the rain hitting the trees and earth, her horse's hooves hitting the muddy ground, or perhaps animals scurrying for cover. She heard the howls of a forlorn animal, a wolf, she thought, and had scarcely turned her head to see when she felt a hard, dull thud on her forehead. Before she knew it, she was off her horse and flying through the air.

She landed hard on the mud, the wind knocked out of her. Somehow she had managed to hang on to her rifle, and she clutched it as she dragged herself to her knees. Star, faithful, stopped and waited. Sybil reached up and felt for her head, wondering how she didn't see the branch. Before another possibility could dawn on her, she felt a boot, hard, in her stomach.

She keeled and rolled over, still clutching the rifle, as realization hit her. It was a man. She looked up, edging away, and saw two dark figures approach. The sky lit up, and she saw the face on the closer one, covered in mud, grotesque decaying teeth spread far apart in a lurid smile.

Without thinking, Sybil brought her rifle around, cocked it, and fired. She missed by several feet, hitting a tree and sending chips everywhere. The man paused, just long enough not to see Star, neighing, rear up and kick. Star caught him flush on the jaw and knocked him over.

Sybil whistled, and Star ran to her, getting between her and the second man. Sybil mounted him as quickly as she had ever done, and Star ran without prodding. The second man, though, had a hold of Sybil's leg. He held on, and horse and rider dragged him for nearly twenty feet, Sybil losing her grip on the reins, until finally he let go and fell face first in the mud.

Sybil climbed fully up on Star, giving him a kick and doubling their speed. She didn't know if it was tears or rain on her cheeks, but she had no time to think of it as she warned herself never to take her eyes off the path again.

A glimpse of a marker flashed in the lightning, and she saw the path. She turned onto a road she knew headed south toward Carmel. She knew there was a lake to her right, but as she galloped ahead, she could see no sign of water—only a vast stretch of blackness, ominous and eerie. Her wet fingers kept slipping down the reins, and with her other hand she clenched her musket; she tried to keep it above Star, but could feel the weight of it pulling her arm down. Water ran down her face, into her eyes and mouth, but she had no free hands with which to wipe her face, so she simply bore the wetness.

After what seemed like hours, on the brink of despair, Sybil broke through the woods and into a clearing. The sky was tremendous. A red glow rose on the horizon, seeming to grow bigger by the second. It held no beauty, though; no spectacle of nature, it was only a blazing reminder of danger at their door. Danbury. That meant Carmel was to her left, only minutes away. She headed straight toward it and redoubled her efforts.

Almost immediately, Sybil came upon her first home. The house was dark, and she rode right up to the door and banged her rifle on the wood without dismounting. She couldn't help thinking of her own family and the fear they had felt when suffering a similar intrusion. Beating her rifle again on the door, she heard a voice pierce the night silence, a scream that scared her until she realized the voice was her own.

"Hello! Wake up! Danbury is burning! Please! Come quick! Hello!"

Lights came on, a face appeared at the window, then a man she recognized from her father's regiment opened the door. He stared at her, shocked. As records indicate, she yelled her fateful warning: "Meet at Colonel Ludington's home by daybreak. Bring your arms! Danbury has been sacked! It is burning! Spread the word!"

Galloping onward, not waiting for his reaction, Sybil felt empowered as never before, by a sense of passion, of patriotism, of camaraderie with the men. This was now her fight, too; she was as much a part of it as they were. On and on she rode, traveling south through the town of Carmel, arriving at home after home, spreading the word. She reached Mahopac, circled the lake to the north, and awakened the households there. She rode back up northeast into Cold Spring, finally arriving in Stonewell. To her amazement, she found lights already on in the houses. The message was spreading on its own.

Resting on Star, she stared for a moment at the bustling village. Then she turned south, heading back home, to complete a ride that would later be found to have been a staggering forty miles in all.

Just two years earlier, Paul Revere had made his famous ride at the request of Dr. Joseph Warren, the Boston Patriot leader. Revere, a vigorous man of forty, rode through the gentle Massachusetts countryside, over roads well lit, well populated, and excellent by the day's standards. He had begun his ride at 11:00 P.M., and rode approximately twelve miles into Lexington, where he enjoyed a late-night supper with Samuel Adams and John Hancock, with "boots off and a glass of flip in hand," as it has been said. He then proceeded into the town of Concord, where he was arrested by a British patrol and had his horse confiscated, in all riding less than fourteen miles in two hours.

Dawn was breaking as Sybil rode out from the woods and into the field leading up to her home. Coming up the drive, she could see from her perch hundreds of men gathered on her father's front lawn. As she neared, the regiment—over 400 men strong—turned and watched. A chorus let loose a cheer, a greeting so filled with unity and admiration that she felt her heart rise. They closed ranks on her and embraced her as an equal. Her father spotted her and in no time swept her off her horse and into his arms, in an embrace she would remember for years. Her mother came running out, then her sisters and brothers, amid the cheers for Sybil. She felt part of the Revolution as she had never before. The fight for freedom was now personal.

General Tryon, drunk, pushed his way through the crowd of cheering soldiers, trying to see what all the fuss was about. Around him on every side houses burned; men drank straight from rum barrels; raucous screams carried through the streets, and smoke choked the air. It couldn't have been easier. Danbury, the touted Patriot stronghold, was taken. Valuable supplies were destroyed. The Hudson Highlands were now in reach, and the Patriots were too far away to do anything about it. His men were drunk, perhaps too drunk; he could have cut it off sooner, but he figured, let the men have their fun. Tomorrow they would get back to business.

Two days before, on April 25, 1777, a force of 2,000 British troops under General Tryon had landed with twenty transports and six warships at Campo Beach, near Fairfield, Connecticut, at the mouth of the Sagatuck River. They had spent the night camping in Weston, eight miles inland, and the next morning marched north through Bethel. General Washington, that fool, had left Danbury unguarded, taking his men to use them in another battle. The supplies were out in the open, and the British would steal every last one of them. Soon, though, when they saw the extent of the supplies and realized how much the burden would slow them down, they decided on the spot not to take them. Instead, they would burn them.

Marching inland virtually unopposed, they arrived in Danbury on April 26 and began burning the American Army tents, the supply stores, and town. They successfully destroyed thousands of barrels of supplies and consumed incredible amounts of rum. They became dangerously drunk, setting many private homes on fire. It was a drunken orgy the likes of which had never been seen before, one in which thousands of drunken redcoats staggered up and down Main Street, singing, cursing, shouting insults, and wreaking dangerous havoc on all who lived there. Their behavior would later be described as one of the most shameful displays of British arms in the war.

On the morning of April 27, Colonel Ludington's regiment approached Danbury with his four hundred men. He was joined by a hundred Patriots from Bethel and by General Alexander McDougall's three hundred colonists, marching in from Peekskill. They marched all day, and by nightfall reached Redding, where they were joined by Patriot generals Wooster, Arnold, and Stilliman. They were now one thousand strong. But the British had over two thousand, and the situation looked bleak. Still, they mustered their forces and began to march.

With what would later be described as a "berserk rage,"[3] the American militia advanced strategically, engaging in one of the first known battles of guerilla warfare. They scattered their men far and wide and used sharpshooters to fire from behind trees and fences and stone walls. The British, drunk, surprised, and quickly over-whelmed, hastened to retreat to their ships. They raced to board, but the Patriots pursued them all the way, and many drowned in their hurry to escape the colonists' onslaught. General Wooster received a wound from which he died a few days later. Benedict Arnold, a great Patriot general at the time, had his horse shot out from under him as he furiously charged the enemy. The British reported fifty to sixty enlisted men and five officers killed or wounded in one two-hour stretch alone. The Americans had been victorious. The Highlands of the Hudson would be free from harm; indeed, no attempt was ever made to attack it in the same way again.

Postscript

When she was twenty-three years old Sybil Ludington married Edmund Ogden, with whom she had a son, Henry. Edmund was a farmer and innkeeper, according to various reports. In 1792 Sybil set-tled with her husband and little Henry in Catskill, where they lived until September 16, 1799, when Edmund contracted yellow fever and died. Henry was only thirteen years old.

In 1803 Sybil applied for and was granted an innkeeper's license, becoming the only woman among twenty-three men in that occu-pation. She ran the tavern herself until 1811, supporting herself and

Henry. Henry went on to become an attorney and assemblyman, and Sybil would spend the remaining years of her life living with him and his family in Unadilla, a town in Otsego County. Henry and his wife had six children, and Sybil, the proud grandmother, helped raise them. She died on February 26, 1839, at age seventy-seven and is buried in the Old Presbyterian Cemetery in Patterson.

Though her story was told publicly for the first time in a memoir of her father published in 1907, compiled by Willis Fletcher Johnson (associated with the *New York Herald Tribune* until he died in 1931), not until 1961 would she receive any recognition. That year, the Enoch Crosby chapter of the Daughters of the American Revolution (DAR) erected a statue of her on the shores of Lake Gleneida. In 1975 a postage stamp in her honor was issued as part of the national Bicentennial series "Contributors to the Cause." Another statue of her stands in Washington, D.C. Numerous articles have been written throughout the years calling her the female Paul Revere, comparing her ride to his.

In 1963 Congressman Robert R. Barry addressed the House of Representatives, wherein he read part of a resolution made by the National Women's Party that he then entered into the *Congressional Record*: "The best tribute we can bring to Sybil Ludington is to go forward ourselves in the present day campaign for the complete freedom of women—with the same courage, the same determination, the same intensity of conviction that the heroic young Sybil Ludington displayed in her famous ride for freedom of the American colonists from the control of the Government and laws of England."[4]

The Battle of Danbury was among the many battles of the American Revolution where the patriotism and courage of its defenders was put to the final test; many would not survive to enjoy the liberty so desperately fought for. While Sybil had risked her life to help the men in Danbury, another young girl in a neighboring colony would write of the death of one of its heroes. On news of the death of General Wooster, a young slave girl sat down in Massachusetts to express the collective grief of a nation during this time in her history. She composed a poem to his widow, a poem that many years later would garner fame, attention, and controversy. That girl's name, all would soon learn, was Phillis Wheatley.

PHILLIS WHEATLEY

Caption TK

Breaking the Chains of Silence

PHILLIS WHEATLEY

*In every human Breast, God has implanted a Principle,
which we call Love of Freedom; it is impatient of Oppression,
and pants for Deliverance.*

—PHILLIS WHEATLEY

Africa, 1761

THE FIRE BLAZED out of control, casting a majestic red throughout the village as men, women, and children fled in terror. She struggled to keep up as her mother yelled her name, falling back every few minutes, only to be pulled forward. The crackle of the fire and the smell of burned flesh kept the terrorized seven-year-old girl going, but she reached a point when she suddenly couldn't go any farther. That is when it reached up and pulled her on, the hand she thought was her mother's. It was too late that she realized it was not. It was a different hand, a white hand, one that would take her from her family, her home, her country, and her freedom.

Phillis stood shackled to the man in front of her as she was forced to board an enormous schooner. All around her, hundreds of

Africans pressed forward, every step carrying them farther away from home and closer to hell. She had looked for her mother earlier, but could not find her then, and still could not see her now.

She clutched her frail little hands in front of her and lowered her head. The wooden plank beneath her creaked and tilted, while the rough water below churned ominously. She had never been on a boat before, much less to sea. Her grandfather had told her all sorts of scary stories, though, and fear filled her heart. The bright sky—where she had stared at the stars with her father only the night before; where she had watched her mother bow to the rising sun every morning of her short life—slowly faded from view as she descended the stairs to the middle deck of the ship. She lifted her head one last time before the hope-filled sky.

Phillis was crammed with nearly seventy-five other girls in a room measuring only thirteen by twenty feet and only three feet, eight inches high. The ship was damp and cold; the smell of body odor and salt filled the air. The others were so close, she could feel their skin rub up against her own. The damp, choking darkness of the room suffocated her every time she tried to breathe. She curled into a little ball in the corner, where she would remain for nearly a month, thinking of her family. The ship pushed off, and the cabin filled with screams, the little girls falling on top of each other, the boat creaking loudly. Phillis looked up and caught one last glimpse of Africa, and felt an awful certainty that she would never see her parents again.

The sad and dreadful history of the African slave trade began in 1442, when a small Portuguese ship captured twelve blacks on a raid off the Atlantic coast of Africa. The slaves were carried back to Lisbon to become the slaves of Prince Henry the Navigator. Soon after, another expedition successfully captured 235 prisoners and carried them back to Portugal as well. By the early 1500s the slave trade was well under way, with the court at Lisbon eagerly pushing the profitable business with Africa. At that point in history both England and France looked down upon human cargo as trade, and Spain and Portugal commanded the field. By 1492, however, with Columbus's discovery of America, the idea of slave labor quickly began to take hold. Columbus and the colonists first focused on the Native Americans, a people they saw as inferior, whose lands were ripe for the taking. Many Native Americans revolted or died from the harsh labor, the brutal treatment, or white man's diseases against which they had no immunity. When this happened, the colonists looked to Africa. Charles V, king of Spain, granted a license to import slaves from Africa to the New World, and by 1540 ten thousand slaves a year were being carried in chains across the Atlantic to the West Indies, while others were taken to South America and Mexico.

The Portuguese monopoly on the slave trade began to break up when the English decided to get involved. In 1562 Admiral John Hawkins led three ships to the coast of Guinea, later called the Slave Coast: for his services, he was knighted by Queen Elizabeth two years later. The Dutch pushed the Portuguese off the African coast in 1642, and by the 1700s the English and French had become the two leading nations in the trafficking of slaves. In the late 1700s Europeans were operating forty slave stations on the African coast, the great majority coming from West Africa, along the three thousand miles of coast from Senegal in the north to Angola in the south.

North America became involved late in the game when, in 1619, a Dutch ship entered Jamestown in the colony of Virginia and sold twenty slaves in exchange for food and goods. By that time a million blacks had already been brought from Africa to South America and the Caribbean. But not until 1730, when staple agriculture—such crops as cotton, rice, and tobacco—began to spread, did North America import sizable numbers of slaves, linking the two countries both politically and economically.[1] The years from 1730 to the outbreak of the American Revolution saw a surge of imports: by 1776 the slave population had climbed to more than 500,000. American traders did not have their own posts in Africa, so they used those of the English. Rhode Island was the colony most active; her ships made about a thousand voyages to Africa in one century, bringing over 100,000 slaves to America. New York, Pennsylvania, and Massachusetts actively "plied the trade" as well, although relatively few slaves were brought to the northern colonies.

The Atlantic slave trade, as it came to be known, referred to the voyage of a trader from Europe to Africa, from Africa to the Americas, and from the Americas back to Europe, with the trip from Africa to the Americas being called the Middle Passage. But while this passage was fraught with danger and death, both for the slave and the trader, the ordeal for the kidnapped slave often began weeks or months before she set foot on the deck of the ship. Slaves brought to the coast from the interior of Africa were forced to march hundreds of miles to the sea in shackles; men, women, and children were bound in iron, their feet in fetters, their necks fastened to one another by rope or twisted thongs. Skeletons littered the earth surrounding the Gambia River.

Those who survived would sometimes have to wait many weeks at the mouth of the river, chained to the ship that waited, patiently, for enough human cargo to justify its setting sail. Many perished during this brutal wait; food and drink were scarce, conditions on the ship a nightmare. The physical conditions aboard a slave ship were not fit for animals, much less humans. The ships, steeped in filth, reeking with the vile stench of human excrement basting in heat, perspiration, fish, and sea mixed together, sat at the docks ready to greet their cargo.

And then the most dangerous, brutal part of all: the Middle Passage, the sea voyage across the Atlantic in a slave ship where men, women, and children were packed like sardines into the lower recesses, not an inch separating one from another. Slaves were forced down into the lower decks, beaten, flogged, and starved. Many died of dysentery, measles, smallpox, yellow fever, dehydration, or a variety of "fevers" that spread through ships like wildfire due to the unsanitary conditions. The Spanish contracts relating to slavery usually made an allowance for a death rate of up to 40 percent during the three-to-four-month voyage. A slave named Olaudah Equiano, in an account of his time on board a slave ship, described the stench as "so intolerably loathsome it was dangerous to remain there for any time," bringing on a "sickness among the slaves of which many died."[2] He continued by saying, "This wretched situation was again aggravated by the galling of the chains . . . and the filth of the necessary tubs, into which the children often fell, and were almost suffocated. The shrieks of the women, and the groans of the dying, rendered the whole a scene of horror almost inconceivable."[3] Men, women, and children were split up, so that even if a family had remained together through their kidnapping, by the time they were aboard the ship, they would be separated. Many children, like Phillis, had been taken from their parents and placed on one of these ships all alone. The African slave trade to the Americas lasted for more than three and a half centuries.

Boston, 1761

Susannah and John Wheatley arrived at the dock just as the slave ship *Phyllis* finished unloading. A handsome, aristocratic couple, they had seen the advertisement for "Slaves to Be Sold" in the *Boston Evening Post* the night before, and Susannah had decided it was time to purchase a young slave girl, one who would care for her in old age. The slaves she already owned were older, not as malleable, she thought. She had cultivated in them neither love nor loyalty; and there was now no chance of their being anything other than domestics. But a young girl—that was a different story. A young girl could be loyal if treated right, if raised to only know Susannah as a mother figure; then, in old age, she would not be alone. She had children of her own—two, in fact—but children grow up, marry, leave home. Susannah wanted the assurance of having someone by her side when the time came.

The Wheatleys lived in an imposing mansion on Boston's residential King Street (the same King Street that would host the Boston Massacre ten years later). John, one of Boston's wealthier merchants, had begun as a tailor and had prospered with his own business. They shared two teenage children, Mary and Nathaniel. The Wheatleys were well established in Boston's upper social circles, having both wealth and Christianity on their side.

They were standing toward the front of the crowd, near the auction block, where they had a clear view of the platform lined with black men, women, and children. It was a sweltering July afternoon, and the crowd was growing impatient for the auction to begin. It was Susannah who first caught sight of the little girl, standing with the others but hidden by the larger girls in front of her. She stood at the end of the line, off to the side, wrapped only in a dirty little carpet about her waist, her two small hands holding it up. She appeared so frail and sickly, her arms and legs thin as a skeleton, her long black hair matted around her face, her eyes facing downward, that it seemed an effort for her simply to stand. The sight tugged at Susannah's heart as she made her way over to inquire.

After receiving no information from the slave master, a man too busy to be bothered with details of the child's life, Susannah bent down to look into the child's eyes: there was a desperation and fear in them, a sadness she had never seen before. She asked the girl her name, but did not receive an answer. An auctioneer, watching Susannah with bemused interest, answered that the child's name was Phillis, pointing to the ship she had just arrived in. Susannah understood immediately: the little girl's real name was unknown, her history lost. (Phillis would never regain her memory of life before her abduction, except to describe her mother as bowing to the morning sun at the start of each day. Historians have only guessed that she was an African of the Kaffir tribe who inhabit the country between Cape Colony and Delagoa Bay, or that she was an inhabitant of the Gambia River colony, or that she was possibly even from Senegal.)

"Can you speak, child?" Susannah asked, bending low enough to meet the child eye to eye.

The girl tried to open her mouth, revealing two missing teeth, but nothing came out. "The child must be only seven or eight years old, John," Susannah cried, troubled by the thought of such a young child traveling as she had, so far from her land, alone in such wretched conditions. "She is just a baby. I am quite frankly amazed she has survived the trip at all."

John looked at little Phillis himself and considered the fate she might come to in the hands of the wrong person. Even he, a slave owner, ached at the vileness of the human bondage these poor creatures endured. He owned slaves, yes; but he would never submit them to the shameless cruelties he had heard existed.

"We will take her," he said to the slave master. "How much?"

Surprised, the auctioneer looked down at Phillis and, smirking, answered, "One shilling." (Later, he revealed that he thought the girl might die on his hands.)

"Sold."

King Street, Boston, *1763*

The Wheatley home on King Street was located in the hub and heart of Boston's intellectual elite, where its wealthiest, most educated citizens lived and socialized, including the Wheatleys. It was a world of glitter and gold, fashion and laughter, nightly dinners, constant entertaining, and endless conversation. An aristocratic family in eighteenth-century Boston has been called "the reputed cradle of all that is refined in American manners and letters."[4] Much of that conversation centered on the slave trade, whose morality was being questioned by increasingly vocal opponents. Slavery was an important and almost daily topic of discussions in Boston, as was talk of restricting it. (By 1770 Massachusetts, Pennsylvania, and Virginia had taken steps in that direction.) Perhaps this is because the colonists were starting to have a taste of their own shackles, as Great Britain's policies toward them became increasingly oppressive. The Stamp Act was but one display of England's repeated attempts to control the colonists; the Boston Massacre another. Realization was dawning in the hearts and minds of the colonists: they disliked being enslaved to King George's policies and whims, and not having a voice in matters directly affecting their lives.

Susannah, John, and both their children had treated Phillis kindly from the start. Her age set her apart from the other servants almost immediately, as did her physical condition. It was quite clear to anyone who looked upon the poor child that she was on the verge of death. Furthermore, Susannah had made it clear from the outset that if she returned with a young girl, then that girl was to be considered hers. Phillis was given small domestic chores as she regained her strength, but most of her time, as planned, was spent attending to Susannah. She never spoke, only listened and watched.

As Susannah whirled down the stairs that night, carefully lifting the hem of her brocaded, floor-length satin gown, she felt irrepressibly happy at the thought of her and John being invited to the Warren's home for dinner. They had made their acquaintance one year ago, and only now had received a proper invitation to dine with them. Mercy Otis Warren had quite a reputation for being exceptionally bright and ferociously patriotic, like her brother, James Otis; the dinner conversation promised to be interesting. When Susannah reached the bottom of the stairs, she called out to Nathaniel and John in the parlor to see if the chaise was ready. After hearing nothing, she made her way into the drawing room, and almost immediately, she spotted her. There, huddled in the corner, covered in white chalk, was Phillis.

As Susannah neared the child, moving quietly so as not to make any noise, she peered curiously in her direction, wondering what in God's name she was doing. Her newly painted lime-green wall was covered in something—she had a sudden thought that the child was destroying her home, and felt fear well up inside her. But then she saw them: letters, English letters, all over her wall. She must have made a sound, because Phyllis jumped back, chalk on her face, a look of sheer terror in her eyes. Nervously Phyllis tried to wipe away the letters, but Susannah stopped her. Susannah's eyes wandered back over the wall: an *A,* a *C,* what looked like a broken *B.* The child was writing the alphabet. She stared, letting the realization sink in.

"Phillis, do you know how to write?" she asked, shocked that the child may have known the English language all this time.

Phillis simply shook her head.

Carefully holding up her gown, Susannah took Phillis by the arm, lifted her up, and tried to wipe some of the chalk off her face.

"Where in God's name did you learn your letters?" she asked, still shocked at the sight.

Meekly, Phillis bowed her head and simply said, "I am sorry."

"You are sorry?" Susannah replied, with a quick sort of laugh, which seemed to show she was not angry. "My dear child," she said now, in an even gentler, easier voice, "you should be proud."

Then, smiling in pride, as though this display of genius had come from her own child, she took Phillis by the hand and said, "Come now, let us get you cleaned up."

From that moment on, Phillis's life would take a different turn. Though Phillis had acclimated to the Wheatleys before this event, regaining strength, working quietly by day, and retiring to her servant's quarters at night, Susannah had recognized that Phillis's writing on the wall was a truly remarkable display of genius. Now, instead of the usual daily work of a domestic slave, Susannah did not "require or permit her services as a domestic."[5] Sometimes she would allow her to "polish a table or dust an apartment," but should Phillis think of an interesting verse or be inspired with a thoughtful phrase, "the brush and duster were soon dropped for the pen."[6] Instead, at Susannah's insistence, Phillis was to spend her time studying, and she spent hours each day being tutored by Mary. She astonished the Wheatleys when, in only six months' time, she had learned to read and write.

She was given her own room and supplied with paper and pencils and, by her bedside, a candle, should she choose to stay up late reading. She was no longer treated as a slave, but rather as a member of the family. As time went on and Phillis grew, so did her intellect, her knowledge, and her writing. She became proficient in astronomy, ancient and modern geography, ancient history, and English and Latin literature. The classics were her favorite, as was the Bible, "the most difficult parts of which she could read within 16 months."[7] In four years she could write fluently.[8] In fact, her translation of Ovid's *Odes*, published in Boston around 1769, was highly commended by scholars of the time.

The first published poem by Phillis dates back to 1767, when she was fourteen years old. This first poem, entitled "On Messrs. Hussey and Coffin," was printed in the *Newport Mercury* on December 21, 1767, and chronicled the narrow escape at sea in a storm by two of the Wheatleys' dinner guests, whom Phillis had overheard telling the story. After Phillis published this poem, the first ever to be written and published by a black woman (not to mention a slave), she became the focus of Boston's intellectual elite, attracting attention from high-ranking clergymen and aristocratic New England individuals, who visited her to marvel at her genius, offer her books, and "steal a peek at the black girl who could write. Phillis wrote five years before the dawn of the American Revolution and the birth of German idealism. She wrote before the mighty outburst of the human spirit which gave rise to Goethe, Schiller and Heine in Germany and Wordsworth, Byron, Keats and Shelley in England."[9] Alexander Pope who reigned supreme in the eighteenth century, and Phillis was an avid reader of Alexander Pope at an early age. Pope believed in imitation and translation, and he was the suggested model for writers at that time.[10] His translation of Homer was her favorite classic, and before long she too began to write verse.[11]

Not only was Phillis visited, but soon she was invited into the most exclusive homes in town, asked to dine at the same table as her hosts, and treated, generally, as an equal. Despite these gestures, however, she never considered herself a true equal—she was a black slave, owned by a family, and no matter how sweetly she was treated when invited into other people's homes, she "always declined the seat offered her at their board, and, requesting that a side-table be laid for her, dined modestly apart from the rest of the company."[12]

Though Phillis was a member of the Wheatley family, she was very much aware of the racial discrimination of the time. She had been admitted to the Old South (Congregational) Meeting House in

Boston on August 18, 1771, and the following year, contrary to the traditional prejudice against blacks, had become a communicant, but she sat separately in church—in the Negro pews. Though she never formally protested, blacks who would not comply with the dictates of the church were forcibly removed, had tar put on their pews, or were even threatened with physical violence. Discrimination was so intense in Boston that by about 1800 the black leader Prince Hall could only advise his brethren to "be patient and bear up under the daily insults we meet on the streets." [13]

Encouraged by the enthusiastic initial reception of her work, however, Phillis continued to write, and in 1770 published another poem, "On the Death of Reverend George Whitefield," which would become the most pivotal work of her career, launching her reputation in America and extending it internationally. The poem eulogized the famous reverend, who had died on September 30, 1770, in Newburyport, Massachusetts. Part of the reason this poem hit such a nerve was its topic: Reverend Whitefield was an extremely popular English-born evangelist who preached throughout the American colonies, even converting and befriending blacks. He was known on both sides of the Atlantic as the "Great Awakener," and was considered personal chaplain to Countess Selina of Huntingdon, in London. As the countess was also close friends with Susannah Wheatley, Susannah had Phillis send her a copy of the poem on October 25, 1770, with an accompanying note. The week before Whitefield's death, he had preached in Boston, and may even have stayed with the Wheatleys in their home. The Wheatleys were frequent hosts to visiting English ministers, members of the countess's circle. If so, Phillis would have met him.

The poem would be published in at least ten editions in Boston, Newport, and Philadelphia, as Whitefield's death had garnered widespread interest, and Phillis's treatment of it, so pious, kind, and laudatory, created an enthusiastic market for her elegy.

Boston, October 1772

Phillis had been sitting in the dark, quiet hallway patiently for almost two hours, waiting to be called in. The bench was hard and cold, and her back began to feel the strain. She tapped her shoes on the marble floor, the echo offering a daunting reminder of the importance of the building, and the reason for her wait. She glanced at the ornate ceiling above her, at the intricate, architectural carvings that formed an arch over her head. The shine on the marble floor reflected the light of the stained-glass window at the end of the corridor. She marveled at the ability of man to create such beauty.

Phillis pressed her sweaty hands over her dress again, trying to both dry her hands and flatten the fabric of her dress. She wondered what Mary Wheatley, her beloved tutor, was doing now. One year earlier, Mary had married the Reverend John Lathrop and moved away from home. Phyllis missed her and their daily studies together. She thought of her often—especially today, as Mary was such a big part of the reason Phillis was there at all.

The sudden click of a doorknob interrupted her thoughts. One of the gigantic doors before her opened, and His Excellency, Governor Thomas Hutchinson of Massachusetts, appeared. Close behind him was Andrew Oliver, his lieutenant governor. Without a word, he motioned for Phyllis to enter. She stood very nervously, afraid her feet would not carry her inside. Then, obeying his request, she picked up the manuscript that lay beside her on the bench, that well-worn collection of thoughts and prayers, verse and poetry, piety and penance, and let herself be led into the room where eighteen of Boston's most revered male citizens sat, ready to question her.

This group of "the most respectable characters in Boston" (as they would later call themselves) had assembled that day for the sole purpose of deposing Phillis on the "slender sheaf of poems" she claimed to have written by herself. It had been two years since she had published her poem to the Reverend Whitefield, and during that time she had amassed a collection of thirty-three poems to create her first volume of poetry. Despite the international acclaim heaped upon her, and the elevated status she enjoyed in local Bostonian circles, both Phillis and John Wheatley had encountered a bigoted response to her creative efforts when they tried earlier that year to publish this collection.

The Wheatleys had advertised her proposal for her first volume of poetry as early as February 1772, in the *Boston Censor,* then again in March, and finally in April 1772. Racist resistance sprouted up on all sides in response to the proposals. Piqued Boston whites, "not crediting the performance to be by a Negro," refused to subscribe to her volume, which they could not or would not believe had been written by a black servant girl who only a few years earlier could not read or write English.[14] Boston publishers did not believe a black girl had truly authored the poems. Her proposals were ignored, and her volume went unpublished. John Andrews, a Boston merchant and fierce admirer of Phillis' works, noted how difficult it was to get the volume of poetry published and attributed this to "its being written by a Negro."[15] Andrews also wrote on May 29, 1772, saying, "It's about two months ago since I subscribed to Phillis' poems but the want of spirit to carry on anything of the kind here prevented it, as they are not yet published."[16] Stung by the rejection, Susannah had decided that the "young, black poet girl would most assuredly be published, and if not in racially prejudiced Boston, then in fashionable, sophisticated London."[17] Susannah had contracted her good friend the countess to help in this endeavor, who had agreed.

Though the countess and others in London were thrilled with Phillis's work, others still clung to their disbelief. It may have been Susannah's idea to obtain a formal declaration of authenticity, one that vouched for the claim that a slave had indeed written the poetry in question. Whoever's idea it was, the group of men assembled were expressly concerned with determining Phillis's authenticity; they were considered the most respected, educated, and revered men of the time, and their support of Phillis, should they offer it, would go a long way toward establishing her work as real. They had gathered for an inquisition, to question Phillis, who was then seventeen or eighteen years old, on her knowledge of Latin and the classics, the Bible and literature and English verse, in what has been called "the oddest oral examination on record."[18]

The annointed group of men included then governor and lieutenant governor of Massachusetts; five judges; seven reverends; three lawyers, including John Hancock (who would later gain fame for his signature on the Declaration of Independence); and John Wheatley himself, who had retired from business one year earlier and had actively been trying to help Phillis publish her poems. Historians have speculated on what actually occurred in that room. It is agreed by all that she underwent a rigorous examination of her intellect, and by the end of the long and arduous interrogation, an open letter to the public was composed, signed, and published by the committee, a two-paragraph attestation that prefaces Phillis Wheatley's first volume of poetry and reads in part:

TO THE PUBLICK

As it has been repeatedly suggested to the Publisher, by persons who have seen this Manuscript, that Numbers would be ready to suspect they were not really the Writings of *PHILLIS*, he has procured the following Attestation, from the most respectable Characters in Boston, that none might have the least Ground for disputing their original.

We whose Names are underwritten, do assure the World, that the Poems specified in the following page were (as we verily believe) written by *PHILLIS*, a young Negro Girl, who was but a few Years since brought an uncultivated Barbarian from Africa, and has ever since been, and now is, under the Disadvantage of serving as a Slave in a Family in this Town. She has been examined by some of the best Judges, and is thought qualified to write them.

The attestation is undated, but it is guessed to have been written before mid-November, 1772. The Wheatleys were wise enough to realize that the attestation alone would not be sufficient, so Susannah contacted the countess and the London publishers. Susannah arranged the dedication to the countess and contacted a printer in London, a Mr. Archibald Bell. One month before her letter to the countess, however, Susannah had written another letter to the Reverend Samson Occum, dated March 29, 1773, stating that "Mr. Bell [the printer] acquaints me that, about five weeks ago, he waited upon the Countess of Huntingdon with the poems, who was greatly pleased with them, and pray'd him to read them; and often would break in upon him and say 'Is not this or that very fine? Do read another'; and questioned him much, whether she was real, without deception? She is fond of having the book dedicated to her, but one thing she desired, which she said she hardly thought would be denied her, that was, to have Phillis' picture in the frontispiece. So that if you can get it done, it can be engraved here. I do imagine it can be easily done, and think would contribute to the sale of the book"[19] It seems the manuscript was in London in early December, 1772, and the printers were simply waiting to receive the painting of Phillis.

Susannah also had John write a biographical sketch of Phillis, outlining the circumstances under which she had studied in their home. John Wheatley's letter to the publisher, signed by him and dated November 14, 1772, tells of Phillis's tutelage with Mary Wheatley, and recalls the speed with which she learned to read and write the English language. He says that "as to her writing, her own curiosity led her to it," and remarks on her "great inclination to learn the Latin Tongue."[20] Further, a preface was also written that explains the circumstance of how a female African slave might actually have written poetry. The preface reads, in part, that the poems were written for "the amusement" of the author, as she had "no intent" to publish them. Only because of the "importunity of many of her best, and most generous friends" had her writing seen the light of day, and, it continues to state, she was "under the greatest obligation" to them. It also states its hope that the reader "will not severely censure her defects," and alludes to the "difficulties she has labored under."[21]

With the attestation, the dedication, the preface, the biographical sketch, and the manuscript of the poems in his hands, Captain Robert Calef, the Wheatley's personal friend, sailed to London on Sunday, November 15, 1772. Arriving in London mid-December, Calef gave the manuscript to Mr. Bell, who in turn showed the papers to the countess, who not only approved of their publication but insisted on having Phillis's portrait affixed as a frontispiece. So important was the attestation in securing a publisher for Phillis's poems that without it, her publisher acknowledged, few would believe that an African could possibly have written poetry all by herself.

London, Summer of 1773

She awoke with a start, confused, uncertain of where she was. Her hands and arms were sweaty, and her heart beat fiercely, pounding away each second with an urgency and fear she recognized too well. For the past three nights, the same dream had startled her out of her sleep. She sat alone in a small, dark, cold room. The room rocked back and forth as she desperately searched for something to hold onto. Finding nothing, she reached for the wall, but the room would only rock harder. She lifted herself up, choking back tears, and reached for the light. She had lunged toward it and screamed for help when the water overtook her, crashing into her face, covering the light, and ending the dream.

She sat up in bed, calming herself, reminding herself she was safe in her own room. But the message of the dream was not lost to her: the fear in her dream mimicked her own real fear now, ten years later, at the thought of climbing aboard a ship and setting out upon the vast ocean. She closed her eyes at the thought of it, as if she could wipe away the terror and dread of her last voyage, knowing too well that the private hell of her past would haunt her forever.

Phillis suffered, in that winter of 1773, unlike any other time since her arrival in America. Her health deteriorated markedly after she became severely ill with complicating consumption and almost died. Her frail body had been ravaged with coughing fits, and her strength was all but gone. Her doctor had recommended a sea voyage, in the hope that a change of environment and the sea air would help her recuperate. Nathaniel Wheatley was scheduled to travel to London on business that spring, so it seemed wise to have Phillis join him on his trip. Both Phillis and Susannah had considered the benefit of Phillis's meeting the countess in person, as the countess had repeatedly voiced her desire to meet Phillis. It had been settled, then: the voyage was to take place on the Wheatleys' own ship *London*, scheduled to set sail from Boston Harbor the next day, May 8, 1773.

After Phillis washed and ate breakfast, she returned to her room and steadily finished packing her belongings into the well-worn bag Susannah had provided. When she was finished, she sat on her bed, picked up her manuscript from her bedside table, and stared at it. On top lay her most recent poem, one she had written with her voyage in mind. "A Farewell to America," which had been printed in many New England papers that week, was especially personal to her because of its topic: she spoke of Susannah and their parting. It read in part:

Susannah mourns, nor can I bear
To see the crystal shower,
Or mark the tender falling tear,
At sad departures hour.
Nor unregarding can I see
Her soul with grief opprest;
But let no sighs, no groans for me,
Steal from her pensive breast.

When she finished reading it, she glanced at another piece of paper underneath it: the Attestation. She read it again, knowing each line by heart already, but always stopping at the part where they called her an "uncultivated barbarian." The sting of those words still made her reel with anger, as did the entire process she had been forced to undergo. Reflecting back on that horrendous day when she was called upon to justify and explain herself to that committee of men, she realized now that in defending her own ability, she had defended the ability of every black person to think and speak and write. She had found her voice and used it; she had defended her right to freedom, much as they colonists were fighting for and defending their right to freedom from England.

Mr. Wheatley's reassuring face throughout the ordeal had given her support, always her staunch ally. She read his letter too, though she knew it also by heart, and thanked God again for giving her to the Wheatleys. But now it was time to go. Carefully, she placed the two letters with her manuscript on top of her clothes, zipped the bag shut, and walked out of her room.

The voyage would last five weeks as planned, with both its embarkation and its passengers widely reported on in the newspapers. Good-byes were said at home, as both she and Susannah did not want an open display of emotion at the dock. Susannah was the only mother figure, the only family, Phillis had ever remembered. The trip held the promise of many dreams to be fulfilled, but as she stood perched on the doorstep of freedom, she felt bewilderingly sad. The Wheatleys had given her comfort, and the closest thing she knew to love and family. She was their slave, yes, but she had never been mistreated; on the contrary, she had been taken into the family circle, unlike many other slaves, and been treated like a white person. She had been safe with them, and safety felt good—freedom, or what felt close to it, now felt scary.

Although she didn't realize it, real freedom was, literally, only a voyage away. The year before, in 1772, the British judge Lord Mansfield handed down the Somerset decision, which effectively freed all slaves in Great Britain. "The decision was widely understood in the following terms: As soon as a slave set his foot on the soil of the British islands, he becomes free."[22] Therefore, when Phillis arrived in London on June 17, 1773, technically she was no longer a slave; she was, for the first time in her adult life, a free woman.

Phillis was already known in certain literary circles in England before her arrival, not only for her 1770 poem "On the Death of Reverend Whitefield," but for other poems published in England as well, such as her 1772 poem "On Recollection," which appeared first in the *London Magazine,* then again in the *Annual Register.* Though she didn't realize it as she left Boston Harbor, the world of London's wealthiest, most royal, privileged, and accomplished citizens was waiting to welcome her as a star, to actively seek out her company and invite her into their homes, where they conversed with her on many topics. Her genius and voice were widely praised, and gifts were bestowed upon her. Though her volume of poetry was not published until the end of the summer, on September 1, 1773, her reputation preceded her. She was hailed and feted by English nobility, gentry, religionists, and abolitionists. Phillis's time in London was almost completely taken up by social invitations, literary gatherings, and parties.

Life in London was a whirlwind from the moment Phillis arrived on June 27, 1773, as invitations and gifts were showered down upon her. Sir Brook Watson, a wealthy London merchant (who would by 1796 become Lord Mayor of London) presented her with a folio edition of Milton's *Paradise Lost*. William Ledge, earl of Dartmouth, secretary of state for the colonies, and president of the Board of Trade and Foreign Plantations, gave her a copy of Smollet's translation of *Don Quixote* and five shillings to purchase Pope's works. Benjamin Franklin visited her. John Thornton, the millionaire philanthropist, became a friend (he was a great supporter of Dartmouth College, where Thornton Hall is named after him). She continued working on her volume of poetry, though it was already going through the printing process. She remained busy with revisions, writing and rewriting her work. She was permitted to interrupt the printing process to add new or revised pieces. After all she had been through in her then short life, her brief time in England was like a dream; as though she had stepped into the white world of privilege, intellect, and beauty as a member of its inner circle, not the outsider she was so used to being. Looking back, it would be the highlight of what would become her tragically short life.

Boston, September 1773

As the Boston coach carrying Phillis turned the corner from Mackarel Lane onto King Street, an autumn gust swept across her face, a chilly reminder of how the glorious summer was most definitely, and sadly, at an end. It was September 10, 1773, three months to the day since she had set sail for England with Nathaniel, and now she was returning alone. Nathaniel had stayed on for personal reasons, marrying Mary Enderby of Thames Street in London. Only the Wheatleys' servant boy, Prince, accompanied her in the chaise sent to retrieve her, she sitting properly behind him. She had not been lucky enough to be in England for the publication of her volume of poetry the week before, but instead had spent the week suffering through the long voyage back to America.

The horse pulled to a stop, and there before her eyes stood the Wheatleys' home, her home. With a mixture of sadness at what most likely lay ahead, and relief at having arrived safely from her long and lonely journey back to America, she descended from the coach and looked upon the home in all its splendor. How beautifully it stood; just as she had remembered it. Prince offered her his hand, helping her down onto the street. Slowly and sadly she walked toward the front door.

News of Susannah's failing health had come as a complete shock. The letter from Mary almost begged Phillis to return, expressing Susannah's deep wish to see Phillis one last time before the end. When Phillis received the letter, she had been in England only one month; she had not yet met the countess, the one person she had so much wished to meet and thank in person. She had prepared for the moment when she would meet her over and over in her mind, what she would say, how she would thank her. But there was no way she would ever deny Susannah her wish—she would return to America the first chance she had. She would never actually have the chance to meet Selina, the countess of Huntingdon, her chief patron and backer. Selina, who was aging and ill, had been restricted to Wales during the time Phyllis was in London. Although the countess had sent an invitation for Phillis to come visit, Phillis's loyalty to Susannah demanded her return to America. In a letter to the countess dated July 17, 1773, Phyllis wrote, "Am sorry to acquaint your Ladyship that the ship is certainly to sail next Thursday on which I must return to America. I long to see my friend there. I am extremely reluctant to go without having first seen your Ladyship."[23]

An engraving of Phillis had been made, with a striking resemblance to the original. She sent a copy of it to Susannah, who in turn set it over the fireplace and exclaimed, "See! Look at my Phillis! Does she not seem as though she would speak to me!"[24]

In this way, then, Phillis's summer had come to an end. And now, here she stood, able to speak to Susannah and remain by her bedside, which she did, caring for her through her daily battle with pain. After fourteen weeks in bed, on March 3, 1774, Susannah died. She lived long enough to see Phyllis's volume of poetry in print, however; in January 1774 the volume was made available in America, sold by Messrs. Cox of King Street and advertised prominently in the *Massachusetts Gazette* and *Boston Weekly News Letter.* She was said to have "extraordinary poetical genius" by the *Providence Gazeteer* on September 25, 1773, and was described as having "singular genius and accomplishments" by Dr. Benjamin Rush.[25] Contemporary critics dubbed her the "girl wonder of the revolutionary age."[26] Even Voltaire spoke of Phillis when he wrote to Baron Constant de Rebecq, "Fontenelle was wrong to say that there never would be Negro poets. There is now a Negree who composes very good English verse."[27]

"Freedom was a vital topic in pulpit and parliament,"[28] and a new awareness of the black race as deserving of freedom was dawning in England. Phillis's strong feelings against slavery are found laced throughout her work, in many different poems. In one such poem, "On Being Brought From Africa to America," she says,

> *Some view our sable race with scornful eyes—*
> *"Their color is a diabolic dye."*
> *Remember, Christians, Negroes black as Cain*
> *May be refined, and join the angelic train.*

Phyllis was a constant witness to the American struggle for independence, and created a canon of her own some have called political poetry. Throughout her work, passionate political statements supporting the American colonial quest for freedom are found. In 1768 in "To the King's Most Excellent Majesty," she praised his repeal of the Stamp Act:

> *Midst the remembrance of thy favors past,*
> *The meanest peasants most admire the last.*

She also wrote a poem called "To The Right Honorable William, Earl of Dartmouth," wherein she clearly states her feelings:

> *No more, America, in mournful strain,*
> *Of wrongs and grievance unredressed complain;*
> *No longer shall thou dread the iron chain*
> *Which wanton Tyranny, with lawless hand,*
> *Has made, and with it meant t' enslave the land.*
> *Should you, my lord, while you peruse my song,*
> *Wonder from whence my love of Freedom sprung,*
> *Whence flow these wishes for the common good,*
> *By feeling hearts alone best understood,*
> *I, young in life, by seeming cruel fate*
> *Was snatched from Afric's fancied happy seat:*
> *What pangs excruciating must molest,*
> *What sorrows labor in my parents breast!*
> *Steeled was that soul, and by no misery moved,*
> *That from a father seized his babe beloved:*
> *Such, such my case. And can I then but pray*
> *Others may never feel tyrannic sway?*

Then she wrote "America," in which she scolded Britain and implored her to treat "Americus," the British child, with more respect. According to the poem, America the child has grown into an independent being who wishes to be free of the tyrannical control her parent exerts over her. Her use of the phrase "iron chain"

44

evokes imagery of slavery too: America longs for its independence, while robbing the Africans of theirs.

Phillis also composed a poem called "On the Affray in King Street, on the Evening of the 5th of March," referring to the Boston Massacre. She was living with the Wheatleys on King Street at the time, and there is a very high likelihood she was an eyewitness to the massacre. Unfortunately, this poem has not been found; but we know she was actively recording American political events. In Providence, Rhode Island, on October 25, 1775, she wrote a covering note to George Washington at Cambridge. Both the note and the poem appeared first in the *Virginia Gazette* for March 20, 1776, and then in the *Pennsylvania Magazine* and the *American Monthly Museum* of April of that same year. The poem read in part:

> *And so may you, whoever dares disgrace*
> *The land of freedom's heaven defended race!*
> *Fix'd are the eyes of nations on the scales,*
> *For in their hopes Columbia's arms prevails.*
> *Anon Britannia droops the pensive head,*
> *While round increase the rising hills of dead.*
> *Ah! Cruel blindness to Columbia's state!*
> *Lament thy thirst for power too late.*

Her letter to George Washington reads in part, "Wishing your Excellency all possible success in the great cause you are so generously engaged in."[29]

He replied to her from Cambridge on February 28, 1776: "Your style and manner exhibit striking proof of your poetic talents; in honor of which, and as a tribute justly due to you, I would have published the poem, had I not been apprehensive, that, while I only meant to give the world this new instance of your genius, I might have incurred the imputation of vanity."[30] He continued the letter by inviting her to visit

him in Cambridge, "which she did a few days before the British evacuated Boston; her master, among others, having left the city by permission, and retired with his family to Chelsea."[31]

One week before Washington sent this letter to Phillis, he referred
to her poem in a letter to his adjutant Joseph Reed, again from Cambridge, on February 10, 1776: "At first, with a view of doing justice to
her poetic genius, I had a great mind to publish the poem; but, not
knowing whether it might be considered rather as a mark of my own
vanity, than as a compliment to her, I laid it aside till I came across it
again in the manner I just mentioned."[32] Reed, upon receiving this
letter, sent Phillis's letter of October 26, 1775, to George Washington to
the papers himself, where they were printed in the *Virginia Gazette* in
April, 1776, on page 1, and in the *Pennsylvania Magazine* that same
month, when that paper was edited by Thomas Paine.

Phillis's antislavery feelings are evident not only in her poetry,
but also in letters she wrote to various people at different times
throughout her life. In the spring of 1774 an antislavery letter she
had written to Reverend Occum was published in several New
England papers. As reported in the Thursday, March 24, 1774, issue
of the *Massachusetts Spy,* the letter read:

> I have this day received your obliging, kind Epistle, and am greatly
> satisfied with your Reasons respecting the negroes, and think highly
> reasonable what you offer in Vindication of their natural Rights:
> Those that invade them cannot be insensible that the divine light is
> chasing away the thick Darkness which broods over the Land of
> Africa. . . . for in every human Breast, God has implanted a Princi-
> ple, which we call Love of Freedom; it is impatient of oppression and
> pants for Deliverance—and by the leave of our modern Egyptians I
> will assert that the same principle lives in us. . . . God grant Deliver-
> ance . . . upon all those whose Avarice impels them to countenance

and help forward the Calamities of their fellow Creatures. This I desire not for their Hurt, but to convince them of the strange Absurdity of their Conduct whose Words and Actions are so diametrically opposite. How well the Cry for Liberty, and the reverse Disposition for the exersize of oppressive power over others agree I humbly think it does not require the penetration of a Philosopher to determine.[33]

Phillis was seen as an example of what a black person could be capable of, touted as an example of black genius, that rare and arguably impossible thing to find.

Still, not until 1789 would the first motion against the slave trade be made in the House of Commons. Two days after the motion was made, the London daily paper the *Diary* reprinted Phillis's poem "An Hymn to Humanity," and one month later it would publish her poem to the earl of Dartmouth.

Not everyone loved Phillis's work. Thomas Jefferson, in whose library a copy of her *Poems* was found, and who was ardent slaveholder himself, disparaged Phillis, writing, "Misery is often the parent of the most affecting touches in poetry. Among blacks is misery enough, God knows, but no poetry. . . . Religion, indeed, has produced a Phillis Wheatley; but it could not produce a poet. The compositions under her name are below the dignity of criticism. The heroes of the Dunciad are to her, as Hercules to the author of that poem."[34] Jefferson was a man whose feelings about blacks were particularly severe and ambiguous. He made many racist comments in his *Notes on Virginia,* written in 1784, and expressed doubt as to whether there was "a black anywhere who was capable of tracing and comprehending the investigations of Euclid", yet he carried on a personal affair with one of his slaves for many years, reportedly fathering her child. Phillis may have been dismissed by others as "a single example of a Negro girl writing a few silly poems,"[35] but her journey from an African slave ship to the royal court in London had been too remarkable for her to allow critics to dissuade her.

The Europeans had been grappling with the question of whether or not the African "species of men," as they were commonly called, "could ever create formal literature, could ever master the arts and sciences. If they could, the argument ran, then the African variety of humanity was fundamentally related to the European variety. If not, then it seemed clear the African was destined by nature to be a slave."[36] Phillis was keenly aware of this sentiment; indeed, as a beloved slave of an aristocratic family in Boston, she had teetered between the two worlds of the white man and the slave her entire life, uniquely positioned to see and hear the rhetoric of freedom— freedom for the colonists and, less so, freedom for the slaves. On the day when she was called into the hall to defend herself against accusations and doubts, she spoke as much on behalf of all Africans as for herself alone. It has been said that her success opened the door for two traditions at once—the black American literary tradition, and the black women's literary tradition. Phillis would go on to travel a road no other black woman in the history of America had traveled: from slave to published author.

Phillis would, in later years, be called the mother of black American literature, with some going so far as to call her the mother of American writers; but her success was not hers alone; she was a woman who succeeded through the help of other women, a feat unheard of at the time. Even Anne Bradstreet had men secure her position, while Phillis's ventures were "rendered possible almost exclusively through the machinations of other women, both financially and intellectually."[37] Even in Great Britain, women authors of this period did not publish under their real names, so Phillis's achievement was doubly meaningful; she was not only a published black female slave, but a known one: "She was certainly the most

ardent female poet of the Revolution, if not, along with Philip Freneau, one of its two most poetic defenders."[38]

When Susannah died, Phillis was already a free woman. In a letter to
General Wooster in New Haven, dated October 18, 1773, she says
that "since my return to America my Master has, at the desire of my
friends in England, given me my freedom." She also makes clear
how anxious she is to receive funds from his sales of her work in New
Haven, "as I am now upon my own footing and whatever I get by
this is entirely mine. It is the chief I have to depend upon."[40]

Many have questioned Phillis's commitment to the fight against
slavery, though, and have criticized her unwillingness or inability to
speak more fervently against the oppression of her people and the
anguish suffered at the hands of white American Christians. Her
poetry reveals her feelings about slavery, although not as forcefully
as one might hope; but her letters are also repositories for how she
felt. The inherent contradiction between the colonists' fierce fight
for freedom and their attachment to the institution of slavery was
not lost on Phillis. William Robinson, a noted Wheatley historian,
has said, "Phillis Wheatley, speaking as a free, black woman, was
being quite personal and meant exactly what she said—that the
gross contradictions of a professedly freedom-loving, Christian slave
master did not require the penetration of a philosopher to determine; that even a twenty year old, African born female domestic
could penetrate such matters. And now, in February 1774, before the
flushed faces of Boston's modern Egyptians she could point to the
reality of the London-published volume of *Poems* as physical proof
of her ability not only to fathom such bigoted contradictions but
even to rise in something close to serene triumph above them."[41]

Postscript

One month after Phillis's return to America, Nathaniel came with his English wife to Boston in September. He sailed back to England a few months later, where he died in 1783, a father of three English-born daughters. He left one third of his estate to his wife and the rest to his daughters, never mentioning Phillis at all.

Mary, Phillis's tutor, became the wife of the Reverend John Lathrop. At about the time of her mother's death, her husband was driven from his Boston Second Society Church, and they were forced to flee. The British eventually burned the building down to use it for fuel. He and Mary, en route to Norwich, Connecticut, his birthplace, stopped in Providence, Rhode Island, where he filled an empty pulpit in the First Congregation Society. He was one of a handful of Boston ministers who preached scorching sermons against the British regarding the Boston Massacre, and actually had one of his sermons published in London in 1771. Mary suffered a long weakness in which she endured great distress, and she died on September 24, 1778, at the age of thirty-five.

Phillis may or may not have lived with John and Mary Lathrop for a short while when she wrote her poem to George Washington, which is dated Providence, October 26, 1775. She had visited with Washington in Cambridge a few days before the British evacuated Boston: "She passed half an hour with him, from whom and his officers she received marked attention."[41]

John Wheatley retired from business in 1771, and certainly Phillis was in his house as late as October 30, 1774, when she wrote a letter to John Thornton in England, saying, "My old master's generous behavior in granting me freedom, and still so kind to me, I delight to acknowledge my great obligation to him. This he did about three months before the death of my beloved mistress and at her desire as well as his own humanity."[42] John Wheatley died in

March 1778, and in his will of March 20, Phillis is not mentioned. He left his estate to his daughter and her heirs.

One month after John Wheatley's death, Phillis married a John Peters on April 1, 1778, when both were listed as "Free Negros." There is conflicting testimony regarding the character of this man, most of the negative views offered by whites, although a good part of it is positive. It was said, "He was a respectable colored man of Boston. . . . He kept a grocery store in Court-Street, and was a man of very handsome person and manners; wore a wig, carried a cane, and quite acted out 'the gentleman.'"[43] Also, it was said that "Peters not only bore good character, but was in every way a remarkable specimen of his race, being a fluent writer and intelligent man."[44] There is also documented evidence that he practiced law in the courts of Boston.

Sadly, though, whatever good fortune John Peters and Phillis may have enjoyed at the start of their union soon unraveled. Forced to flee Boston in an effort to escape the besieging British, they went to Wilmington, Massachusetts, where they lived in gnawing poverty and conceived three children. "Soon after, in 1784, her husband had become so shiftless and improvident, that he was forced to relieve himself of debt by an imprisonment in the county jail."[45]

Phyllis continued to write, however, and even managed to publish proposals for a second volume of poetry to be dedicated to Benjamin Franklin, to contain thirty-three poems and thirteen letters. She advertised it for "twelve pounds, neatly bound and lettered, and Nine pounds sew'd in blue paper. . . . The work will be put to the Press as soon as a sufficient numbers of encouragers offer."[46] The proposals ran in the *Boston Evening Post* and *Genera Advertiser,* beginning in October 30, 1779. Sadly, they failed to attract enough interest, and the volume was never published.

Destitute, Phyllis returned to Boston with her children, where she was able to stay with a kind niece of Mrs. Wheatley, an Elizabeth Walcutt. She lived with her and her daughter, Lucy Walcutt, for six weeks, helping Mrs. Walcutt in the day school the woman ran on Purchase Street, until her husband came to retrieve them. In 1784 she published an elegy "to the memory of Dr Samuel Cooper," a longtime friend who had died one month before. And when the Revolutionary War ended, she celebrated by publishing a poem called "Liberty and Peace."

She tried one last time—three months before her death—to interest the public in her volume of poetry, advertising in the September 1784 issue of the *Boston Magazine*. Again, she suffered rejection, and her work was never published. She spent the last few months of her life cleaning homes in the slums of Boston, and soon became severely ill. By this time, two of her children were dead.

Records indicate that the last months of her life were filled with exceptional hardship: "The sensitive Phillis, who had been reared almost as a spoiled child, had little or no sense of how to manage a household, and her husband wanted her to do just that; he made his wishes known at first by reproaches and followed these with downright bad treatment, the continuation of which so afflicted his wife that she grieved herself to death."[47]

On December 5, 1784, Phillis died at the age of thirty one with the last of her children. Her obituary was printed in several papers, and read in part, "Last Lord's Day, died Mrs. Phillis Peters (formerly Phillis Wheatley), aged thirty one, known to the world by her celebrated miscellaneous poems."

Her husband's fortunes continued to decline, as historians have concluded from the flyleaf of Wheatley's treasured gift book, Milton's *Paradise Lost:* "This book was given by Brook Watson, formerly Lord manor of London, to Phillis Wheatley—and after her death was sold in payment of her husband's debts. It is now presented to the Library of Harvard University at Cambridge, by Dudley L. Pickman of Salem. March 1824."

Throughout her life, Phillis fended off offers to return to Africa and partake in missionary work as a preacher. As early as 1771, the Reverend Samson Occum advanced notions of this to her in a letter to Susannah: "Pray, Madam, what harm would it be to send Phillis to her Native Country as a Female Preacher to her kindred, You know the Quaker women are allowed to preach, and why not others in an extraordinary case?"[48]

Phillis Wheatley wrote at least one hundred forty-five known poems, including over two dozen variants from the 1773 volume alone, and almost two dozen miscellaneous poems. The complete body of her work has been estimated to number over one hundred pieces of work, and she lived to see more than fifty of them in print. Also extant are nearly two dozen notes and letters. The large number of reprints her work has undergone (twenty reprints of her volume) is a testament to her poetry's continued and growing interest.

ABIGAIL ADAMS

Caption TK

First Adviser

ABIGAIL ADAMS

This is a stand-in for a quote which is, hopefully, forthcoming.
It should take up this much space

—ABIGAIL ADAMS

Massachusetts, 1797

THE PATH LEADING to Abigail Adams's home was completely covered in knee-deep, glistening white snow. As the boy trudged over the road on foot, with only a lightweight jacket on and a pad and pen in hand, he could see the lights of her home up ahead, warmly reflecting the land. He was only a hired hand, he told himself as he walked, but she had offered to help and seemed sincere. As he nervously took his last steps toward her door, he paused, scared to knock, fighting an urge to turn and run. After all, she was the wife of John Adams, the president of the United States. Maybe he had misunderstood. Why did she care if he ever learned to read and write?

The cold of the whipping wind was painful on his face, but the idea of making his way back through all that snow got the better of him: he braced himself and knocked.

Abigail heard something at the door, so faint she at first took it for a branch, or perhaps falling snow. But when it came a second time, she stopped and approached, thankful she'd been close enough to hear it. She used both hands to grasp the iron knob and yank back the stout oak door, frozen shut, as always, in the winter. There, small against all that shining, open space, stood James, head down, too timid to look up. She immediately remembered their lesson. She had put it out of her mind, not thinking there was any possible way a ten-year-old boy could make the long journey through waist-high drifts.

He looked painfully embarrassed, and at that moment Abigail felt her heart might break for the boy. She knew exactly how he felt. She sorely remembered the young girl who had wanted so desperately to learn, sitting at her brother's table, watching him do his studies, night after night being left out of the conversations and the lessons that fascinated her as nothing else had. In a world where school was reserved for boys, Abigail had always felt the sting of not being included in the boys' studies; unlike other girls her age, she had cared. As she let her eyes rise to his tiny trail of footsteps, already being covered by the snowfall, the meanness of cutting a person off from learning was almost more than she could bear.

"James, I am so happy you have come. Come in and warm up. I did not think you would venture out in this weather."

"No, ma'am," James sheepishly replied, as he walked into the hall, "I would not forget, ma'am."

Abigail shut the door and brushed the snow from his shoulders. She removed his thin, ragged coat and hung it to dry, then took off his wet shoes and socks and put them near the stove. She noticed James look up with eyes only slightly raised. She followed his eyes across the room and turned to see her young grandson, ten-year-old William, visiting with Abigail as he often did, enter the room. He stared at James with wonder. James stared back, then lowered his head.

"William," Abigail said, "this is James, my new student."

William stared.

"James," Abigail spoke kindly.

James looked up at her.

"This is your first lesson: never lower your eyes to anyone."

James immediately lowered his eyes.

"Do you understand?"

James slowly looked back up. This time he did not let his eyes lower. William walked over.

"How do you do?" William said.

"How do you do?" James replied.

"William, please put a kettle on the fire, dear. We need to fix James a cup of tea."

William ran off to do what he was told, and Abigail led James down the hall into her library. Abigail and James settled comfortably at her writing table, and moments later William brought some tea. James sipped tentatively.

"I see you have brought paper and pen," Abigail gently commented.

"Yes, ma'am."

"Well, then, let us get to work."

Inequality was rampant in the country, and its first and clearest manifestation was in what Abigail considered to be the antithesis of freedom: slavery. As the years passed, Abigail became increasingly preoccupied with her country's right to govern itself, a right that for her included blacks. It had been twenty-four years since she and John Adams had married, and in that time she had firmly established herself as a woman and a wife whose patriotism became the defining point in both her and John's life. After years of studying, reading, and thinking endlessly on the twin matters of freedom and equality, after having experienced firsthand the sting of being excluded from a real education because of her sex, Abigail had no patience for those who allegedly fought for freedom for the country while at the same time denying freedom to its own members. As she voiced to John on a number of occasions, "You know my mind upon this subject. I wish most sincerely there was not a slave in the province. It always appeared a most iniquitous scheme to me—fight ourselves for what we are daily robbing and plundering from those who have as good a right to freedom as ourselves."[1] As far back as when John wrote an article in the *Boston Gazette,* "Tracing the Rise and Fall of Human Freedom in the Face of Tyranny," which garnered him acclaim and launched his career as a public figure, he argued pointedly those sentiments that Abigail had argued passionately to him.

Though Abigail's influence over John would grow significant with time, to the point where he listened and deferred to many of her views, had she been told as a young girl that this would be so, she might not have believed it. Born as Abigail Smith in 1744, she was raised in the seacoast town of Weymouth, Massachusetts, in a large, rambling home perched on the top of a hill. She and her older sister, Mary, and her younger siblings, Elizabeth and William, spent their childhood in the rich landscape of farmlands, fields, and valleys. The children's mother, Elizabeth Quincy Smith, and their father, Parson William Smith, were an industrious, learned pair, her father having been educated at Harvard. His love of books and his library were well known among the townsfolk, and he succeeded in passing his love of reading on to all four of his children. Members of his congregation would often stop by the home, and lively literary discussions were almost always being held in one room or another. Religion and education were of foremost importance in the home, but as girls, Abigail and her sisters had been excluded from the formal schooling their brother William had received. Abigail lamented the fact that females were usually offered little to learn that was worth remembering, "dooming them to a life of talking about insipid and trifling topics, while males had the advantage of training and experience from which to make worthwhile comments."[2] But Parson Smith knew of Abigail's love of books, and made all three large libraries in the family available to her: his own, grandfather Quincy's, and Uncle Isaac's. Her grandparents lived in the neighboring town of Braintree, in a home called Mount Wollaston, high up on a hill overlooking the ocean, and Abigail loved to spend time there with her grandmother, who always praised her intellect and curiosity. There she would sit for hours, devouring books on every subject imaginable, and as she grew older, she did not hide her disappointment that she had been denied a formal education like her brother's. Her father had taught her and her sisters to read and write, but their mother would not allow Abigail and her sisters to attend the local dame school, no matter how much they begged. The bite of exclusion left its wound on Abigail; she would ever after be an ardent defender of equality in education, not only for women but also for blacks.

After dedicating many months of study with James, Abigail sat reading in her library one night when another knock came at her door, this one hard and persistent. She opened it to find a respectable neighbor, the father of two young boys in the evening school she had enrolled James in, looking back at her. His pinched, Puritan face looked disapproving in the cold.

"Mrs. Adams?"

"Won't you come in?"

"No, I'm afraid I won't be staying."

Abigail looked back, puzzled.

"I've just stopped by to report that many of us in school feel deeply troubled by the presence of others studying with our children."

"Others?" Abigail asked, not thinking.

Then it dawned on her. He was referring to James. She had received reports that he was already excelling far beyond many of the other boys.

"Pray, has the boy misbehaved?" Abigail inquired.

"Oh, no," replied the man.

"Well, then, why are there objections? And why haven't the others come, too?" she continued. The man stood silently facing Abigail, looking into her eyes as though searching for a recognition she was most clearly not going to give.

"I am here to request you withdraw the boy immediately, or the other boys will refuse to attend, and the school will close. Surely you understand?"

Abigail burned with anger at the blatant prejudice right before her eyes. It was 1797, and she could hardly have picked a more precarious time to engage in confrontation. Her husband, John Adams, had just won the presidential election, beating Thomas Jefferson by a mere three votes. His position against slavery, one heavily influenced by Abigail, was well known and in sharp contrast to that of Jefferson, a slaveholder himself. This issue had roiled many in the country and the Congress, and it was clearly not going to go away.

"No, I don't understand," Abigail answered, feeling her face flush with anger. At fifty-three years old, Abigail no longer had the shyness she once displayed as a young girl. The gentleman's face turned red, but no words came out of his mouth. He was obviously not used to being challenged, especially by a woman.

"The boy is a free man as much as any of the young men, and

merely because his face is black, is he to be denied instruction? How is he to be qualified to procure a livelihood? Is this the Christian principle of doing unto others as we would have others to do to us? You can send the boys to me, and you may tell them . . . that I hope we shall all go to heaven together."[3]

The man turned on his heel. Abigail watched him go, then slowly but firmly shut the door behind him. This, she would relay to her husband afterward, was the last she heard of the situation; James was permitted to remain at the school.

Braintree, Massachusetts, 1764

As a young woman of twenty, Abigail had already cultivated many of the attributes that would later make her a valued political counselor to her husband, the man who would go on to become the second president of the United States. Always frail as a child, Abigail shied away from the outdoors, instead choosing the life of the mind, spending her young days and nights immersed in reading and learning and thought. She studied political theorists, philosophers, and poets on her own and developed views early on about education and equality for women. When she first met John as a fifteen-year-old girl, she had no reason to believe he would be anything but the local lawyer he aspired to be, nor that her views, through him, would find a larger stage. At their first meeting he was a twenty-four-year-old graduate of Harvard College who did not express interest in knowing her further. In fact, John would confide in his diary that he found Abigail and her sisters neither "fond, nor frank, nor candid." He was a man who had been steeped in learning from a young age, an ardent inquisitor whose mind was as sharp as a blade, and whose passions were cerebral. She, while not having been given the luxury of an education like his, was a natural intellect who, in many ways, was self-taught through a childhood of rapacious reading. Though this shared intellectual passion would be one of the main bonds the two would share throughout their lives, at first glance neither felt the pull of attraction. As fate would have it, two short years later they would be reintroduced by Robert Cranch, Abigail's sister's fiancé, and this time they fell deeply in love. Their courtship would last three years, though very little of it was recorded by either of the pair. The letters that do exist show a genuine warmth and sense of humor, and an ever-increasing desire to spend their lives together. John frequently addressed Abigail in his letters as "Dear Diana," after the Roman goddess of the moon, or "Miss Adorable," and he signed his own letters "Lysander," after the Spartan hero. For her part, she loved his passion, conviction, and heart; he loved her intelligence, wit, and cheerfulness. On October 25, 1764, when she was almost twenty years old, Abigail was married by her father at the Weymouth parsonage, surrounded by a small circle of family and friends.

The house where John and Abigail lived when they first married was in Braintree, Massachusetts, a place that would later be renamed Quincy after her grandfather. It was a modest gray clapboard farmhouse, a "humble cottage," as Abigail called it, at the bottom of Penn's Hill, a home John had inherited which was part of the Adams family property. It was located between Plymouth and Boston, surrounded by beautiful green fields and farmland. With four rooms downstairs and two bedrooms on the second floor, the space was fine for Abigail and John. A parlor and large front room that John made into a law office and library comprised the main living area downstairs. A large kitchen with an enormous fireplace stood toward the back of the house, along with a little room off the kitchen for their young servant girl. The house was quite different from the large one where she had been raised, in the neighboring village of Weymouth; but though it was smaller than what she was used to, she did not feel deprived in the least; on the contrary, she was thrilled with her new role as wife and the chance to make her own home. She also discovered a new passion and pleasure, one she joyously shared with John: farming the land. The new couple spent significant time together planting, growing crops, clearing the property, and turning their new land into a working and productive farm. It was here they would start their family, Abigail giving birth to their first child in 1765, a girl named Nabby. And while they would go on to have three more healthy children—John Quincy in 1757, Charles in 1770, and Thomas in 1772—Abigail would also give birth to a girl named Susannah in 1768 who, only thirteen months later, would die, a loss so painful for Abigail and John that it would not be spoken of for years to come.

By 1774, as political events exploded all around them, John found himself more and more in the fray as his and Abigail's budding patriotism continued to swell. It was that year, when John was elected to the first Continental Congress, that Abigail's role as trusted counselor began to take shape in a different way than it had before. Up until this time, John had used Abigail as a trusted confidante in all of his political decisions, and Abigail had increasingly cultivated her philosophical thoughts on government and politics in the years since she first married John. But the arena in which he exerted influence had been smaller. Now, with his ascendance to Congress, his chance to sway public and private opinion and to legislate would grow dramatically. The stakes were markedly higher. John's position as one of only thirteen men chosen to represent the nation in this new thing called the Congress placed him squarely in the eye of the storm: his thoughts, his words, his passions, would now be looked at by a nation urgently in need of guidance and direction. At this moment in history, independence was still a matter of great dispute. Many in Congress and in the country felt that the twin ideas of equality and independence were absurd and dangerous. Having the first Continental Congress meet in Philadelphia in 1774 was itself a dangerous experiment, one in which all who participated risked almost certain death. Furthermore, it meant John would now be forced to remain in Philadelphia while

Abigail stayed home with the children, the beginning of what would be, unbeknownst to them, almost ten years apart.

Braintree, Massachusetts, 1775

After an eighteen-month separation, with John toiling away in Philadelphia and Abigail remaining in Braintree with the children, one winter night in December 1775 John made an unexpected visit home. From the very first days of their marriage, John and Abigail enjoyed a quite ritual of spending their evenings either strolling their property or sitting together in their library, reading, writing, and discussing the pressing issues of the day. Abigail cherished the times when she and John would discuss their opinions. She understood that her husband considered her an intellectual equal and, in fact, had been attracted to her for that very reason. This in turn had empowered her studies, and learning and reading filled the lonely hours when John was in Philadelphia. She had always listened to his ideas, but by the time the American Revolutionary War had begun, Abigail had evolved into more than just a sounding board. She had developed strong and passionate ideas of her own and was a formidable counselor. John sought Abigail's opinion with increasing frequency; and, as history would reveal, from those early days of the First Continental Congress and ever after, John listened.

On this cold December night, at home by the hearth with his "dearest friend" and adviser, John was as eager to discuss political principles with Abigail as she was to discuss them with him. Settled before a fire in the library, the children in bed, she prepared herself for the evening's conversation; she was bursting at the seams with questions for John.

She was bothered by the tax on liquor imposed on Massachusetts, as it seemed to draw trade away from her state. She suggested that all of the colonies be taxed, not only to encourage free trade, but also because of her antipathy toward the use of liquor. She also questioned the wisdom of using silver and gold as payment in trades, noting that this use served to make a dollar in silver a great rarity. Abigail's remedy was ingenious: "If any trade is alloud to the West Indies would it not be better to carry some commodity of our own produce in exchange?"[4]

After debating these issues for quite some time, the two compatriots sat in silence, John deep in thought. It was clear to Abigail that there was more on his mind than the usual issues of governance, and she ventured a guess with her question.

"There have been many rumors flying about, my dear, as to the position our Congress will take with Parliament. I, for one, have very strong ideas on the subject."

"You, my dear, have strong ideas on every subject worthy of thought," John replied with a devilish grin.

"I should hope you mean that as a compliment," she playfully answered, knowing perfectly well he did. "Are you considering an official document? What kind of language will you use? What is the general sentiment in Congress regarding how far to break with England? Will you finally outlaw slavery? Might you include women in your thoughts on equality? May I tell you what I think is absolutely necessary to include—"

"One moment, Abigail, really," John laughingly injected, exasperated with her quickness. "You barely give me the chance to answer your ten thousand questions." After a brief pause he lifted his head solemnly. "Abigail, there is much work to be done, as you well know. Congress is splintered on all sides. We have a country whose very existence is at stake. The time has come to declare our purpose or shrink from the fight."

On that particular night, what John had on his mind was the impending duty he and two of his fellow representatives were assigned. John had been one of three men placed on a committee whose task was the creation of a paper articulating unequivocally those principles of sovereignty upon which to officially found the nation. Congress had wrestled with divergent voices for some time at this point, but had emerged from the debate determined to declare its sovereignty. By early 1776, those in Congress recognized the need to reconcile philosophical ideas of freedom and natural rights with political action; John Adams, Edward Rutledge, and Richard Henry Lee had been chosen to put those ideas into words in a preamble to a document later to be called the Declaration of Independence. John had been chosen to write it, and as he sat at home with Abigail, this task was pressing on his mind.

Abigail's influence over John was especially strong during the early part of 1776, when, for Abigail, there was never a question of whether America should break with England. Though prominent men in Congress still wrestled with that issue, Abigail had seen clearly that unless a people were truly "free," there would be no way to forge a new government. She had argued her case to John many times and engaged in endless hours of correspondence with him, outlining her reasons, her arguments and theories. She had written, "Let us separate, they are unworthy to be our Breathren. Let us renounce them." In a typical letter to John during his time in Philadelphia before the outbreak of war, she had interrogated him, "If we separate from Britain, what code of Laws will be established? How shall we be governed so as to retain our Liberties? Can any government be free which is not administered by general stated Laws? Who shall frame these Laws? Who will give them force and energy?"

Abigail had used in her arguments, the theories of John Locke, Michael Harrington, Thomas Gordon, John Trenchard, and James Burgh political philosophers who regarded the rights they were after not simply as constitutional rights but as natural rights, "which it was the very purpose of government to protect."[5] She and John debated these principles passionately, each helping the other flush out the flaws, the weaknesses, and the reasonableness of what they declared. On this night by the fire, the two compatriots struggled yet again with just how far to go. For John, answering what he called Abigail's "ten thousand questions" helped him formulate his own ideas as well. It was a crucial time, with John being asked to help lead the nation into being. In the words he would finally use to declare his nation's independence and stir his country to passion, he echoed the strong sentiment of separation from Great Britain that Abigail had argued forcefully to him.

John and Abigail continued to discuss politics after he returned to Philadelphia a few months later, in February 1776. In whatever spare time he had, John wrote to Abigail, giving her the information she so fervently sought on the progress of Congress. Her craving for information and knowledge was compounded by the culture surrounding her at that time. The colonists were increasingly talking about the state of nature, the origin of government, the limits of authority, and the rights of man. John, clearly understanding Abigail's need to be involved in important dialogue, had in fact upon his return to Philadelphia sent her a copy of Thomas Paine's pamphlet *Common Sense,* saying it was "a vindication of doctrines to which they were both committed." At the time of the pamphlet's arrival, independence was still a matter of theory, even disputed by some. Abigail was grateful to receive it and could only wish "it would be carried speedily into Execution."[6] Interest in Paine's theory of equal rights was spreading, as witnessed by the sale of over 120,000 pamphlets within the first three months of publication.

It has been said that Paine "in one stroke propelled Americans into the great discovery of human equality toward which they had been moving unwittingly ever since they first denied Parliament's right to tax."[7] Abigail herself had this to say for the pamphlet: "I am charmed with the sentiments of *Common Sense* and wonder how an honest heart, one who wishes the welfare of their country, and the happiness of posterity, can hesitate one moment at adopting them; I want to know how those sentiments are received in Congress? I dare say there would be no difficulty in procuring a vote and instructions from all Assemblies in New England for independency, I most sincerely wish that now in the Lucky Minuet it might be done."[8]

The winter of 1776 had been filled with excitement for Abigail, in large part due to the arrival of *Common Sense*. Abigail, privy to the inner workings of Congress and its painstaking steps toward a document finally and formally declaring independence, felt vindicated by Paine's pamphlet and proud of herself for having seen so clearly so early on. Confident now that it was just a matter of time until independence was declared, exalted at such an idea, her mind returned to that other topic burning incessantly in her mind, and she decided to broach it, again, with John. She sat for a while, considering what to say.

Only a few months earlier, during John's visit home, Abigail had raised the issue of women's rights in this soon-to-be new nation. He had listened to her suggestion that women might stand to benefit from the notion of independence as well as men, but had been unwilling to turn his mind and attention to such an ancillary proposition as women just yet. Day after day, through the long, wintry months of February and March, she endured without John, alone in her home each night, writing him letter after letter filled with an unveiled passion and cry for liberty at all costs. But though John encouraged her to speak her mind, he also sometimes seemed bothered, as though he wasn't sure how much he wanted to hear. In the quieter moments of night, as she lay in bed, she sometimes doubted herself and the wisdom to speak so freely. Who was she, after all?

Now, however, sitting in her study on this beautiful spring evening, reveling in a newly awakened feeling of hope, her confidence and spirit lifted. She felt as though she had emerged from the long, dreary winter stronger than when it began; as though all the thought and energy she had given to the notion of liberty and independence had not been for naught, with Paine echoing all she had said. It was March 31, 1776, when Abigail put pen to paper and composed a letter, a letter that would garner fame for its vision and eloquence, famously beseeching her husband to "Remember the Ladies." She wrote:

> I long to hear that you have declared an independancy—and by the way in the new Code of Laws which I suppose it will be necessary for you to make I desire you would Remember the Ladies, and be more generous and favourable to them than your ancestors. Do not put such unlimited power into the hands of the Husbands. Remember all men would be tyrants if they could. If perticuliar care and attention is not paid to the Ladies, we are determined to foment a Rebelion and will not hold ourselves bound by any Laws in which we have no voice, or Representation.[9]

Abigail received a response, but John's amused answer was not what she had hoped for. He wrote back, saying:

> As to your extraordinary code of laws, I cannot but laugh. Your Letter was the first intimation that . . . a . . . Tribe more numerous and powerful than all the rest were grown discontented—This is rather too coarse a compliment but you are so saucy, I won't blot it out.

He had continued:

> Depend upon it, we know better than to repeal our masculine systems. Altho they are in full Force, you know they are little more than Theory. We dare not exert our power in its full Latitude. We are obliged to go fair, and softly, and in Practice you know We are the subjects. We have only the name of Masters, and rather than give up this, which would completely subject Us to the Despotism of the Petticoat, I hope General Washington, and all our brave Heroes would fight.[10]

Abigail's fierce resolve was evident in her next letter to him, a resolve that had clearly learned how to eloquently express itself. This time she was not willing to let go so easily.

> I cannot say that I think you very generous to the Ladies, for whilst you are proclaiming peace and good will to men, emancipating all nations, you insist upon retaining an absolute power over wives. But you must remember that Arbitrary power is like most other things which are very hard, very liable to be broken—and notwithstanding all your wise Laws and Maxims we have it in our power not only to free ourselves but to subdue our Masters, and without violence throw both your natural and legal authority at our feet.[11]

Though it seemed to Abigail that John was not willing to listen to her on this particular topic, his actions on May 26 reveal otherwise. In a letter to Brigadier General Joseph Palmer he discussed his views of government, who had the right to vote, and under what circumstances. "Shall we say, that every individual of the community, old and young, male and female, as well as rich and poor, must consent . . . to every act of Legislation?" And if this were impossible, as he assumed Palmer would say, then what about the "right of man to govern women without their consent?"

He ends the letter with a prophecy that reveals the degree to which he must have considered Abigail's words: "Depend upon it, Sir, it is dangerous to open so fruitful source of Controversy and altercation, as would be opened by attempting to alter the Qualifications of Voters. There will be no end of it—New claims will arise—Women will demand a vote."[12]

In this exchange, the depth of respect John felt for Abigail's views and the influence they had on him in his official duty as a member of Congress are exceptionally clear. While it would be many years until the wisdom and fairness of Abigail's arguments relating to women would be seen by a nation, at least part of Abigail's wish came true. On July 4, 1776, the famous declaration to the world, written by Thomas Jefferson, put into words the mind-boggling new idea that had now taken hold of the minds and hearts of the men and women in America: that "all men are created equal." The publication and the signing of the Declaration of Independence truly marked an end to what some historians have termed the war of ideas, and paved the way for the long and vicious fighting that we now call the American Revolutionary War.

Braintree, Massachusetts, 1778

After a separation of three years, in the autumn of 1777 Abigail waited with anticipation at the thought of having her husband back home. He had planned to resume his law practice and settle into life with her and the children in Braintree. After thirteen years of marriage, she had at this point been separated from John for three of them. John had promised that next time he was home, it would be for good.

Then the letters arrived. John had been elected joint commissioner to France. He was to join Benjamin Franklin and Arthur Lee, already in Paris, to negotiate a French alliance with America. He was to sail on the frigate *Boston,* a journey that would take months at sea, a wartime passage particularly dangerous for its weather and its time. Abigail pleaded to go with him.

But it was not to be. The passage, she knew, would be too dangerous for her small children. Besides, she herself was mortally afraid of the sea. She let John convince her that she and the children were best off at home. It was a crushing disappointment to her. She could not bear the thought of being separated, and moreover she had always wanted to travel abroad. But what really broke her heart was little Johnny. He had begged to go along, an adventure for an eleven-year-old boy that would hold high drama, excitement, and the chance to be with his father. Both John and Abigail, after much discussion, had seen the value inherent in such a trip—educationally, diplomatically, and experientially—and in the end they agreed.

A bitterly cold day dawned with a sadness unlike any Abigail had known before. Father and son were already downstairs in the kitchen when Abigail descended from what had been a restless sleep. The two spoke in hushed whispers, a father-son team already bursting with anticipation of what lay ahead. Trying hard to conceal her sadness, Abigail made inquiries as to their belongings, papers, luggage. She spoke distractedly, as if going through the motions of an unreal event, trying quietly to absorb how her long-awaited reunion with John had turned into yet another separation, one that promised this time to be much longer and more dangerous than all the others—a separation that was now claiming little Johnny too.

After all the food, clothes, bedding, supplies, and animals—six live chickens and two fat sheep—were packed onto the coach, John turned to his children to say good-bye. Embracing thirteen-year-old Nabby first, he reminded her to write him regularly, keep him abreast of news, and of course, to mind her mother and do her chores. Ever the quiet, reserved one, Nabby gave her father only a slight smile and quick hug, although her letters afterward would reflect a deep sadness and fear she might never see her father or brother again. John knelt down to little Charles and Thomas, hugging them both at the same time. It was soon little Johnny's turn to say good-bye. He approached his mama and embraced her, whispering in her ear never to worry, that he and Papa would be fine, that he loved her and would write to her always, which he did. But on that day, she did not realize it would be four months until she would hear a word from either of them. Saying good-bye was, Abigail wrote in her diary, like tearing her heart out, but she did not show it.

John brought Abigail aside, out of sight of all the rest. Though they had said their real good-byes the night before, he now wanted one last private moment with her. Reaching down, he pulled a tiny locket out of his breast jacket pocket. In it sat a picture of a lonely woman, watching a ship sail off. She leaned on a round piece of wood on which was inscribed, "I yield whatever is right." This last token was almost too much for Abigail to bear. She had deliberately chosen to say her good-byes here, at home, not to have to see them set sail on a ship into the black sea. John must have seen the dread in Abigail's eyes as he quickly turned to leave.

As Abigail gathered her remaining children around her, holding their little hands tightly, she watched with a "full heart and weeping eye"[13] as her husband and son rode out of sight. Not knowing when or whether she might see John again, she clung to the one passion that had given her the strength to endure: the idea that John was fighting for freedom, for her country. She repeated to herself that she was sacrificing her husband to her country, and her fiery patriotism gave her strength.

Braintree, Massachusetts, 1784

Abigail had seen John for only a few months in 1779 when he returned from Europe with Johnny, after a year and a half abroad. After a mere one-month reunion, news came again. This time John was appointed sole minister plenipotentiary to France. With this news and John's eagerness to accept, Abigail's plans to resume life in Braintree were once and for all shattered. To make matters worse, this time John would not only be taking little Johnny again, but also nine-year-old Charles. She was being asked to relive the pain of parting all over again, a parting now claiming two sons. She had spent years dedicated to freedom for her country, she had actively encouraged John to work for its cause; but at times such as this, when it seemed she was being asked to sacrifice her family, she wondered, how much more of a price would freedom exact?

The five years of John's absence passed slowly, witnessing Abigail turn forty and become more independent than ever. She considered herself widowed, and as such, took great pains to keep order for her family. Busy as she was raising Charles, Thomas, and Nabby (Charles returned home after three years away, sooner than either his father or his brother) as well as tending to her extended family of sisters, brothers-in-law, nieces, nephews, and cousins, Abigail also had responsibility for her family's finances. She leased out her farm rather than run it herself, which proved to be a profitable decision; she managed the family finances, becoming skilled at financial trading, exchanging hard currency (silver) for the paper money issued by the Continental Congress; she ordered cloth, rugs, china dishes, and glassware from Holland and Spain and resold them at a profit to eager customers in Braintree; she acquired several small farms when they were sold at good prices; and she stayed well informed of current events by John's political associates and through her own independent friendships, particularly with her closest friend, Mercy Otis Warren.

Abigail and Mercy had first met during the spring of 1773, when Abigail had accompanied John on one of his many trips to Plymouth to attend a court session there. Mercy was the sister of James Otis, one of John's heroes, and the wife of James Warren, a leading Massachusetts radical. John often visited the Warren home when in Plymouth, and had brought Abigail with him on one of his trips. It was in their home, during one of their frequent political meetings, that Abigail and Mercy met. They developed an instant attraction to each other, both ardent patriots and considerable intellects in their own rights, a status unheard of among women at that time.

Soon after the visit, Mercy initiated a correspondence with Abigail. Abigail was flattered and thrilled by an opportunity to converse with a woman of Mercy's reputation. Mercy had herself become an active propagandist for the Patriot cause in 1772, when she published a play entitled *The Adulateur*. She would eventually become a well-known literary and political figure, writing plays and poetry with clear political intent. Mercy was forty-five at the time, and Abigail had been only twenty-nine. But they shared great minds and a passionate interest not only in the politics of the day but also in the state of affairs for women. It was to Mercy that Abigail would eventually reveal her innermost feminist thoughts.

Through the difficult, lonely years between 1779 and 1784, with John away in Europe, Abigail found in Mercy not only a fellow patriot and intellectual companion but also a woman who thoroughly understood her plight, as Mercy herself was suffering through a lengthy separation from her own beloved husband, James. The Revolution and its war demanded much from its sons, but it also took much from its daughters; the two women considered themselves practically "war widows." The body of letters between Abigail and Mercy reveal an intimacy and friendship deeper than most women shared at the time, most likely because of their ability to connect on many more levels than women traditionally had access to. They could talk about typical domestic concerns, such as where to buy fabric; they could commiserate as mothers, each sharing her fears and joys concerning her children; they could offer one another support as the wives of men deeply involved in the revolutionary cause; and they could enjoy an intellectual camaraderie, since both were not only passionate about politics and the Revolution but informed.

Abigail not only continued her appeals to women, she also did not stop inquiring John as to his political maneuvering and developments and, most importantly, never stopped advising him as to issues of state. Her letters to him during his years in Europe are rife with opinions, entreaties, suggestions, and reminders, all dealing with political theory and principle.

Now, in 1784, John had written for her, asking that she and Nabby travel overseas and join him in Europe. Abigail felt a mixture of joy and fear. The thought of being with John again filled her with a happiness she hadn't known in years, but as the reality of leaving her home and her little boys set in, she suffered many fitful nights agonizing over what her decision should be. Finally, she agreed.

As she placed the last of her belongings on the front step, Abigail turned toward her home for what felt like a last good-bye. She scrutinized her kitchen one last time—her equipment was in order, her linens packed away, her garden meticulously tended—and let herself wander to the back of her lawn for a last look at her farm and her animals and her pasture. She had loved this home, a place filled with so many memories, a place that had shielded her from outside harm, a property that had yielded harvest for her family for what had been almost fifteen years. She had witnessed war, known love and friendship, grown from a young girl into an experienced wife and homemaker. She had given birth to five children in this home, burying one and raising four. She had educated herself in this library and become a true farmer on this land—and now she was leaving. She stood in her garden, frozen, as if glued to the ground. It was Nabby's voice that finally broke the silence.

"Mama, I have been calling you. It is time to go. Aunt Mary has arrived. The boys are waiting, too."

At the mention of the boys, Abigail felt her stomach tighten and a lump come into her throat. This was the moment she had been dreading from the time she knew for certain that she and Nabby would be boarding the frigate *Active* and setting sail for England to reunite with John.

When John first sent Abigail his request for her to join him in Europe, he had asked her to bring Nabby and leave Thomas and Charles with her brother-in-law Robert Cranch, the schoolmaster. Charles, who was twelve at the time, had already made the trip to Europe once, and neither John nor Abigail felt it fair to ask him to do it again, nor did they want to interrupt his education. If she brought ten-year-old Thomas with her, then Charles would be left home alone. Heart-wrenching as this decision was for her, she had to agree with John that the boys would be better off at home. She arranged to leave them in her sister Elizabeth's care, where she knew her sister and brother-in-law John Shaw would be certain to continue the boy's education and preparation for Harvard.

Abigail turned the corner of the yard, and there, standing together, in their breeches, open shirts, and ruffled hair, were her two little loves, Thomas and Charles. She paused, looking up at her sisters, Mary and Elizabeth, in whose eyes she could see the gentle strength and faith that she had become used to seeing over all their years together. She looked at Mary, into the eyes of her favorite sister, her close friend and ally in all she did and said and thought. Now, at this moment, when she needed Mary's strength as never before, the look she received reassured her as always that all would be all right and that all was in the hands of God. She slowly knelt down to the boys and embraced them for what she dared to imagine might be the last time.

"You be good boys and mind your aunt and uncle. Nabby and I will write to you every day. Study hard, do your chores, write to me of all your news."

They nodded, Charles becoming tearful and Thomas quietly playing with a stick he had picked up from somewhere outside. Abigail hugged each boy so hard and for so long that it was not until Mary made a noise with her throat that Abigail raised herself up. She gave Elizabeth a tight hug and thanked her yet again for ensuring the care of her sons. She then turned to Mary and her brother-in-law Richard Cranch, and the two sisters tearfully laughed as they embraced and reassured each other they would all be together again very soon. No longer able to stand the pain, Abigail turned quickly away from the carriage as Elizabeth and the boys climbed into it, abruptly called Nabby to her side, and, forcing herself to watch the coach lest her boys think she didn't care, watched as it rode off down the road, leaving a whirling circle of dust behind.

The last memory of that day was the voice of her two little boys yelling good-bye, trailing the clatter of the coach from behind, voices that grew fainter and fainter as they rode farther away.

The danger inherent in her voyage was well known to Abigail, and the real possibility that they might not return hung in the air like a thick cloud of smoke, choking her every time she dared think of it. She had agreed to pack up and leave all to fate: she gathered her strength, her bravery, and her determination and boarded a ship out of Boston with Nabby, embarking on June 20, 1784, an overseas voyage to visit the man whose devotion to politics would not let him come to her.

Upon hearing the news of his wife's decision to join him, John Adams had confided in his friend, the unofficial American chargé d'affaires at The Hague, when he said, "I hope to be married once more myself, in a few months, to a very amiable lady whom I have inhumanly left a widow in America for nine years, with the exception of a few weeks only. Ask Madame Dumas whether she thinks she has Patriotism enough to consent that you should leave her for nine years pro bono publico? If she has, she has another good title to the character of an Heroine."[14]

The *Active* was a small American merchant ship. There was one large cabin where the passengers took their meals and spent most of their time. Two smaller cabins served as staterooms for the women. Abigail and her maid shared one; Nabby and the only other woman on board shared the other. The men slept in the main cabin. The women forced to keep their doors open in order to have any fresh air, had little privacy. Almost immediately, seasickness set in with the women on board. As the tiny ship was tossed about the Atlantic, with "everything wet, dirty and cold, ourselves Sick," the reality of the voyage she had undertaken began to dawn upon Abigail. For a woman who had in her forty years never spent any time on the sea or in boats, the journey from Massachusetts to the shores of England promised to be, at the very least, arduous. Despite her and the crew's best efforts to clean the tiny ship, the filth of the boat only made her seasickness worse, as it caused the most "loathsome" smells to fill the air: cargo fumes, leaking fish oil, and potash. To make matters worse, the damp chill from the Atlantic had caught inside Abigail's bones, making her rheumatism worse. She was forced to stay in a bed that itself was also damp, day after day, and she began to feel as though she were locked inside a "partial prison." She was shown her room: an "eight-foot-square stateroom, with its small, solitary window fenced with iron, opened into the men's cabin, which also happened to serve as dining quarters. It was shut only when it was time to dress or undress, otherwise she would have suffocated, she was positive, or at least have been poisoned by the foul air that clotted her every breath." [15]

After some time, however, both she and Nabby not only acclimated themselves to life at sea but also began developing a new appreciation for its beauty—the vast, limitless blue water, the sparkling sky overhead, the wildlife that joined them on their voyage.

Finally the day came, four weeks after they had set sail, when they were able to see land. As she watched in awe, Abigail could see the shore from a distance, and a joy rose in her heart at the thought of soon being reunited with her husband and son. Perched near the edge of the boat, she eagerly viewed the approaching shore with a mixture of trepidation and excitement, pondering the journey she had undertaken and the new one that now seemed upon her.

After a six-hour ordeal in which the *Active* found itself caught in an unexpected storm, the little ship landed on the shores of Deal safely. Abigail had crossed the Atlantic, a feat she had both feared and craved, and as she, Nabby, and the other passengers made their way from Deal to London in a coach over rocky roads, she reflected yet again on the vicissitudes of life. Arriving in London, Abigail thought the city both "magnificent and beautiful." But while touring London proved exciting, Abigail could barely contain her impatience for John and John Quincy to arrive. She had only seen John Quincy for a brief three-month interval over the past six years and five months. The last time she laid eyes on him, he had been a twelve-year-old boy; now he was a seventeen-year-old man. She worried she might not recognize him. As she sat in the hotel room waiting for her son's arrival, memories of him flooded her mind, one in particular she had never been able to rid herself of. She had often wondered if he, too, remembered that night the way she did. She closed her eyes, instantly recalling the roar of the cannon and the way the earth shook. She had awoken with a start that night, quickly falling out of bed, and by the time she had reached for her nightdress and lit a candle, seven-year-old Johnny was already there, standing in her doorway.

"Mama, are you all right?" he had asked, fiercely protective of his mother. Grabbing him in a quick, tight embrace, Abigail had struggled to stay calm.

"I am fine. Where are your brothers and sister?" she had asked.

"Still asleep. Can I stay with you?" The silence had felt eerie in the wake of the explosion.

"I must go downstairs to make sure everything is in order. You stay here and—"

"No, I want to come with you," Johnny had protested, his voice filled with strength.

She marveled at the courage of her oldest son. Even then, he had taken it upon himself to be the man of the house whenever he knew John was away on business, as he had been that night.

"We must go quietly."

She held Johnny's hand tightly as they ventured down the stairs. Seeing and hearing nothing amiss, Abigail peered through the large window in the living room. All was dark. How she wished her husband were home from Philadelphia. Suddenly the stillness was shattered by another explosion of cannon and shells, this one not so near. She and Johnny stood frozen, as though bracing themselves for something—although they knew not what. After a long wait, Johnny suggested they go outside. Abigail was inclined to say no, but something in the noise they had heard sounded so far off, she had agreed.

The air had been heavy with heat. They crept quietly in the darkness. They walked a hundred yards, but could see nothing of any significance.

"Shall we climb Penn's Hill to get a better view?" Abigail suggested, answering herself by the quick footsteps she took in that direction.

Finishing the fearful climb up the huge rock that made up Penn's Hill, they reached the top, out of breath, and stared in horror. In the distance, across the shimmering bay, they watched as a mass of black smoke reached into the sky, spreading its darkness over what had, moments before, been Charlestown. There, holding little Johnny's hand, the two of them had witnessed firsthand what would later be named the Battle of Bunker Hill (or Breeds Hill). (Years later, John Quincy said it was a scene he had never forgotten.)

A sudden knock on the door jolted her out of her memory, and for a split second she forgot where she was. Then, as if hit with a bolt of lightning, she realized it was probably him at the door. Nabby came bounding out of the bedroom, a look of exquisite glee and excitement on her face. After all these years, they were going to see their beloved Johnny.

Trembling, Abigail opened the door to a tall, handsome young man she did not know. She was afraid to speak, for fear it was not truly him. "O, my mama and my dear sister!" was all that he said as she, Nabby, and her little Johnny tearfully embraced, with tears of joy and sadness mingled together.

One week and a day later, as Abigail sat writing at her desk, there was another knock on her door as she heard it open. She turned to see John, who stood nervously by the door. Abigail's reunion with him was so overwhelming that she was not even able to write about it. All she recorded was a note, "Poets and painters wisely draw a veil over those scenes which far surpass the pen of the one and the pencil of the other."[16]

After a joyous and emotional family reunion, on August 8, 1784, Abigail and John traveled to France, where they settled into a magnificent old limestone mansion in the suburb of Auteuil, just outside of Paris. They would remain here for almost one year, and it was during this time in Paris, one of the happiest the Adams had ever known, that their relationship with Thomas Jefferson grew into a deep friendship, both between him and John, and, separately, between him and Abigail. They spent much time together, Abigail and Thomas, strolling through the parks, dining, attending theater, discussing politics. Abigail immensely enjoyed Jefferson's company, his wit, his brilliance, calling him "one of the choicest ones on earth."[17] For his part, he was completely enthralled by Abigail's intellect, political acumen, and knowledge. They shared many of the same passions, most obviously their patriotism and love of their country, and their fierce belief in its autonomy. It had been a long time since Abigail had experienced that sense of empowerment when she spoke, as though all she said held importance and mattered. With Jefferson she felt a renewed sense of belonging to the struggle that had defined their lives; no longer was she home in the background writing letters, but here, in person, in the midst of activity, sought out by Jefferson, who immensely respected her views. When the time came for Abigail and John to leave Paris for London, it was 1785, and they did so with a heavy heart.

After a time in London, it was with great joy they were reunited with Jefferson when he came to London and stayed with them, rekindling the friendship and bond they had all enjoyed years earlier. When the time came for Abigail and John to sail back to America in May 1788, they parted with Jefferson as the dearest of friends. Neither could have then known that in three short years their deep and abiding friendship would come to an end; for, unlike the revolutionary activity in America that had brought them together, a new and dangerous uprising was on the verge of taking place in France, one that would rip them apart. The world was on the cusp of witnessing an event that would call into question those principles the colonists had so fiercely and successfully fought over: the French Revolution.

Inspired by America's success in determining self-rule, the French would revolt against the monarchy of King Louis XVI, demanding equal rights. At first many in America cheered this move; but as the Revolution became more brutal, many of the early supporters recoiled in horror. When both King Louis XVI and Marie Antoinette were beheaded, John Adams said, "I am a mortal enemy to monarchy, but I am no King killer."[18] Abigail and John understood the French Revolution's roots but feared the bloody violence used to effectuate its goals. Jefferson, on the contrary, was an ardent and outspoken supporter of the revolutionaries, seeing in their fight a mirror of the one America had waged a decade earlier. As the violence grew, so did the debate in America as to its merits; but for Abigail and Jefferson, their difference of opinion in this matter would become the tip of the political iceberg down which they were about to slide. Passionate as ever over her convictions, politics became personal as the two friends embraced different emerging philosophies.

This schism was a taste of what would slowly grow into a full-blown difference in political thought between Abigail and Jefferson. In April 1789, one year after Abigail's return from Europe, she and John learned that John had been elected vice president, an honor and acknowledgment of his years of work and service during the Revolution. Shortly thereafter, Abigail was forced to leave her beloved Braintree, the home to which she had just returned, and follow John first to New York, then on to Philadelphia, where the federal government had been moved. While John's service as vice president would last ten years, Abigail would not live with him in Philadelphia for the last five years of his term due to concerns for her health. As they had done during earlier separations, they wrote to each other constantly, John still seeking Abigail's advice and thoughts on issues of grave significance and analyzing solutions together. The years in which John served as vice president brought with them unbelievable progress, as they produced among other things the groundwork for a judicial system, ratification of the Constitution, and approval of the Bill of Rights. But the immense gains of a nation had a price, both personal and political, for those involved.

During the years between 1789 and 1797, political parties formed in America, reflecting the intense difference of opinions on how the country ought to be run. This difference centered primarily around the extent of power endowed to the federal government, with the Republicans feeling the states ought to control more of their own decisions, and the Federalists wanting awesome power for the central government, including the creation of a central bank. Thomas Jefferson, serving as secretary of state, headed the Republican Party, while the Adamses were clearly Federalists. This change in political landscape coincided with events in the French Revolution and, making matters more complicated, with France and Britain's declarations of war on each other. There was widespread fear of America being dragged into the conflict, with the Republican Party fiercely anti-British and the Federalist Party opposed to France. By 1797, John Adams's term as vice president to George Washington was over, leaving him in a position to run for the presidency against his old friend and new political rival Thomas Jefferson in the new election. Adams won by three votes, making Jefferson his vice president.

Abigail did not witness John's inauguration in Philadelphia on March 4, 1797, as she remained in Braintree for health reasons (Braintree was now renamed Quincy), but immediately afterward John wrote her, "I never wanted your advice and assistance more in my life. The times are critical and dangerous and I must have you here to assist me."[19] Abigail obliged him, traveling in April to Philadelphia, where she would live with him in the president's mansion for the next three years, until they moved once again to the new capital in Washington in 1800. After all these years, Abigail's behind-the-scenes influence was about to grow even larger, with her role as presidential confidante noted with astonishment, particularly by political opponents. Others reacted to her influence differently, trying to recruit her help in their cause. Abigail, for her part, was not intimidated by those who disapproved of her influence: "I will never consent to have our sex considered in an inferior point of light. Even if a woman does not hold the reins of government, I see no reason for her not judging how they are conducted."[20] After all these years, Abigail's determination that women be counted along with men remained as fierce as ever. As the president's wife, she continued to do what she always had—advise her husband on all things political. There was no way, after all these years, with John finally at the helm of government, she was now about to lower her voice. But while she was grateful that John had been granted the honor of serving his country, the tenure of his presidency was difficult for Abigail in many ways, not the least of which was the domestic political intrigue between Alexander Hamilton and her husband, which would mar his term.

While life as first lady was grand in many ways, she was weary, too, repeatedly writing her sisters how much she missed her humble farm and how she longed to spend more time with her family. Nor did her friendship with Jefferson repair itself during the tenure of the presidency; on the contrary, the strained relationship faltered even more.

While historical accounts differ as to Jefferson's role in the many troubles of John Adams's time in office, it is clear that Jefferson's Republican Party, specifically Alexander Hamilton and James Madison, were out to get John Adams from the start. His tenure as president lasted one term and was marred with conflict and controversy. Even though he had avoided war with France, his (and Abigail's) support of the Alien and Sedition Acts had been very unpopular, as had his resistance to maintaining a standing army. He had suffered the disloyalty of his own cabinet, been deprived the benefit of a vice president whose views were similar to his own, and been the object of Alexander Hamilton's scorn and treachery. Throughout it all, Abigail stood steadfastly by John, defending him and his principles to all with whom she spoke.

Adams lost the next election to Jefferson in 1801, and in one of his last moves before leaving office, he appointed Chief Justice John Marshall, a man whose political bent was clearly opposed to Jefferson's, to the Supreme Court. This was the only move Adams had made, Jefferson would later say, that "was personally unkind."[21] But whether it was an act of spite or not—he denied to Abigail years later ever having even known about it—one of the first acts of Jefferson's presidency was to recall John Quincy from his appointment as commissioner of bankruptcy, a move that looked "so particularly pointed" that even some of Jefferson's friends commented on it. Under these circumstances, Jefferson's friendship with both John and Abigail came to a bitter end.

It was not until 1804, when Abigail read of the death of Jefferson's daughter Polly, that her heart sank with grief. She had just suffered the loss of her own, beloved Charles to alcoholism. Her heart-break prompted her to pick up pen and paper and write to Jefferson, who was still president at the time, after a three-and-a-half-year silence. Without mentioning to John that she was doing so, she expressed her deep sadness and regret at hearing the news: "Reasons of various kinds have withheld my pen, until the powerful feelings of my heart have burst through the restraint, and called upon me to shed the tear of sorrow over the departed remains, of your beloved and deserving daughter, an event I most sincerely mourn."[22]

Jefferson responded with sincere gratitude, expressing regret "that circumstances should have arisen to draw a line of separation between us."[23] Conveying his feelings of sadness at the loss of her friendship, he said he would now take advantage of an opportunity he had long wished for. He decided to open old wounds and launched into polit-ical events and their "unfortunate bearings" on private friendships: "The injury these have sustained has been a heavy price for what has never given me equal pleasure."[24] Yet he could not refrain from men-tioning some of their old political disagreements, especially those affronts he considered to have been committed against him by John. By appointing some of his "most ardent political enemies," John had guaranteed that Jefferson must do without "the faithful cooperation" of his own views. His remarks so incensed Abigail that she responded in kind with her own argument on behalf of John and his actions. This initiated what would become a five-month correspondence cen-tered on political issues, not personal niceties, all unbeknownst to John; a correspondence wherein Abigail eloquently and forcefully told Jefferson not only what she thought of his political point of view but, more amazingly, what she thought of his personal behavior.

She continued in her next letter to Jefferson to "freely disclose" what she felt had "severed the bonds of former Friendship" and placed Jefferson in a light "very different" from that in which she had once viewed him: his release of a man named James Callender, who had been jailed under the Sedition Act for "the basest libel, the lowest and vilest Slander" against her husband.²⁵ The law in question was the Sedition Act of 1790, and the dispute questioned with whom power to prosecute First Amendment violations should rest, the federal government or the states. Jefferson explained he had discharged every person punished under the Sedition Act because he considered "that law to be a nullity as absolute and as palpable as if Congress had ordered us to fall down and worship a golden image."²⁶ He had freed the offenders without asking "what the offenders had done or against whom they had offended."²⁷ In his point of view, the right to control the freedom of the press was the state's, not the federal governments.

Abigail would not capitulate. Clinging to the Federalist notion, derived from English common law, that the First Amendment did not deprive Congress of power to influence speech and press, she wrote, "If there are no checks to be resorted in the Laws of the Land, and no reparation to be made to the injured, will not Man become the judge and avenger of his own wrongs, and as in the late instance [referring to the duel between Hamilton and Burr] the sword and pistol decide the contest?" She continued, "I have understood that the power which makes a Law, is alone competent to the repeal. If a Chief Magistrate can by his will annul a Law, where is the difference between a republican, and a despotic Government? That some restraint should be laid upon the assassin, who stabs reputation, all civilized Nations have assented to. No political character has been secure from attacks, no reputation so fair, as not to be wounded by it, until the truth and falsehood lie in one undistinguished heap."²⁸ Though their political exchange continued, eventually Abigail felt that "faithful are the wounds of a friend. I would forgive as I hope to be forgiven."²⁹

Not one year later, in a twist of fate, those words would come back to haunt her when she suffered another loss so great she barely knew how to describe it: the loss of her cherished friendship with Mercy Otis Warren. Mercy's book *History of the American Revolution* was published in 1805. In it, Mercy pointedly criticized John's presidency and politics. Though a political rift had grown around the differences in party opinion, both Abigail and John were hurt and furious; Abigail felt tremendously betrayed by her old friend. The friendship, which had lasted thirty-two years, had been one of the most intimate Abigail had ever known; yet, ultimately, it could not withstand such political difference. It was John this time putting pen to paper in anger and denouncing Mercy's treatment of him as unjust, inaccurate, and biased. Mercy responded in kind, and the two old friends traded insults and accusations that burned a hole in the fabric of friendship that had lasted all these years. Here again was another instance of political difference overshadowing heart, but for these political creatures, politics and heart were one and the same. In the end, it would seem, Abigail could not or would not separate the two. She who had devoted her life to her country's cause, in so many ways, could now in the twilight of her years look back on all she had gained with the knowledge of all she had lost. The Revolution had demanded of them all something different; Abigail truly felt she had given her all. The memory of the grand fight and what came after still made her beam with pride, but no longer without sad reminders of the high price she had paid. While she was a woman of extraordinary intellect and will, she was also a woman of heart, and her sadness over the loss of such close ties stayed with her until the end, right alongside the memory of what she and John had accomplished together.

Postscript

Abigail's last years were a true mix of heartbreak and joy. While she had John home with her again after all these years, the separation of her family members continued. In 1809 John Quincy was appointed ambassador to Russia, and though she knew he would be gone for a desperately long time, Abigail encouraged him to go. Two years later, she suffered the death of her beloved sister Mary and Mary's husband, Richard Cranch, within days of each other. And two years after that, Abigail would experience the deepest sorrow of her life.

In 1813 Abigail's only daughter Nabby died of breast cancer at the age of forty-eight. This loss was almost more than Abigail could bear, for her daughter's life had been so brief and laced with such hardship. She found consolation in the two small children Nabby left behind, as she buried herself in their care, staying as busy and productive as ever. Abigail continued writing letters, as her daughter-in-law Louisa wondered how she "never appeared at a loss for a subject."[30] Abigail acknowledged "At the age of seventy, I feel more interest in all that's done beneath the circuit of the sun than some others do at, what shall I say, thirty five and forty?"[31]

That great and burning intellectual curiosity would continue to bring her contentment in old age, and she was given the gift of living long enough to see John Quincy, in 1817, be appointed secretary of state by then-president Madison and return home from Russia. She enjoyed a wonderful reunion with him and his family, but sadly, she would not be granted much time: one year later, in 1818, she contracted typhoid fever. She put up a brave struggle against the disease and for a few days seemed to be winning, but it was to be her last. Surrounded by family members, with John at her bedside, she died on October 28, two weeks before her seventy-fourth birthday. John quietly said, "I wish I could lie down beside her and die too."[32] But that was not to be. He would go on to live eight more years, talking about his remarkable wife and her remarkable wit and intelligence, her stubborn independence, her courage, and her love for her family. He was blessed with the honor of witnessing John Quincy become the sixth president of the United States, a moment Abigail would have relished with deep pride. On the Fourth of July, 1826, on the fifty-year anniversary of the signing of the Declaration of Independence, John

Adams died at the age of ninety-one. Mysteriously, Thomas Jefferson died on that exact day, too.

Looking back on her life, one filled with tremendous accomplishment, Abigail acknowledged in the end that friendship and family had given her richness like nothing else. It was, therefore, a true blessing for Abigail that she and her oldest, dearest friend Mercy Otis Warren forgave one another, a reconciliation that took place in 1812, when Abigail was sixty-eight years old. These two intellectual powerhouses had chosen different ways to express their passionate belief in liberty, but each had been heard, each had been listened to. Though Abigail would enjoy great fame, partly due to her husband's position of power, Mercy would fade into obscurity, known to only a handful of the most ardent students of American history. But Mercy's influence had rippled through prerevolutionary America, where her daring, her patriotism, and her words helped ignite the spark that would lead a nation to war.

James Adams had this to say of the two female powerhouses: "But if I were of opinion that it was best for a general Rule that the fair should be excused from the arduous Cares of War and State, I should certainly think that Marcia (Mercy) and Portia (Abigail) ought to be exceptions, because I have ever ascribed to these Ladies a Share and no small one neither,—in the Conduct of our American affairs."[33]

So it was that a "founding father" acknowledged his wife's involvement in the political fervor of those days. It was clear to all at the time that Abigail had been more than simply a first lady, more than the wife of one president and the mother of another—she had been a good adviser, her words and her writings echoing through, and making a difference in, the mind of the man who stood before a nation and helped bring it into being.

MERCY OTIS WARREN

Caption TK

Her Pen as Sword

MERCY OTIS WARREN

🖎

The feelings of the heart will dictate the language of truth,
and the simplicity of her accents will proclaim the infamy of those
who betray the rights of the people.

—MERCY OTIS WARREN

Boston, 1776

THE COLONISTS LOOKED ON in despair as the ragged British soldiers ranged across the streets of Boston. These soldiers had been let loose in the city, a swarm of men, officially prisoners of the American army with nowhere to go. After their defeat in Saratoga, they had descended on the city, wreaking havoc with an arrogance reserved for victors. Boston's residents had been forced to endure their filth and smells, their obnoxious behavior, their rioting. To make matters worse, the Tories of Boston, who had lain low in submissive silence, now "came out of hiding, celebrating their own restoration in the city."[1]

Howls of laughter rang through the air as General Burgoyne's army sat transfixed in the makeshift theater he had set up for their amusement. Burgoyne had come to America one year earlier with

Sir William Howe and Sir Henry Clinton, sent by Her Majesty to support General Gage, commander in chief of Her Majesty's forces in North America. These three would dominate the British command for most of the war; indeed, Burgoyne was directly responsible for planning the attack that would ignite the Battle of Saratoga in 1776, a battle that ended in terrible defeat for the British. Along with his military and political aspirations, Burgoyne harbored a yen for writing, fancying himself a literary talent. In fact, after his humiliating defeat at Saratoga, while he and his troops languished in Boston as prisoners of war, he composed a play, *The Blockade of Boston,* ridiculing the colonial soldiers and exalting the British. The play was a hit with the British population, and the residents of Boston had been forced to endure this spectacle.

Across town, in her favorite armchair, sat Mercy Otis Warren, reading Burgoyne's script, sent to her by a friend, for herself. She had devoured its every word, every joke. The anger she had felt by the first page had turned into righteous indignation. Rising from her seat, script in hand, she made her way to her desk. She would not allow the general to get away with this. She would not allow him to demoralize the citizens of Boston one moment longer. She did not have muskets at her command, but she had something equally powerful: her pen. Not wasting one minute more, she sat down and began writing. If it was a fight he was after, she would give him one.

Mercy had written many plays, but had never written anything as swiftly as she wrote *The Blockheads: or, The Affrighted Officers: A Farce.* For the first time, she used female characters and wrote conversations between characters in prose. Her political satire wove its way straight into the hearts of its readers, with a brilliant realism that caricatured her victims perfectly, thwarting the effect of Burgoyne's attack. The play, in three acts, painted a realistic picture of General Gage's soldiers stuck in Boston at the mercy of Washington's army, deprived and scared. She endowed her soldiers with the "barrack room language of the day."[2] One soldier says, "I would rather s-t my breeches than go without these forts to ease myself."[3] She depicts their panic-stricken flight onto ships, where they crowd together in fear, as though she had viewed this herself (which in fact she had, when she rode in from Waterloo for the purpose).[4] The language in the play is authentic, which accounts for its realism and its bite.

Mercy exhibited little restraint with her pen, as she sarcastically labeled her British characters with names such as Captain Bashaw, Lord Dapper, Shallow, and Dupe; Meagre, Surly, Bonny, and Simple. When one of the women characters falls in love and is ready to leave home to follow the man, Dorsa the maid warns her, "One thing I would mention (excuse my boldness) this Lord Dapper suffers under the disgrace of inability." Dorsa prods on, saying, "I would rather marry my old grandfather."[5]

Dialogue like this delighted American soldiers as the pamphlet passed from hand to hand in their tents.[6] Soldiers relaxed to roars of laughter, a psychological boost, as the war had just begun. What had started out for Mercy as a love of poetry and literature turned into a means of winning the war.

As the play was published anonymously, none but a few knew it was Mercy who had penned the words. Of course no one at the time could know that Mercy was the voice behind this satire. Writing for publication was a strictly male venture; any woman who attempted to write would use a pseudonym or no name at all. Also, the Patriots of the era found it much safer to publish anonymously. So Mercy allowed *The Blockheads* to be attributed to other writers, as she would *The Motley Assembly* written three years later.

The Blockheads was printed on Queen Street in Boston and distributed widely. The play depicted the British soldiers as dangerous fools; using her already well-known satirical voice, she castigated and embarrassed the redcoats and their fight against America. The effect was immediate: it rallied the demoralized colonists and fueled outrage against the British. The psychological effect was huge; with their pride restored, the colonists continued the fight.

Born on September 25, 1728, in Barnstable, Massachusetts, Mercy Otis Warren was the third of thirteen children. Her grandfather had settled there in 1678, and built a farmhouse thereafter known as the Otis farm. It was an incredible piece of land, situated in what is now Cape Cod, replete with all the natural beauty of beach property: scrubby dunes and pine and oak, nestled into land adjoining green pastures and valleys, with ponds glistening on the sides of walking paths. Mercy would call the home of her childhood "a well to do habitation."

Of her large family, two of her brothers, James and Joseph, were known for their patriotic activities during the Revolution; but it was with James that she would share an intense love and friendship, one that defined her life from childhood. Three years her senior, James spent almost all of his time with Mercy, as the two shared an intimacy with one another from a very young age. Life in Barnstable offered few distractions other than the natural landscape surrounding them; and while they had many siblings to choose from, it seems they found each other's company the most desirable. By all accounts she had very little camaraderie with her sisters, who spent their time happily in the domestic sphere with her mother. But in James's company she seemed to thrive, stimulated by the conversation and learning they shared. In 1766, when his patriotic career was at its start, James would write her, "This you may depend on, no man ever loved a sister better, and among all my conflicts I never forget yet I am endeavoring to serve you and yours."[7] He was her favorite brother, her best friend.

James would become a brilliant, classical scholar, tutored by the Reverend Jonathan Russell; and as Mercy had been allowed to sit in on his lessons (an almost unheard of event in those days) the reverend became her director of reading. He loaned her *Raleigh's History of the World* and encouraged her in the study of history, for which she had a passion. It was her brother James, however, who would take the leading role in her education, dissecting political and historical issues with her, helping teach her to write. When James left for Harvard in 1769, at age fourteen, Mercy was eleven. She missed him terribly but continued with her studies, becoming and remaining his equal intellectually.

Lively, informed conversation was a mainstay of the Barnstable home. Books were valued by Mercy's father, a well-regarded, self-taught district judge. Her mother was a good woman, who concentrated on raising her large family and teaching her daughters domestic concerns. Mercy thrived in this environment, an ardent book lover from a very young age, a girl whose unceasing curiosity was impossible to quell—not that it seems anyone tried. The patriotic fever that was gripping the nation made its way into her family, capturing her father's heart and attention and, increasingly as the years went on, becoming the main conversation in an already political home. Though education and intellect were not valued for girls or women at the time, Mercy was fortunate in having a father who allowed her to study, and a brother who taught her all he knew.

The fates would send her a similar man as a husband: at the age of twenty-six she married Mr. James Warren of Plymouth in 1745. He graduated from Harvard in 1745, one year after her brother, with whom he was very close friends. The two men would remain close throughout the following years, when both they and Mercy would help ignite revolutionary passion throughout Massachusetts.

She lived with him in the old Warren farmhouse in Plymouth, which he inherited upon his father's death. It stood three miles outside of Plymouth, at the end of a road lined with huge trees and scrubby growth and brushed by sea breezes. The house was a modest dwelling, with one room on each side of the front door, but its surroundings were magnificent. Perched between fields and marshes on one side and the beach on the other, it offered a view onto the bright green marshes where the Eel River lay. The estate comprised acre upon acre, overlooking Clark's Island and Manomet Point, with woods to walk through and paths lined with big, beautiful old trees. Mercy named the estate Clifford.

Her husband had stepped into his father's place as high sheriff, appointed by His Majesty's governor, a post he remained in until the outbreak of the Revolution. He also became a merchant of Plymouth, involved in foreign and domestic shipping ventures. But as political events heated up, he found his name on almost every committee of public safety. At the time of the Stamp Act, he was chosen a member of the General Court from Plymouth; at the death of Joseph Warren in the battle of Bunker Hill, he was made president of the Provincial Congress; while the American army was at Cambridge, he was paymaster-general. He was asked to be a delegate to the Continental Congress, but declined out of a devotion to the navy and a reluctance to stay away from Mercy too long. He was always on the side of revolt, though, always awash in the flame that was kindling through the colonies.

Though Mercy began her married life in Clifford, she and James made their true home in town, on the corner of North and Main Street, a house that still stands today. A large, shingled home with an ancient staircase and rambling space, it was here Mercy would raise her five sons, taking trips to Clifford or visiting her husband when he was in Cambridge. Her first son, James, was born in 1757; Winslow followed in 1759, Charles in 1762, Henry in 1764, and finally George, in 1766.

In this home Mercy also gave birth to her writing career, passing much time in the early days of her marriage composing verse (she was married three years before she had any children). This was where she sat on that sweltering day in August, composing an answer to Burgoyne's play. This was not her first play, nor would it be her last. Her printed satire had been stirring up resentment since 1769, when she had begun to write with a new and clearly defined objective. She had embraced the cause of her brother, her husband, and her father, and made it her own. Her writing had become her exclusive weapon against an enemy entrenched in her midst, one she had vowed to spend her life trying to root out.

Plymouth, Massachusetts, October 1772

Mercy poured John Adams another cup of tea and sat back down beside him, in front of the blazing fire. Her husband sat to her left, and Samuel Adams reclined across from her. It was a cozy gathering of intimates, deceptively serene from the outside; had these four met at a different time in history, their meeting might not have been more than a typical autumn's evening passed by the warmth of a fire with some good company. As it was, however, the meeting was anything but serene. Mercy's fireside had become "a lesser Caucus Club for the revolutionary group."[8] The two Adams men had braved a wet and uncomfortably cold night to travel out to the Warrens' home in Plymouth, where Mercy and her husband waited eagerly for their arrival. There was serious business to discuss.

The problem was communication. Patriot groups in the thirteen colonies were spread apart, with no organized means of communicating critical information and plans. As the British noose grew tighter every day, Patriot leaders such as Samuel and John Adams felt the increasing need to form organized resistance and a much-needed united front. The ominous decade between 1760 and 1770 had ended with the British presence stronger than it had been, still desperate for control. The Adams men had thought long and hard about a solution to this problem. So had Mercy and her husband.

Though the howling wind outside made the candlelight flicker, the fire provided enough light to reflect the faces of Mercy's guests. She knew John Adams well, better than she knew Samuel, and the earnest look in his eyes told her he was captivated. He sat forward in his chair, his head bent to one side, his eyes focused straight ahead. She had seen this gesture before, and now took it as a sign of sincere interest. Samuel was harder to read. He was gazing into the fire, head in hands, and had not said a word for a while now, a silence unusual for the young Patriot so prone to conversation. She waited anxiously for their reaction to the idea her husband had just outlined, an idea she had known he would propose, one she felt strongly about from its start. She had discussed it with him as the two wrestled with the problem they were all trying to solve.

When the two men finally spoke, it was clear they were thrilled; in fact, it is said that Samuel Adams, upon his return to Boston later that night, put the plan into action immediately. That night in Mercy's home, at the suggestion of her husband, James Warren, the idea for the Committees of Correspondence was born. Committees were to be appointed throughout the colonies to establish and maintain communication, with respect to plans and grievances, in the form of letters.[9] Each committee would be responsible for disseminating crucial information; in this way, the colonies could know what was happening in one another's province. Furthermore, the colonies could then pass along proposals for action and keep abreast of action in neighboring towns. While the debate over whether James Warren or Samuel Adams created the idea continued years afterward, it was clear it had emerged from an experiment with the "circular letter" four years earlier. In 1768 Mercy's brother, James Otis, and Samuel Adams had drafted a letter reiterating the notion of "no taxation without representation," and calling for a new boycott of British goods. Circulated through the legislatures in each colony, it had been adopted by the Massachusetts assembly early that year. The British, infuriated, had demanded a retraction. The colonists refused. Shortly thereafter, the tension erupted in what is popularly known as the Boston Massacre. With the memory of the massacre still fresh in their minds, the four friends considered this new idea of formal letter writing committees as just the weapon they needed, not only to communicate with one another but also to keep revolutionary furor alive and well. In this way, the Patriots began their formal organization in 1772, and the idea would last long into the war.

The Committees of Correspondence was but one of the novel and brilliant ideas that came out of the home of Mercy Otis Warren over the period in which the ardent revolutionaries of the day gathered night after night in private to discuss, plan, and prepare. The years between 1760 and 1770 saw the Warren's home increasingly become the destination for groups of ardent patriots, men of a growing nation, called together by circumstance; many possibilities discussed in her home afterward grew into reality.

Mercy participated with the men as an equal, displaying her vigorous, brilliant intellect, her exhaustive knowledge of politics and history, and of course her fierce patriotism, which put her squarely at the center of discussions with her husband and other men, such as John and Samuel Adams. The most prominent men of the time wrote to Mercy frequently, asking her opinions on political matters. She carried on an active correspondence with the leaders of the time, men who actively sought her advice on matters big and small: Elbridge Gerry, Thomas Jefferson, Henry Knox, Alexander Hamilton, James Winthrop, John Dickinson, and sometimes George

Washington, to name a few. In future years it would be said that her "fame rested on her powerful intellect and political influence, two characteristics which have made men of that day stand out and be awed over."[10] While she began to create a place for herself among men of influence, daring to enter their sphere as an equal, her brother's influence continued to work its magic on her, holding her in its grip, carrying her along.

During the years between 1760 and 1769, James Otis's strength and stature turned him into a leader. Through the force of his words and his passion, his patriotism would inflame a city, and eventually a nation. He continually shared his thoughts, his fears, his strategies, with Mercy; their bond had continued and grown into adulthood. He worked tirelessly, drafting and publishing pro-American pamphlets, using fierce and pointed language to crystallize the question: Liberty or death? At that time, the answer was by no means clear to everyone.

War with England was feared, especially as many still considered her their real or mother country, and of those colonists in favor of independence, many were not as unequivocally passionate, arguing less strident measures and a gradual break from England as safer. There were those who thought the idea of taking on the mother country in so defiant and outspoken a manner was actually criminal, its own kind of treason. Among those who held this view—and there were many—nothing would have been more pleasing than James Otis's capture. It was these colonists whom the British would consider allies and who did, in fact, fight for the British in many of battles. But one mistake the British would make was in overestimating their numbers. As more and more propaganda and rumors spread about British corruption and incompetence, more and more Loyalists converted over to the side of their Patriot brothers.

James Otis's writings were filled with anti-British rhetoric so pointed that he was instantly thrust into the limelight, especially as his words began to take hold. Several incidents took place during that turbulent decade that would fan the flames of liberty on their own, infuriating the colonists and pushing them further away, psychologically, from loyalty to England. But even then, how these events were interpreted mattered. What made Otis so particularly effective was his satirical voice, one he had learned to use to his best advantage—the same voice that would make his sister effective years later. His biting satire painted the characters ruling the government and controlling the colonists as pompous, self-interested criminals. His spin on the events of the day in favor of the Patriots and vehemently opposed to the British caused many colonists to reconsider their Loyalist views. At a time when every day brought with it a horrible rumor about the British troops' treatment of colonists, when fear filled the air already, Otis's words began to ring true. Mercy watched his literary output, and she learned. His words were making all the difference. And soon hers would too.

The events of that decade would cement Otis and Mercy's commitment to revolution. In 1760, as advocate general, Otis had been given responsibility for prosecuting crimes on behalf of the crown. That position would not last long; his career would take a new path when the Writs of Assistance was issued, an English-contrived legal document whereby customs officers were empowered by the courts to enter a man's house at will and search for concealed goods. Many colonists, infuriated at this blatant violation of their civil rights asked Otis to argue on their behalf. That meant relinquishing his position as defender of the crown and arguing against it instead. He resigned his office and took the case.

On February 24, 1761, in an epoch speech, Otis spoke for four hours, arguing against Jeremiah Gridley, his old master in the law, astounding the five judges and the crowds with his legal arguments, his eloquence, and his passion. The trial took place in the Council Chamber of the Old Town House, where, looking down on rebels and horrified Loyalists, the full-length portraits of Charles II and James II hung in splendid gold frames.[11] The hall, filled with deeply anxious citizens, including Mercy, sat in amazed silence as Otis spoke from a heart filled with such passion, with a mind so brilliant and learned, that they were stunned into silence.

The Council Chamber was as the equivalent of the House of Lords in Great Britain or the State House in Philadelphia. In this chamber, around a great fire, sat five judges with Lieutenant Governor Hutchinson as chief justice, "all arrayed in their new, fresh, rich robes of scarlet English broadcloth, immense judicial wigs." John Adams would recall Otis years later: "He was a flame of fire; with a promptitude of classical allusions, a depth of research, a rapid summary of historical events and dates, a profusion of legal authorities, a prophetic glance of his eyes into futurity and a rapid torrent of impetuous eloquence, he hurried all before him. American independence was there and then born."[12]

Otis's passionate cry echoed through the chamber. Though the judges, all five representing the crown, were dumbstruck by the performance, they delayed decision to a future date, one that of course would never come. That was the end of the Writs of Assistance, however, and the beginning for Otis. He was unanimously elected to the House of Representatives, where he was viewed as a leader by all. He had converted himself from a thinker to a man of action,[13] and as the years progressed, he would take hundreds of people with him, Mercy included.

Events continued to heat up. In 1765 the colonists were hit with the Stamp Act, and though it would later be repealed, it forced the

Patriots to begin to organize. An intercolonial congress was attended by delegates from nine colonies, presenting a united front. Two years later a circular letter was passed, suggesting the advisability of a uniform plan of resistance to things such as the Acts of Trade, instituted by the British to tighten the noose around New England merchants even further: "They could not manufacture for export, could not buy and sell where they wished, could not transport cargo for themselves or others except within narrowly prescribed limits."[14] Of the 17,000 citizens in Boston at the time, a growing number were unemployed. Boycotts of British goods spread through the city, and by 1769 a British naval force arrived offshore, comprised of seven vessels. All business was at a stand still.

Throughout these horrific events, Otis worked feverishly on the home front, stirring patriotism among the colonists with his informative, sagacious satire against the British. It was clear to him early on that war was inevitable; it was also clear to him that without a united front against the British, the colonists were doomed to fail. Though the physical war had not yet arrived, Otis saw himself fighting another war already in their midst: the war for control of the colonist's hearts and minds. As he taught Mercy, the public needed to understand the danger of not taking a stand; this was necessary for winning the war he knew would come. Had events not taken a drastic turn for him, as they did in 1769, his leadership most likely would have continued into and through the revolutionary war. As it happened, Mercy would have to take his place.

Mercy was home in Plymouth with her five children when she heard the horrifying news. A gang of Loyalist supporters of Hutchinson had beaten her brother badly in Boston, inflicting a head injury he would never truly recover from. It was the beginning of a slow and painful mental decline for James Otis, one that Mercy was forced to witness and bear. She, who loved him unconditionally as sister, friend, and student, who had remained by his side for as long as she could remember, now stood in this terrific fight they had undertaken, alone. Or so she felt. But the danger signs of mental breakdown had in fact been growing stronger for some time before this incident, and many had witnessed the change that had overtaken her brother.

Otis's utterances had grown more erratic and unguarded, his behavior more puzzling. He would walk out of meetings with no warning and no explanation; his thoughts would trail off into others, unrelated. The night he was injured was yet another example of behavior no one was able to explain. He had strode into a British coffeehouse on State Street where he knew his archenemies, the four commissioners of custom and then-governor Bernard, usually stayed; this, the night after he had identified them in the *Boston Gazette* as the men who had accused him of treason. Sure enough, Jack Robinson, one of the commissioners, sat in the coffeehouse as Otis strode in. In moments the lights went out, Robinson and his friends beating Otis, seriously wounding him in the head.

Lieutenant Governor Hutchinson's role in this was not overlooked by a grief-stricken Mercy; the long history of personal animosity between the two had now reached its crest. (Hutchinson would be an archenemy to Otis and the entire Otis family for many years.) It would take two years of grieving, but she finally accepted that, while Otis had physically recovered, his political career was over. She emerged from her deep suffering a changed woman. Resolute in her determination to carry on her brother's work, Mercy wielded her pen now only for political purpose, using satire as her vehicle. She had studied her brother, and she had studied Molière; she was particularly influenced by the latter, as witness she wrote to Abigail Adams: "I think the follies and absurdities of human nature, exposed in ridicule, in the masterly manner it is done by Molière, may often have a greater tendency to reform mankind than some graver lessons of morality."[15]

*

By 1772 Mercy had become one of the most effective satirists in America, through a multitude of poems written on various subjects, not all political in nature. She had also become Boston's "leading patriot muse,"[16] although her work was always published anonymously. Her friend Hannah Winthrop's husband, Professor Winthrop, encouraged her to write *Lamira*, about a selfish woman who cares only for clothes as the Revolution heats up all around her. John Adams had encouraged her to write "Squabble," a poem about the Boston Tea Party, saying, "I wish to see a late glorious event celebrated by a certain poetical pen, which has no equal that I know of in this country."[17] Her poems, published in the *Boston Gazette*, were immensely popular, and "Mercy found herself, at forty-six, the center of a small whirl of fame."[18]

But two years earlier she had found a new literary genre, one she had put to good effect when she penned her first dramatic satire, a play that launched a new level of literary warfare. With Molière in her mind and Otis in her heart, she undertook her first satirical play, *The Adulateur: A Tragedy; As It Is Now Acted in Upper Servia*. Its first installment was printed anonymously in the *Massachusetts Spy* in March 1772; the second installment appeared a month later. Instantly popular, the play was read by an avid public, provoking hysterical laughter among Boston's citizens, who immediately knew the characters portrayed.

The main perpetrator, Ropatio, depicted Hutchinson as a demented and pathetic figure, concerned exclusively with his own welfare. He and the men holding office acted like spoiled bullies. Not surprisingly, Otis and Samuel Adams were the heroes, the two true Patriots, also easily recognizable. The names she gave to this "rulling clique stuck, so that Hutchinson was referred to as Ropatio both in private letters and conversations ever after." Mercy's goal had been accomplished; in a handwritten note, she said of the play, "The above dramatic extract was deemed so characteristic of the times and the persons to whom applied, that it was honored with the voice of general approbation."[19] This was true, but at least some would call the play "more weapon than art."[20]

Mercy was far from through with Hutchinson, though. Fueled by injustice and anger, her next play, *The Defeat*, came out in two installments in the *Boston Gazette* that same year, 1773, and was based on secret information she attained about Hutchinson's betrayal of the colonists. Benjamin Franklin, in London as a "colonial spy," had gotten his hands on some letters written by Hutchinson, in which the governor spoke badly about the colonists, ridiculing their desire for freedom. Franklin sent these letters under a secret seal to Thomas Cushing of Boston, who in turn gave them over to, of all people, his good friend James Warren. Needless to say, the letters were now exposed to Mercy and her radical Patriot brothers, who met in her home to decide how best to handle the whole affair. Although Ben Franklin had meant for the letters to remain secret, Mercy and her party felt otherwise. The letters were published, with Samuel Adams only too willing and happy to take responsibility.

It was not enough for Mercy that the incriminating letters be published; she had to write a play for the occasion, driving another nail into Hutchinson's coffin. In *The Defeat* reprises Ropatio as its leading figure, who relates his plan to charge the improvements on his house to taxes. But his conscience begins to gnaw away at him:

I tremble at the purpose of my soul
The wooden latchet of my door never clicks
But that I start—and ask—does Brutus enter?[21]

The attack—especially as accompanied by the incriminating letters—so effectively targeted Hutchinson that the result was mind-boggling in immediacy and its sweep. Hutchinson was chased out of town before a year was out, never to return to America, banished as his great-grandmother Anne Hutchinson had been. (He would die in England in 1780.) In a display of twentieth-century political warfare, Mercy Otis Warren had accomplished what few others before her had: the complete unraveling of a reputation through the written word. She understood instinctively how to portray her characters to best effect, how and when and where to publish the material, and what the people needed to hear. She had learned from the master.

Mercy would produce one more anonymous play before the outbreak of the revolutionary war. *The Group: A Farce,* the most popular of her political satires, was published just days before the battle of Lexington and Concord. Appearing as an anonymous pamphlet published by Edes and Gill in Boston on April 3, 1775, it dealt with the Tory leaders who ruled over Boston at the time. Hutchinson's brother takes his place in this play (as Judge Meagre), and his wife's brother, Peter Oliver, is Chief Justice Hazlerod. They and their corrupt companions—Hum Humbug, Esq., Sir Sparrow Spendall, Hector Mushroom, Beau Trumps, Dick the Publican, Simple Sapling, Esq., Monsieur de Francois, Crusty Crowbar, Esq., Dupe, and Scriblerius Fribble—form the rest of the cast. To "the ancient enemy of Otis" she gave the name Brigadier Hate-All, a character who feels no love for his country or his wife, and whose war plans are known by the Patriots in Boston. The play concerns itself only with conversations between men. The politicians gather in their Tory headquarters to discuss the state of public affairs and how it affects them personally. Again, as with her other plays, the Whig public gleefully enjoyed this piece, "shelling out 9 coppers for the pamphlet." Whether this play was ever produced is still a matter of speculation. Whether performed or not, it was a "crowning coup d'etat" for a woman whose mission in life had become publicly shaming those who rejected the cause of liberty—no small feat, considering the Patriots lived in daily fear of being captured and sent back to England. In this climate, Mercy's writing and anti-British propaganda could have landed her or her family in jail, or worse. Her anonymity certainly sheltered her, but it also led to other problems as well.

As her works were printed without her name, plagiarists were easily able to claim credit. A memorandum in Mercy's handwriting in the Massachusetts Historical Society referring to her first play reads, "Before the author thought proper to present another scene to the public, it was taken up and interlaced with productions of an unknown hand. The plagiary swells *The Adulateur* to a considerable pamphlet." [22]

The author of this extraneous scene about the Boston Massacre was never discovered, but Mercy obviously did not object to the addition, as she let the material remain. But when credit was claimed years later for her play *The Group*, she would act decisively, calling upon John Adams to help her preserve authorship. Whatever the many dangers in writing such political material—from discovery by the authorities to plagiarism and distortion of her work—she plowed on. The fight for freedom had become her life, and this was the way in which she knew how to fight. In an era when no other women produced writing so publicly, she barreled ahead in the name of freedom, producing some of the best propaganda this country has ever seen. "How Mercy acquired all this technical skill, working quite alone, would be hard to explain."[23]

The years between 1779 and 1787 brought with them heartbreak in the forms of war and smallpox. Mercy saw little of her husband anymore, as he served the Revolution as a staunch and dedicated patriot. She survived the separation by traveling to visit him, frequently stopping in Braintree for visits with her close friend Abigail Adams, the two women practically war widows. But often she would sit home alone in her northeast corner room in Plymouth, and watch and listen as Washington's army fought to the death.

But the years also brought with them new heights of joy, culminating in the signing of the Declaration of Independence. As James Warren said to John Adams, "Your Declaration of Independence came on Saturday and diffused a general joy. Every one of us feels more important than ever; we now congratulate ourselves as Freemen."[24]

It had been a fight to the death, and the country and its men were tired.

It was in such a mood that James Warren, in 1781, would seize the opportunity to buy Milton Hill, Hutchinson's beloved American estate. Thus would their paths cross again. The irony that Mercy would now live in Milton Hill did not escape her attention or anyone else's. Nestled fourteen miles outside of Boston, it was, like her other homes, surrounded by incredible vistas. But nonetheless, it had been his. While James was enthralled at the prospect of owning Milton Hill, Mercy's feelings must have been more mixed. She expressed her pleasure to him, though, knowing how excited he was about the purchase. But as the years followed, with tragedy after tragedy befalling her and her family, some could well wonder whether the ghost of the man she had smote with her pen had not come back to even the score.

It was a grand estate, and James had grand plans for it, not the least of which was a writing sanctuary for Mercy. But as history would sadly show, most of his plans for the home were never realized. In May 1781, while the Warrens were midway through the move from Plymouth to Milton, Mercy's oldest son, James Jr., was wounded, shot in the knee aboard a battleship: "One of the first events to take place in Milton was the opening of doors to a stretcher bearing the oldest son of the house."[25] At age twenty-four, his leg amputated, James became a cripple in body and soul. Not until four years later, with the help of a loving and wise cousin (the daughter of the insane James Otis, Mercy's favorite brother), he begin to heal.

One year later, misfortune would strike Mercy's family again when Charles, her third son, came home from Harvard with tuberculosis. He would spend the next years of his life at Milton, progressively weakening. By 1785 Mercy acquiesced to Charles's great desire to visit his brother Winslow in Lisbon, arranging a voyage for him and accompanying him to Boston, where he embarked on what Mercy must have realized would be his last trip. She gave "a thousand last directions to the servant who was sent to travel with him,"[26] as he was too sick to travel by himself. He would die on November 30, 1785, alone, without ever reaching his brother.

&

In 1783, in the midst of all this suffering, Mercy suffered another blow, this one so great that even she could not find words to describe her pain and sorrow: her beloved brother was killed. James Otis had been standing in the home of Joseph Osgood, a prosperous farmer in Andover with whom he lived, when a thunderstorm approached. In an instant, lightning "struck the chimney, ran along a rafter, and slithered down the doorpost to the spot where Otis was standing and waiting for it."[27] The news reached Mercy at what was already a painfully difficult time. Her heartbreak knew no words. John Adams would write about the loss of Otis, "I have been young and am now old, and I solemnly say I have never known a man whose love of his country was more ardent and sincere; never one who suffered so much; never one, whose services for ten years of his life were so important to his country as those of Mr. Otis from 1760–1770."[28] Some anonymous hand would pen the following poem:

> *When God in anger saw the spot*
> *On earth to Otis given*
> *In thunder as from Sinai's mount*
> *He snatched him back to Heaven.*[29]

When Mercy finally spoke of her brother, she spoke of him as one with the Revolution. It was as if his life and hers were inextricably woven with revolution; as if they did not or could not exist separate and apart from the events of the time. She wrote to his daughter, "While the pen of a sister, agitated by the tenderest feelings, can scarcely touch the outlines, history will doubtless do justice to a character to whom America is more indebted for the investigation of her rights and the defense of her liberties than perhaps any other individual. It was the masterly precision of his pen, and the early and vigilant exertion of his abilities, that laid the foundation of a glorious revolution which will be recorded among the most interesting events in the annals of time."[30]

In the years preceding his death, in a fit of despair, Otis made a bonfire and burned all of his letters, documents, speeches, and books, creating a vacuum in history that has been impossible to fill.

But it would also be said of Mercy, years later, that had she not been a woman, she might well have earned the appellation of the Patriot as did her brother. Their lives had been woven inextricably together; their fight for liberty was infused with a passion that took over their lives. As John Adams observed, "The Revolution took place in the hearts and mind of the people." Mercy understood this, aiming her words at a public, with a precision meant to pierce their hearts.

Milton Hill, 1784

Mercy had been writing for hours. Dusk had come and gone, and the maidservants had retired, as had her close friend and visitor Catherine Macaulay. It had been a long time since she had felt the ardent passion now running through her veins or the fervent desire to put pen to paper with purpose. As she sat in her little sanctuary upstairs, the place she had carved out for herself in the midst of the chaos and sadness of her own home, the words that flowed out onto the page surprised even her; for unlike her previous work, where she had disparaged the enemy, she now found herself working on a volume of history and scrutinizing the actions of a friend, one of her best friends, John Adams.

Her idea to write a history of the American Revolution originated during her years in Milton, where she was able to look back on the war and its causes and reflect on all that had happened. In doing so, she found herself writing with a new voice and a new eye, that of the critic and historian. Initially, her ambivalence about this new role expressed itself in a letter to John Adams, one in which she questioned her ability and right to create a historical document due to her being a woman. Interestingly, it was John Adams's reply that offered her the words of support and encouragement she so desperately needed to hear.

The irony that her book, when finally published in 1805, would cause the end of their friendship was not missed by anyone who knew them. That female voice that Adams had been so instrumental in raising would rise in protest and criticism, painting a picture of the events of their time drastically different from what Adams himself had seen. Adams had praised her genius and encouraged her writing throughout her life, but her decision to criticize his political acumen and principles was a slight from which he could not recover. But by 1805, when the book finally saw the light of publication, Mercy's authority as a leading figure in Patriot circles and her position as an eyewitness to history was unquestioned.

The idea for the book was inspired by Mercy's friendship with Catherine Macaulay. Though she had always kept a close group of women friends within reach—women such as Martha Washington, Mrs. Hancock, and Hannah Winthrop, the wife of Dr. John Winthrop of Harvard, a professor of mathematics and natural philosophy—two women stood out among the rest for the intellectual camaraderie they offered her. Abigail Adams of Braintree and Catherine Macaulay in England. The latter had a profound influence upon Mercy, more than any other woman of the time. She was one of the most brilliant historical and political writers of the English Whig circle. Mary Wollstonecraft called her "the woman of greatest ability who England had produced."[31] She set an example for Mercy when at age thirty, she wrote and published her monumental *History of England from the Accession of James I to that of the Brunswick Line.* She won abundant laurels in the social and intellectual world, was feted in Paris, and became a minor celebrity of the day. It was this book, so famous in its day, that would inspire Mercy to write her own *History of the American Revolution,* a work she toiled on indefatigably for the last half of her life.

The friendship began when in the 1760s Macaulay became an ardent supporter of the American cause.[32] She sent the first volume of her history to James Otis, inscribing it, "To you Sir, as one of the most distinguished of the great guardians of American Liberty, I offer a copy of this book."[33] When Otis had his breakdown, it was Mercy who informed Catherine, and from this time forward the two women became friends. They shared more than an intense passion for patriotism and writing, though; each woman had grown up on a farm, extremely close to a brother whom they had studied history with, and together developed the principles by which they were afterward always known.

But Catherine's espousal of the American cause became too flagrant for her British countrymen. She wrote a pro-American pamphlet in 1773, and that was the beginning of the end of her popularity. England, which had grown more war-minded, relegated her to the sidelines until soon thereafter, when she married a man half her age. She was now publicly ostracized, no longer the celebrated political voice she had been years earlier. Throughout her fall, Mercy defended Catherine to John Adams, himself a friend and supporter of the woman: "Doubtless, the lady's independency of spirit led her to suppose she might associate for the remainder of her life with an inoffensive, obliging youth with the same impunity a gentleman of threescore and ten might marry a damsel of fifteen."[34]

Catherine would visit Mercy during the difficult winter of 1784 at Milton Hill, one year after Otis had died, when Mercy had all but given up writing plays. The extent of her influence was still felt by Mercy, as seen in a letter she wrote to her son: "The celebrated Mrs. Macaulay Graham is with us. She is a lady whose Resources of knowledge seem to be almost inexhaustible. . . . When I contemplate the superiority of her genius I blush for the imperfections of Human nature and when I consider her as my friend I draw a veil over the foibles of the woman."[35]

This friendship would help get Mercy writing again, her visit awakening in Mercy those feelings of patriotism grief had almost succeeded in quieting. After Catherine's visit, Mercy wrote feverishly, putting down thoughts for her volume of history as well as composing *The Ladies of Castile,* a play about political revolution in Spain, with women at its center. She portrayed two women forced to bear their husband's deaths. One commits suicide, but the other finds strength and rallies a nation to war. The character Maria becomes a symbol for female strength and action, not just at home but in the political arena as well. As soon as Mercy finished this play, she composed another, *The Sack of Rome,* again dealing with political intrigue and its repercussions. With all her protests to the contrary, Mercy would have loved to have seen her plays performed onstage. Since there was no theater in Boston, in 1787 she wrote to John Adams in London, where he was American ambassador, asking his help in having it produced. But he wrote back that it would be impossible, noting, "Nothing American sells here."[36]

Just as her husband had hoped, Milton had become a place where Mercy wrote. Through all the darkness of those years, she had never stopped writing. Though she did not produce a play between 1779, when she wrote *The Motley Assembly,* and 1785, when she would pick up her pen in political farce and compose *The Ladies of Castile,* she wrote numerous letters to friends, especially the famous Catherine Macaulay, and continued work on her *History of the American Revolution,* published ten years later.

By 1788 Mercy and James's lives had taken many unexpected turns. It was in this year that James would give up Milton Hill and his dreams for it, and move back to Plymouth with Mercy. While personal tragedy had darkened and quieted the two Patriots, that year an altogether unexpected event would wrench the two from the calm of domestic life and throw them back into the spotlight, especially Mercy. The victorious end of the war had been celebrated throughout the colonies; freedom had won. But it was not long before the financial cost of the war began to be felt, especially by those soldiers and farmers who had risked their lives for it.

The financial chaos that followed the war impacted the small farmers in the western and central part of the state most: "The revival of the courts and the debtor's prison, the higher taxes, the almost total disappearance of hard money from the scene bore down heavily on men who had come home empty handed from the army."[37] "They banded together and demanded paper money, reduced taxes, a moratorium on debts and stops on the Court of Common Pleas—all the things they could not have."[38] Their chief grievance was with the courts that were sending them to prison for debt. Their leader, Daniel Shays, staged a revolt, famously known as Shays' Rebellion. Though eventually the rebels lost, returning to their state to serve their prison sentences for debt, the lines had been drawn between those who had sided with the rebels and those who had not. Mercy found herself passionately on the side of the rebels, condoning the riot; the "respectable" classes of men in the city were furious that the new government should be threatened in this way. Thus the Warrens found themselves in the new position of being politically unpopular with their neighbors and their friends. According to John Adams, "any movement that attacked the courts was inexcusable to him."[39] But this view would put him at odds not only with Mercy but with his other close friend, Thomas Jefferson, who felt "a little rebellion now and then is a good thing."[40]

Shays' Rebellion thus reawakened Mercy to her political self, preparing her for the next and last fight of her political career. Shortly after the farmer's revolt, the government set out to replace the Articles of Confederation with a federal constitution. This constitution was seen by many, including Mercy, as inadequate and unfair, protecting only a new commercial and landed class of citizens that had emerged out of the wreck of the Revolution. The struggle had begun to provide a new fundamental law for the United States; but Mercy and her followers did not believe this constitutional law spread its wings over everybody. "At the age of sixty, Mercy entered the fight with all the fervor of her wartime days."[41]

The fight as it developed was of a new sort, different from what the colonists had been used to. Rather than rallying against an outsider, they were now, on the contrary, poised for battle between themselves. For the first time in the country, two political parties sprung up, arrayed against each other. Federalists and Anti-Federalists, or Republicans. Those who favored the Constitution and with it a central, strong government were considered Federalists, and those who sought more power in the hands of the people, Republicans. In a bitterly fought contest that at times threatened the well-being of the union itself, the two sides went to bat against each other. The Republican's main objection to the Constitution as it stood was its lack of civil protections and redress for the bulk of new Americans: "The men who put their names to the new constitution were, it seems safe to say, at that time identified with the aristocratic interests."[42] The Republicans saw many inequalities and privileges that had been established in favor of a new ruling class, with power centered more in government than in the hands of those who populated the land. Mercy and her husband became outspoken critics of the document, with many intelligent and educated merchants following their lead. Forsaking history, satire, and blank verse, Mercy now returned to the good old pamphleteering of her brother's days, writing of the danger of the Constitution's being adopted the way it then stood. Her propaganda was intellectual and obtuse, but she worked hard and published her views, as much the political warrior as ever.

The two sides would, in the end, compromise to a constitutional amendment in the form of the Bill of Rights. When this was done, the Anti-Federalists of the day and their leaders—Mercy and James Warren in Massachusetts—retired from the battle. Mercy had once again injected herself into the discourse of a country whose birth she had helped conceive. Her love of liberty had remained as strong as ever, even after the war was over, even after their independence was won. She, who considered herself among those who had helped lead a nation into being, had now helped ensure a Bill of Rights for those who would make their home in this country.

Postscript

Mercy devoted her life to principles of liberty and equality. In 1790, back in Plymouth, she would carry on her literary tradition by publishing a volume of poetry of her earlier works, entitled *Poems, Dramatic and Miscellaneous, by Mrs. M. Warren.* This was the first time she had dared to put her name to something, and it was published immediately in Boston after the new government took place. The book was dedicated to George Washington, president of the United States. She chose for the contents *The Ladies of Castille, The Sack of Rome,* and a collection of earlier works. She was sixty-two years old. By all accounts she "prized the volume with her name on it; it made her happy and proud."[43]

But in 1791 this newfound happiness, given to her after so many years of heartache, was cut. She would receive news that her beloved son Winslow had been butchered in a battle with the Indian called Saint Claire's Defeat. Her despair was gut-wrenching, as it had been when she lost her brother Otis. She would resort to poetry again, writing two ballads about Winslow and a letter in which she expressed her anger and sorrow, but she refrained from publishing these. She ended one letter to a friend, after Winslow's death, by saying she "wished to submit in silence,"[44] something Mercy had never been accustomed to.

In 1800 Mercy suffered yet another loss: that of her youngest son George, who died alone in Maine at the age of thirty-four. It had come as a complete shock to her and her husband. This was the third time she had lost a son to death. Her son James Jr., who had never married, came home to Plymouth and remained with Mercy, helping her write when her eyes became infected. Though she had finished most of her volume of history in 1791, Winslow's death forced her to put the manuscript down for what would amount to almost ten years. She had planned on dedicating the work to him. By 1805, however, her *History of the Rise, Progress, and Termination of the American Revolution* would finally be printed as a book. She would write in the preface, "The decline of health, temporary deprivation of sight, the death of the most amiable of children, 'the shaft flew thrice, and thrice my peace was slain.'"[45] Yet she persevered until the end, when with the help of her last beloved son, she would complete the book. She was seventy-seven when it was finished. She notes in the preface, "I am a woman in whom historical events had stimulated to observation a mind that had not yielded to the assertion that all political attentions lay out of the road of female life."[46]

The publication of the book didn't come without cost. In 1807, after years of diverging political views with her close friend John Adams (he had been an ardent Federalist through Shays' Rebellion, and had persisted in his Federalist point of view throughout his presidency), they got into a bitter fight over her treatment of him in her book. The chasm between them, opened during Shays' Rebellion, grew further when, afterward, he refused to write a letter of recommendation for her son Winslow. Though she had communicated with him during his presidency, and their words had remained cordial, the warmth of intimacy was no longer there. Mercy was thrilled when Thomas Jefferson robbed Adams of a second term in 1800, as her and her husband's politics had grown more aligned with that of Jefferson, a Republican. Neither the history of all their years toiling together for the Revolution, nor the memory of the journey they had shared, could bridge the gap that now threatened her friendship, not only with John, but increasingly with Abigail. The intimacy she had shared for so many years with the Adamses now seemed all but forgotten.

It was against this backdrop that Mercy's book was published, a book that included a less than favorable review of John's political position and performance as president. Enraged, he wrote a series of letters to her, admonishing her for her betrayal and belittling her work. Infuriated in turn by this attack on her work, she entered into a verbal war with the man who had been her mentor, encouraging her in all she had done, including and most pointedly this book.

It would be years before the friendship was repaired, another high price paid by both for their politics and principles throughout life. James Warren and Abigail Adams were unavoidably pulled into the conflict; James Warren's friendship with John was already diminished by political difference, and Abigail Adams's loyalty had always and exclusively belonged to John. But when the friendship did heal—the two old friends were finally reunited at the prompting of their mutual friend, Elbridge Gerry—loving words were exchanged that at least brought a measure of peace to these four before they left this earth.

James Warren died in 1808, and six years later on October 19, 1814, at the age of eighty-six, Mercy died too.

"In point of influence, Mercy Otis Warren was the most remarkable woman who lived in the days of the American Revolution," says Elizabeth Ellet, a nineteenth-century writer and historian. "Seldom had one woman, in any age, acquired such an ascendancy over the strongest by the mere force of a powerful intellect, and her influence continued to the close of her life."[47] Even her close friend's great-grandson, Charles Quincy Adams, noted, "She was one of the remarkable woman of the heroic age of the United States."[48]

FPO-
art tk

Lydia Darragh

Caption TK

Spy Games

LYDIA DARRAGH

✒

*Spare no pains or expense to get Intelligence of
the Enemy's motions and intentions.*

—GEORGE WASHINGTON

Philadelphia, Autumn 1777

THE OAK FRONT DOOR shook with a thunderous crash. The banging grew louder with each moment as she hurried from the kitchen, where she had been hiding. She peered out a small window adjacent to the door: it was too dark to see clearly, but the figures of men at her door loomed dangerously close.

"William!" she yelled for her husband, but received no answer.

Another loud bang jolted her, and she jumped. Voices ordered her to open the door. The British.

Terrified, she slowly lifted the latch on the big wooden lock, sliding it sideways. She cracked the door open. Three large figures in red coats and glimmering gold buttons faced her.

"Madam, we are here on official business with the army. Open your door," one of the officers said. The tallest of the three, he stood directly in front of her, scrutinizing her with a sinister glare. A gust of bitterly cold wind blew into the house, and she shivered.

She didn't know what to do. She prayed William would arrive. The British had been here one month now, and had mercifully left her and her family alone. She had watched them daily, as General Howe and his troops had come and gone from their headquarters just across the street, but had not had contact with any of the enemy up close yet, except at posts and sentinels in the city. Somehow, seeing these men so menacingly close jarred her in a way she would not have expected. She had been given no warning of such an intrusion, no reason to feel she might receive a personal visit—unless, she thought with a pang, they had found out what she had been doing. Unless they knew.

Before she could say another word, the door was thrust back by the man who had spoken, his face creased by an angry scowl. She backed away as the three men entered her home, slamming the door with a crash behind them.

"Is your husband home?" the tall one asked, a leering look in his eye. She had seen this man before she thought, but where?

"Yes," she quietly answered, avoiding his glare, "he is."

"Go get him!" he boomed. "And then pack your belongings. We will be taking over your home tonight."

She stared in disbelief.

"Sir, I—"

"There is nothing to discuss, Mrs. Darragh. Go get your husband, please—you shall do as we say."

✍

On July 20, 1777, after two and a half years of fighting, General Sir William Howe, commander in chief of all British forces in America, sailed out of New York Harbor with a large fleet on a secret mission.

On August 25 he would land his army above Elk Ferry, at the head of the Elk River, near Maryland, where his objective, it would become clear, was to capture Philadelphia, then the capital. Washington hurriedly marched his army south from Middlebrook, New Jersey, to protect the city. He took a position at Brandywine Creek and went to battle, suffering defeat on September 11, with the loss of seven hundred men. One week later, on September 20, Washington and his troops would fight again in Germantown, and again suffer defeat, leaving the path open for Howe and his 14,000 troops to enter and take over the capital.

When Howe first arrived in Philadelphia on September 26, 1777, the city was one of the main urban centers among the colonies; indeed, it had become one of the "principal English cities in the world."[1] It had a flourishing commerce, an increasing population, and an easy rectangular design that accommodated the more than 350 houses built on its roads in the two years after it was founded in 1682. Though many of its sidewalks were paved with brick, and many of its homes were built beautifully for the affluent, with generous proportions and materials, most of its roads were unpaved, and most dwellings were of moderate size and stature. The "built up parts of the city were not much farther west than Fourth Street,"[2] and upon Market and Chestnut Streets houses were sparsely built as far west as Seventh Street;[3] the entire city measured two miles wide and only one mile long. New York would not equal Philadelphia in prestige until after the Erie Canal was finished in 1825.

As was the custom throughout the war, each time the British entered a town or village or city and needed to set up headquarters, a home was chosen for the purpose. This was no exception: Howe immediately descended on one of the more affluent neighborhoods and took over the home of Washington's friend and ally, General Cadwalader, a man to whom Washington at the time owed a great debt: Cadwalader had earlier provided Washington with the critical information that led to an American victory at the Battle of Princeton. Cadwalader's house stood opposite Lydia Darragh's, on Second Street, to the west. Her home, the Loxley House, was located on the east side of Second Street, number 177, below Spruce Street, at the southeast corner of Little Dock Street.

Both Lydia and Cadwalader's homes represented the average home of a relatively well off citizen in Philadelphia, designed usually with four rooms, an attic, and a kitchen out back, although Lydia's house boasted a large room toward the back of the house as well. Each room would have its own fireplace, on an angle in the corner of the room, all sharing the same chimney. Many homes had a brick exterior, with painted wood trim. Houses at the time had simple frame structures, low ceilings, small windows, and a big open fireplace in the kitchen for cooking and warmth.

It was here, in her kitchen, that Lydia, William, and her four children huddled together by the fire, desperately trying to plan. When William came around to the front and greeted the officers, they had ordered him directly to "find other quarters" for his family. Of her four children home, her eldest was twenty, but the little ones were only fourteen, eleven, and nine. They had been given one hour in which to make arrangements, and now, as they whispered among themselves, a deathly fear of what might happen should they leave their home that night began to sank in. The night was bitter cold; "the city was crowded and they knew not what to do."[4] Lydia's stomach clenched as she gathered her youngest, little Susannah, in her arms, stroking the child's hair. She could not leave her home and drag her children out into the freezing night, for they had nowhere to go.

Gathering her courage, she decided to take matters into her own hands and speak to someone herself, to plead with them not to force her and her family from their home. She stood firmly and, determined as she had ever been, walked briskly out of the kitchen toward the officer guarding the front door. She gingerly approached and, in a voice of politeness and respect, offered him some warm tea. Much surprised by this gesture, seemingly quite appreciative, he started conversation with her. After only moments, they discovered they were both from Ireland. This was a good moment, she thought, and taking advantage of this connection, Lydia pleaded her case to him, begging him and General Howe to reconsider the fate of her family. Sympathetic to her plight, he offered to speak to General Howe and advocate on her behalf. (Though it is not certain to whom she spoke, what is known is that Lydia Darragh pleaded for her family, begging the officer to allow them to remain. Some speculate she spoke to Lieutenant Barrington, a relative from her father's side of the family serving the British in the war.)

Howe would agree to let her and her older children stay, but the younger ones were sent to live with relatives in the country, with Howe's men taking over the one large room in the back of the house for use as their council chamber. General Howe must have realized the risk in allowing an American family to stay in quarters where confidential information would be discussed, but the Darraghs were well-known Quakers who "seemingly abided by their sect's policy of strict neutrality, despite their older son's enlistment."[5] As a group, Quakers were self-proclaimed neutrals in the war for independence, ardently against war in any form, as it was considered to be contrary to the life and teaching of Jesus. Many Quakers were falsely believed to be Tories when they absolutely refused to fight in the war for independence. What the British did not realize at the time was that they had unwittingly moved their operations into the home of a woman committed to the Revolution.

Lydia had broken with her Quaker mandate to stand apart from the war. She had divorced herself from the Quaker ethos of neutrality, actively deciding to become a participant. Though she was almost fifty years old, frail, soft-spoken, and feminine, she was firm in her belief that the British did not belong in America, and determined as ever to do what she could to help drive them out. As history would later show, allowing Lydia to stay close to British military planning would turn out to be a mistake for the British, one from which they would not recover.

Lydia Darragh, the daughter of John Barrington, was born about 1728 and raised in Dublin, Ireland. Little is known of her childhood except that she was part of a large and loving family. After meeting and falling in love with her family tutor, William Darragh, the thirty-four-year-old son of a clergyman, she married on November 2, 1753, in the Friends Meeting House in Dublin, at twenty-five years of age. As a woman, she was described as "soft spoken and willowy, of fair complexion and delicate appearance. She had light hair, blue eyes and was extremely neat."[6] Another friend described her as a "small, weakly woman."[7]

She and William came to America shortly after their wedding and, like many Quaker settlers before them, went to Pennsylvania, eventually settling in Philadelphia. They were well-known members of the Monthly Meeting of Friends in Philadelphia, the Quaker organization in the city, and regarded by their community as devout believers. The Quakers as a community held strong ties to the city of Philadelphia, as their founder William Penn had been given the land that would become Pennsylvania, and built and named the city around 1682: *Philadelphia* means "city of brotherly love," the embodiment of Quaker ideology.

Though Quakers were Christians who believed in Jesus, they did not require their members to adhere to any one formula or belief, as faith to them was an inner experience of the love of God and love of man, practiced in the spirit of Christ. Since a Quaker's connection with God was direct, there was no need for a bridge in the form of a minister or priest; thus they formed a society, rather than a church. Fervent believers in the freedom of speech, religion, and education, their creed was simplicity—in dress, lifestyle, and surroundings.

Lydia and William were both raised with this ideology and embodied it in how they chose to live. William worked as a tutor in America, continuing his practice of helping people, and Lydia would give birth to nine children, four dying in infancy prior to 1777. Those who survived were Charles, born in 1755; Ann, 1757; John, 1763; William, 1766; and Susannah, 1768. Even with her home filled with five babies, Lydia tried to help people outside. As early as 1766, an advertisement in the *Pennsylvania Gazette* appeared under her name, announcing, "The subscriber, living on Second Street, at the corner of Taylor's Alley, opposite the Golden Fleece Tavern, takes this method of informing the Public that she intends to make Grave-Clothes and lay out the Dead, in the Neatest Manner, and as she is informed a person in this Business is much wanted in this City, she hopes, by her Care, to give satisfaction to those who will be pleased to favor her with their Orders."[8]

It is unknown whether she received work from this advertisement, but it seems she certainly tried. What is also unknown is at what point she and William departed from their Quaker creed regarding neutrality in war. By 1777, however, with the British occupation, their city would scarcely resemble that of ten years earlier. Whether it was due to the British occupation and the drunken revelry it inspired, or to some earlier and deeper commitment to freedom and independence, Lydia would decide to break with the dogma she was raised with and inject herself body and soul into the fighting and heartache around her.

In September 1777 panic had gripped the streets of Philadelphia; rumors spread that the British had crossed the Schuylkill River and were headed toward Philadelphia. After Washington's defeat at the Battle of Brandywine on September 11, 1777, his beleaguered army skulked off with a few provisions. They had no shoes, blankets, or food, and the prospect of winter loomed only months away. The situation had become so critical for the Continental Army that Washington sent Alexander Hamilton into the streets of Philadelphia to beg its residents for donations. At the same time Congress, which had recently returned to Philadelphia from Baltimore, evacuated the city upon news of an imminent British arrival with "the utmost precipitation and greatest confusion."[9]

The British marched triumphantly into Philadelphia on September 26, 1777, completing a series of victories over Washington and his army. Though Washington would rally his men one week later, on October 4, in an attempt to retake Philadelphia, fate would not be on his side. He attacked the main British camp at Germantown, just north of the city, in the quiet of dawn; but between the dense fog of the morning, the drunken state of many soldiers, and the confused battle plan, the three-hour fight would produce many casualties but no victory for the Americans: they would fail to win back their city. The American troops would retreat to White Marsh to regroup.

With almost one-third of Philadelphia's population having fled in panic, mostly neutrals and Loyalists were left behind, citizens who welcomed the redcoats with open arms. The British were treated wonderfully by these wealthy families, many among Philadelphia's finest. They were feted, dined, and treated like royalty by those fiercely loyal to the crown. The young ladies of the city quickly shifted their allegiances to the newly arrived army, as the city's small number of Patriot citizens lay low. It was soon obvious to all that Philadelphia under Howe's occupation was fast becoming a den of iniquity. Gambling and drinking clubs were organized at various taverns. A thriving theater was set up to present plays as diversions for the wealthier citizens. Private entertaining went on almost constantly as the Loyalists engaged in a revelry unsurpassed during the war. The wealthy were caught in a social whirl—dinners, dances, balls, soirees, concerts, assemblies, plays. When the British received social invitations from Philadelphia families, they would return the favor the towns people to the weekly parties held at Smith's City Tavern. As someone at the time would say, "It seems that Philadelphia had captured Howe, rather than that Howe has captured Philadelphia."

Lydia was one who would not flee in panic, but would remain, even when she saw Howe take over her neighbor's house across the street, setting up headquarters not one hundred yards from her home. As a well-known Quaker, she and her family could feel reasonably safe from attack; as long as they kept to themselves, she reasoned, they would probably be all right. But as the days and weeks of living under British occupation passed, Lydia's feelings about the Revolution grew stronger. What right had these men to rule her land from across the sea? The colonists were entitled to freedom; indeed all human beings were entitled to freedom—that was one of the tenets of her Quaker dogma. It must have been painful for this Quaker woman to watch her beloved city fall into such glutinous hands. Ostentation and ornament, revelry and pomp, were now the ruling passions of the day. She felt disgusted at the British habits she both witnessed and heard about, and embarrassed at her fellow citizens' behavior now that Howe was in charge. Furthermore, her son Charles had passionately argued the Patriot cause before he enlisted; he had been willing to risk his life for the notion of freedom, even though he could have used his Quaker status as a shield. She had been using her Quaker status that way, she realized, hiding behind the ideal of neutrality instead of acting to help. She may have been a Quaker, but she could ignore the rightness of the fight no longer: she would do what she could to help in the fight for freedom, even if that meant using her Quaker status as a weapon.

Even before General Howe barged into her home that night, Lydia had a unique vantage point from which to observe British activity, as their headquarters stood across the street. She had taken advantage of her location by diligently watching British activity through her window and relaying to William all she saw, whereby he would "copy it into code on tiny pieces of paper," in shorthand. Her fourteen-year-old son, John, carried many of these messages out of the city on some faked errand for his mother, the notes hidden behind the large buttons of his jacket. Since the buttons were covered with cloth of the same material as the coat, she would cover and recover the buttons as needed. John would slip off to the American camp and deliver the messages to his elder brother Charles, an officer with Washington's army, now encamped at Whitemarsh. Occasionally she "sent little messages by other hands" as well.[10]

Operating her own spy ring from the safety and relative obscurity of her home had felt good to her, and she would continue to do it for a while. But after the British commandeered her house for their own purposes, bringing their intelligence even closer to her watchful ears and eyes, it was only a matter of time before Lydia used her unique access to accomplish what many of Washington's paid informants had been sneaking around the city trying to do: get information. On the night of December 2, 1777, Lydia would seize her moment, as the stakes in this dangerous game grew markedly higher.

Philadelphia, December 2, 1777

Lydia lay in bed, but could not sleep. Here she was, a prisoner in her own home, sent to bed by British guards, ordered around in her own home. She was shut into a bedroom that she dared not leave, told that she and her family must stay out of sight, as the council room was in use with a special meeting. What was happening tonight, that she and William had been ordered to remain in their bedroom?

The officers wished to use the room free from interruption, she had been told, but "a presentiment of evil weighed down her spirits"[11] and clogged her mind. She found herself in the grip of a deep restlessness. Finally, she could take it no longer. Rising from her bed, she walked to the window, searching in vain for signs of life outside, but the dark, wet streets of Philadelphia were empty. Only a few lampposts flickered in the night, their wicks leaking smoke, making the "darkness more visible."[12] Fearfully, she walked across her room to the door and turned the knob.

The door creaked as it opened, breaking the silence in the hall. No sounds could be heard from the parlor. Tightening the belt to her robe, she took a step into the hall. A flickering light from a candle downstairs cast shadows on the wall near the stairs. Cautiously, she crept toward the light, her heart beating violently.

She knew something was happening—she could feel it. Silently she crept down the stairs, turning into a closet whose wall she knew backed up to the council chamber, separated only by a thin board partition covered with wallpaper. Stepping inside the closet, she rested her ear flat against the wall. She struggled to hear. The sound of muted voices was discernible as she listened intently. A moment later she heard the order that would take her breath away: "The troops should march out late in the evening of the fourth, attack Washington's army, and with their superior force and the unprepared condition of the enemy, victory is certain."[13]

Lydia fell back from the wall, reeling at the words. The fourth was only two days away. They must be planning an attack on Whitemarsh. Washington and his men lay there this very moment, unsuspecting. She listened for more, but heard only sounds of the meeting breaking up. She flung the closet door open and rushed back up the stairs, praying not to be detected. Hurrying back into bed, her heart pounding, she stared at the ceiling in disbelief. William lay fast asleep. The loud clatter of boots and voices rang through the air.

Moments later, a knock fell upon her door. She lay very still, ignoring it. After two more sharp taps, she got out of bed and answered, acting as though she had just been woken. The British officer told her they were leaving and ordered her to lock the house and put out the fires, believing her ruse.

Back in bed, Lydia pondered the command she had heard, unable to sleep. If the Continental Army were attacked, it would be terrible. She thought of Charles, with Washington's army at Whitemarsh, poorly clad, half starved, camped outside on this freezing night with so many other young boys like him. In the morning and throughout all of the next day, she did not say a word to William. Though he had acted as a willing accomplice on prior occasions, her work as a spy had been her passion, not his; the danger inherent in what she had just heard was unlike anything she had known or seen before. She knew William would not want her involved in this business, and the only way she could be of help at this point would be to get this information to someone. But William would never approve of her traveling alone through enemy territory; the countryside, riddled with British cavalrymen looking for spies, carried a danger unto itself. The sentinels had been scrutinizing travelers since the reports of spies roaming the land. Any excuse she could offer for traveling alone down such roads would be checked carefully, she knew. The weather was bitterly cold for December; the ground in the city was already covered with light snow, which meant heavier drifts on the country roads. And lastly, there was the danger to herself and her family should she get caught. Though her son John had helped her get her messages to the front before, this time she could not use him: the stakes were too high, and the window in which to act too short. If anything happened to him, she would never forgive herself. She had heard stories of British cavalrymen chasing down and capturing suspected spies; she knew of many men who had been hanged for mere suspicion. As an older woman, she felt she would arouse less suspicion than her son. Also, she was the one who had heard the information, and she remembered perfectly what the officer had said. She was confident she could do this herself, without help from her husband or her son.

By the time she went to bed on the night of the third, she knew what she had to do and had a plan as to how to do it. She didn't know if it would work, and the stakes were dangerously high; but she had to act. And in the morning, she would.

The American Army under Washington had arrived at Whitemarsh on Sunday, November 2, 1777, with a beaten force of approximately 15,000 men. After a wretched defeat at Brandywine on September 11, 1777, Washington's troops had rallied once more on October 4, days after the British captured Philadelphia, to rid the city of the enemy. The battle that ensued at Germantown, commonly called the Paoli Massacre, left the Americans with many casualties. Defeated, and almost broken, the men had retreated to Whitemarsh, only thirteen miles from Philadelphia, where they would try to regroup. Chosen for its thickly wooded hills and its swamp and brook in front, Whitemarsh proved to be a good choice for their interim stop.

Here, however, Washington would have to endure the knowledge that Howe and his arrogant, reckless troops were carousing around Philadelphia. Though a devastating blow for the army, this fact hit Washington personally as well, for he loved Philadelphia.

Indeed, during his life it would become a home away from home for him: he would live there six years, spending more time there than anywhere other than his home state of Virginia. He could not afford to lose more men or morale, especially as there were those already questioning Washington's adequacy for the job. He was gaining a reputation for not being able to make a decision, and he was aware of this. As he and his troops lay hidden at Whitemarsh, they were still vulnerable. Washington needed his men to dig in, and he needed morale to remain high, but he needed something else even more: he needed information. He needed his spy networks to pull through.

By November 1776, after Washington and his troops were pushed out of New York, taking refuge beyond the Delaware River in Pennsylvania, Washington "at last began to establish a series of intelligence nets that would assure him a steady flow of information, no matter how far he had to retreat. The new intelligence system was first set up in New Jersey, where the immediate need was greatest; then around New York and Philadelphia, where there was certain to be fighting sooner or later; and finally, not until 1779, in Iroquis country in wild western New York. Most of the men and women who engaged in this espionage were ordinary farmers who had volunteered for the emergency. Their missions were so perfectly concealed that the identities of most are unknown to this day."[14]

The first clear demonstration of how much American intelligence was improving was the capture of Trenton, where Washington's spy John Honeyman foiled the British. Soon after Trenton, secret missions revealed information that enabled the Americans to win the Battle of Princeton. After both these triumphs, Washington realized the unsurpassed value of intelligence, and "a whole new set of intelligence snares was laid."[15] So important did formal spy networks become to victory that Washington began to put his spies on payroll, as his expense accounts show: "Wherever their army lies, it will be of the greatest advantage to us to have spies among them."[16]

In the spring of 1777, intelligence coming out of New York seemed to show the British busy constructing boats for an expedition against Philadelphia, one in which to "subdue that city." In response, Washington engaged General Thomas Mifflin, a former Quaker, to act as a spy. Sending him off to Philadelphia, he ordered him to set up a spy network there; Washington wanted a system in place should the British succeed. He told Mifflin to "look out for proper persons for this purpose who are to remain among them under the mask of friendship."[17] These agents were to be spotted in Philadelphia itself and the country around it. By this time, and for the remainder of the war, Washington would fully master the intricacies of military intelligence; he would realize he must have spy rings ready, no matter what city the British might occupy. By July 1777 Washington was able to tell Congress, "I keep people constantly on Staten Island who give me daily information of the operations of the enemy."[18]

On September 26, 1777, when the British arrived in Philadelphia and took over the beloved capital, Washington's network was already in place. Reports poured in to Major John Clark, who had by this time taken over Mifflin's Philadelphia network. Getting critical intelligence was as crucial as ever, as the army lay in danger of constant attack. Though hidden by Whitemarsh's thickly wooded hills, and surrounded by a breastwork (a defensive wall put up quickly in battle) barring the only good ford, there was always the chance the British would break through. Washington knew the British would attack; he knew they had three thousand troops ready for this purpose. But he didn't know when. After the defeats at Brandywine and Germantown, a third defeat at Whitemarsh would have been disastrous. And without this crucial information, he couldn't possibly keep his 15,000 troops, already battle-worn, at high alert for months on end. All he could do was sit back, and hope and pray for information.

Philadelphia, December 4, 1777

Lydia awoke with a start as the sun slipped above the horizon. William lay still beside her, sleeping in the warmth of their bed. She climbed down, a frosty chill gripping her feet as they touched the floor. Quickly and quietly she dressed in a typical day's garb: a gray wool dress, wool stockings, and pointed leather shoes. She covered her head in the same white kerchief she wore every day, its lappets hanging over her ears. She had only to gather her hooded wool cloak and be off.

She clutched the empty flour bag in her hands. She had lied to William the night before: she had said she would leave early to fetch flour at the Frankford Mill and visit the children at her relatives', if there was time. She said her good-byes, and now only hoped he did not wake with a changed mind. He had been unhappy about her traveling alone and had wanted her to take the maid. She had refused. She left the bedroom and made her way for the front door.

The streets were dead quiet; except for a few sentinels posted on corners here and there, half asleep, no one was outside this early, and the air was bitter with frost. She suddenly worried if this made her suspicious, but she was already outside and walking, her feet far ahead of her mind. She buried her hands deep in her pockets, feeling for the pass General Howe had given her to visit the children.

It would take one dreadfully cold hour to reach Germantown Road, where she met her first patrol. A short, mean-looking soldier stood at the gate and examined her and her bag through tired, miserable eyes. She recited her story of going to the mill for flour and going to visit her children, and he asked to see her pass. Her hands, clenched together inside her muffler, separated as she reached into her pocket with her right hand, red and stiff from cold, and drew out her pass. He studied it, and she averted her eyes. It seemed a long time that she stood there, waiting for permission to cross, but after a few moments longer he handed her back the pass and waved her on, seemingly unsuspicious. Tightening her hands around the empty flour bag, she passed through the gate, heading north on Front Street to Germantown Road.

Pickets and sentinels had been set up across the lines outside of Philadelphia; she would have to pass through many of these to get to the mill. It was common practice for Philadelphians to walk out of town to the mills in the countryside. Indeed, because of this, Washington had sent many of his spies into this area, "realizing what a fine excuse this was for spies wishing to pass the lines—but this was something General Howe would not think about in time."[19] Lydia had not been sent, however. She had no connections, no person waiting at the other end. She had only this one day in which to travel; if she had heard correctly, the attack would take place that night. Painfully aware of the time and the risk of getting caught, she thought only of her son and the other boys, set to be ambushed by the British. She would never be able to live with herself if she didn't at least try.

After passing down Front Street, she crossed over to Frankford Road, finally reaching the creek. Arriving at the mill, she put her bag down as planned and requested that it be filled. She had walked five miles by this time, and was now safely out of British-held terrain. The sun steadily climbed in the sky, and the gusts of wind felt bitter on her face; the ground crackled with broken ice beneath her shoes, and her feet ached. The mill had been standing in this place since 1698, she thought; it was a place built by the settlers as part of their new country. It was part of her American heritage, part of the new life they had made. She paused briefly, inhaling a few deep breaths. She longed to stop and sit, but knew she did not have time. She would have to get there and back before sundown. She pulled her cloak closer to her, shivering with cold and fear.

Lydia turned westward along Nicetown Lane, heading for the intersection of Old York and Germantown Roads, where the Rising Sun Tavern stood, a known American outpost and message center, a sort of rendezvous for American women spies operating in or near Philadelphia. She had three more miles to go.

It was here on this road, on her way to the tavern, that she would see her first fellow traveler—if that indeed was what he was—a man on horseback approaching in her direction. She froze, as though fixed to the spot, and could not get her feet to move forward. She suddenly stood still. "Any unexplained civilians wandering down Nicetown Lane from the East were certain to be stopped for interrogation that morning,"[20] and she was no exception. Her mind began racing with thoughts and explanations of why she was here and where she was going; she suddenly thought of William and for a brief moment of how she would survive a capture. The horse's hooves beat the ground furiously as the man rode closer. As he approached she saw the figure was not only an American officer, but a man she recognized, Colonel Craig.

"Why, Mrs. Darragh, what are you doing so far from home?" he asked, greatly surprised to see her there.

She had walked almost six miles now, and suddenly she felt an overwhelming sense of relief. Here was a chance to share the information she had heard.

"Would you please walk beside me?" she asked; she noticed her voice shook, a dire urgency in her face.

He got down off his horse and led it beside her.

In low tones, she relayed the sum and substance of the intelligence she had heard. Clearly and precisely she reiterated what she knew, as he listened intently to her every word.

Her story finished, he looked down at her, a mixture of pride, awe, and affection on his face. "You must need a rest, Mrs. Darragh. Come with me."

He brought Lydia to a nearby farmhouse and ordered the owner to feed her and let her rest. Then he rode off in the direction of the American headquarters. After Lydia rested in the farmhouse for a few hours (no one knows exactly what transpired there), she would make her way back home, still freezing and exhausted as she turned east down Nicetown Lane toward the mill. She still had almost seven miles to walk, and she knew not what might lie ahead. (There is controversy over whether the officer she ran into was Captain Craig or Allan McLane. Robert Welsh states that the information was given to Lieutenant Colonel Craig. Welsh's narrative was copied in full by Alex Garden, who substituted Allan McLane for Craig, without authority. Lydia herself told her daughter Ann that it was Craig whom she ran into and gave information, and she also states that she swore him to secrecy as to her identity out of fear for her safety.)

Though she did not know this at the time, Lydia had walked directly into the net of American intelligence patrolling the area that morning, actively seeking information in the wake of rumored reports of an attack on Whitemarsh. While these reports had been coming in sporadically over the weeks leading up to the fourth, they had been vague. On November 26, General John Armstrong wrote President Wharton of Pennsylvania, "Every intelligence agrees that General Howe now, no doubt with his whole force, is immediately to take the field in quest of this army."[21] On December 1, 1777, Major Clarke alerted Washington, "Orders were given to the troops to hold themselves in readiness to march. They either mean to surprise your army or to prevent your making an attack on them."[22] On December 2, another warning came in: "The enemy intend to make a push out—and endeavor to drive your Excellency from the present encampment."[23] Though Washington did not know the exact date and route, he did know British troops were being paid and issued new uniforms. On December 3, Captain Charles Craig reported that three thousand troops with six guns and boats had crossed the Schuylkill and meant to strike the American rear. At six o'clock that evening, the report of an American spy who had left Philadelphia at noon that day came in: "Troops have received orders to hold themselves in readiness when called for, and to draw two days provisions."[24] By the end of the day on December 4, 1777, a final, clear warning came in: "An attempt to surprise the American camp at White Marsh was about to be made."[25]

The spymaster Colonel Craig was only one of a group of men canvassing the area, desperate for information. Somewhere in that general area were Captain McLane, Major Benjamin Tallmadge, and the well-known intelligence officer Colonel Elias Boudinot. Indeed, when Craig left Lydia, he rode directly to the Rising Sun Tavern, where Elias Boudinot, chief of Washington's spy ring in the area, sat dining. It was most likely upon meeting Boudinot that Craig then communicated the intelligence he had gathered from Lydia.

Boudinot had begun his career as a spy the previous spring in New Jersey, where he combined military intelligence with the care of prisoners. Now, his task was to take in and evaluate information as soon as it was received, not to go scouting himself: he had paid informants to do this. Although the Americans at this point had a line of observers for several miles across all possible enemy approaches, it seems Washington sent these men in search of "the naked facts without comment or opinion."[26]

From Boudinot's memoirs published in 1906, a different version of what is most likely Lydia Darragh's story can be gleaned; while he does not name her, he too reports the same intelligence received by a woman that afternoon in the same vicinity. "Although American forces supposedly maintained at least three women spies in the

area,"²⁷ there is no record of their names or whether the woman
Boudinot speaks of was a paid female informant. It seems most
likely that Craig was the one to give Boudinot the crucial information regarding the time of attack; however, Boudinot's recollections
speak of a woman in the area that same day. Boudinot wrote simply
that on the afternoon of December 4, 1777, as he dined with officers
in the Rising Sun Tavern, a woman he described as "little, old, poor
looking, and insignificant" entered.²⁸ The stranger immediately
began to talk to Boudinot about flour, soliciting leave to "go into the
country and buy some."²⁹

"We asked her some questions," he wrote, and the "conversation
dragged on";³⁰ this may have been the woman's attempt to determine
whether Boudinot was a Tory or a patriot, a distinction not always
clear. The Continental Army wore various-colored uniforms, or
sometimes none at all. Some of the Hessians were in blue. There is
also speculation about whom Boudinot referred to when he used the
pronoun "we"; it is quite possible he meant Colonel Craig.

In Boudinot's version, after a short while, the mysterious
woman handed him a "dirty old needle book, with various small
pockets in it."³¹ He told her to go away and come back for an answer
later. Boudinot writes, "I could not find anything till I got to the last
pocket, where I found a piece of paper rolled up into the form of a
pipe shank. On unrolling it I found information that General Howe
was coming out the next morning with 5,000 men, 13 pieces of
cannon, baggage wagons, and 11 boats on wheels."³²

There is no evidence that the woman Boudinot speaks of is
Lydia. But his description of her as "little" matches her friends'
description of her as "small and slight." At the point at which he
would have seen her, she would certainly have been poor looking:
after hours trudging down wintry lanes, she would have been tired
and worn out. Her plain Quaker dress may explain his use of the
word "insignificant." Still, it has always been felt that Lydia never

reached the Rising Sun, because she most surely would have told her daughter Ann when dictating her narrative. Also, if Lydia had a dirty old needle book when she set out on her mission, she neglected to mention that as well. Though Ann never mentioned the needle book, she also never mentioned that Craig took her mother to a nearby farmhouse after meeting her, where she could rest and get something to eat. This part of the story was told by Lydia's biographer Welsh, the first to publish information on Lydia in 1827. If Welsh's account—said to be given to him by old, dear friends of Lydia—is true, then it may stand to reason that the woman who approached Boudinot with the dirty old needle book was a woman from the farmhouse where Lydia rested, sent as a precaution to ensure her message got where it needed to go. Lydia may herself have written the message in the old woman's book, or simply told the woman what to write, but it "strains credulity to suppose that two patriotic ladies were wandering about wintry roads outside Philadelphia at the same time, both with the same important military intelligence, both babbling about flour, unless there was some connection between them."[33]

Boudinot said that upon comparing this information to the other he had received, he determined it to be true. What other information he received he does not say; it is fair to assume that he is referring to Colonel Craig's intelligence from Lydia, as two women having the same information on the same day in the same place would certainly be a strange coincidence.

In both versions, immediately after receiving the news Boudinot made haste, riding off to Washington as fast as he could to deliver the critical information that the British were set to attack that night. He delivered the information to Washington on December 4, 1777, and "from Washington's manner upon receiving the news, the supposition would be that he had not previously been informed as to when the attack was to be made."[34] Indeed, not until Boudinot gave the information to Washington did Washington order the line thrown up along the whole front at the foot of the hill. The Continental Army was now mobile and ready for anything.

↪

Lydia would return to the mill, pick up her flour bag, and return home, undisturbed. It would be an agonizingly difficult walk home, as she was encumbered with a twenty-five-pound bag of flour, on a walk in total equaling a little more than twelve miles. She would survive the harsh cold and the long miles and succeed in communicating the information she overheard. Once home, all she had to do was wait. Safe in her own home that night, a deathly fear and anxiety gripping her, Lydia was unable to sleep. Awake and alone, she sat "by the front window, wrapped in a warm cloak, watching as the soldiers marched by on their way to attack Washington."[35] It was almost midnight, and as their field wagons and artillery rolled through the streets of Philadelphia, a gut-wrenching feeling gripped her heart as she visualized Charles at Whitemarsh, unsuspecting. She prayed that Colonel Craig would reach Washington or someone close, but it would be days until she would learn what happened, days spent in an agony of uncertainty. Even when the troops returned, she was uncertain of the result. There were many rumors, but she dared not ask a question.

The British did indeed set out at 11:00 P.M. on the night of December 4, traveling in the wrong direction, as if they were heading toward the Schuylkill River. But the Americans were not fooled. Forewarned, they had prepared for attack, surprising the British early the next morning with "a reserve in position to the rear."[36]

The British knew instantly that their strategy had failed. The soldiers were spread across battle lines, ready and poised for a fight. The two armies dug in, remaining fixed in position for the next two days, without either army making a move. Finally the British abandoned their posts and headed toward Germantown; but rather than breathe a sigh of relief, Washington had his men cover the left side of their camp, the place he had originally expected they would attack. The British searched for an opening, but could not find any; "Howe, who had led his troops to slaughter at Bunker Hill, knew better than to try a frontal assault on entrenched Americans."[37]

Finally, about noon on December 8, General Howe gave up, his loss having exceeded one hundred. The British army marched back to Philadelphia, "like a parcel of damned fools," said one of its disgruntled officers.[38]

News of the British failure reached Lydia, as it did many in the city. When she heard that Washington's army had been prepared, she felt an overwhelming joy, a feeling of gratitude and irrepressible pride. Washington's army suffered casualties, though, and it would be some time until she would learn Charles's fate; but the American troops, forewarned, had fended off defeat.

Back in Philadelphia, Howe was disheartened by the outcome at Whitemarsh, furious at what he realized was a slip in intelligence. The Whitemarsh fiasco not only greatly discouraged him in Philadelphia, it also discouraged the enemy in London. Cornwallis, who left Philadelphia for a brief visit to London, reported that the conquest of America was impossible.[39]

⚜

Howe's initial response was to scout out the streets of Philadelphia in an effort to discover where the leaks had come from. Both he and his officers scavenged around town, seeking information. It was not long before Lydia received a request to speak with a British officer, one of the figures she had seen often in her home. He called her into the council chamber, locking the door behind them. Motioning for her to sit down, he offered her a chair. The chair was her own, and the irony of his offering it to her did not escape her. Feeling faint, she sat quietly and politely, as she would be expected to do. Dressed in her plain gray, her white kerchief covering her head, her hands folded in her lap, she tried to keep an unassuming countenance throughout the meeting. But "the room was dark and he could not see the pallor of her face."[40] Had anyone seen Lydia at that moment, the thought that this little Quaker woman had provided critical information to Washington would have been ludicrous. She was well aware of her image; indeed, she had used it to her advantage when she made the trip. Still, as she sat before this officer, she felt nervous; she sensed his agitation and anger, and instinctively knew why she had been called in.

"Mrs. Darragh, we are investigating a leak of information in town."

She stole a glance at the officer, and for one brief second felt as though she would not be able to speak a lie and look him in the face at the same time.

"Was anyone in your family awake the night of our last council?" he continued.

"No, they were all in bed asleep," she replied.

"I need not ask you, for we had great difficulty in waking you to fasten the door after us," he answered. She remained quiet, and soon the meeting was over.

Later, when retelling the story, she would say, "I never told a lie about it."[41]

She had avoided detection yet again. Lydia had fooled the British officers at their own game and, with a knowing satisfaction, kept her secret for many years to come. Her work in espionage would be remembered as having come at a crucial time, and was part of a larger invaluable spy network whose intelligence would prove a major factor in America's victory. Though some of Boudinot's officers were considered "staff intelligence officers," many were not. He received and relied on information from various sources, not the least of which came from women. In a war and world where clear lines of demarcation divided men and women into military and nonmilitary roles, espionage was gender-neutral. Many women were better poised to gather intelligence by virtue of their access to officers, and because less suspicion surrounded them. Numerous examples survive of women gathering intelligence and passing crucial information on to Washington and officers in charge all throughout the war. Though Washington had told Mifflin months earlier that no more untrained amateurs were to be used—"Give the persons you pitch upon proper lessons"—it would be an amateur, moreover a female amateur, who communicated that last, most important message on December 4, hours before the British attacked. It was Lydia who would venture out, alone, that bitterly bleak and cold morning of December 4, with nothing but a warm cloak, an empty flour bag, and a mission, not part of any formal spy ring, not officially trained by any men, only a woman fiercely committed to the idea of freedom. Her information would ultimately and indirectly provide Washington with the critical information needed to preserve his army. A small, determined woman, she believed in her country's right to independence and was willing to risk her life to help fight for it.

Postscript

After the winter of 1777–778 (a jovial easy one for the British, as they partied it away in Philadelphia, and a famously nightmarish one for the Americans at Valley Forge), Howe returned to London in late spring, to be replaced by General Clinton. Clinton received orders to evacuate Philadelphia, and soon after did. In June 1778, the party was over for the British. Lydia was thrilled when they left, as she regained her home, her children, and her autonomy.

Charles, who survived the attempted attack at Whitemarsh, fought for Washington until the end of the war and was made a lieutenant. However, he would be exiled from the Quaker clan in which he had been raised. On April 27, 1781, the Monthly Meeting of Friends adopted this minute: "Charles Darragh, of this city, having been reputed a member, has been treated with for engaging in matters of a warlike nature, but disclaiming a right among us, the meeting judges it expedient to testify that we do not esteem him a member of our society and are appointed to deliver him a copy of this minute."[42]

Two months later, at another meeting of the Friends, it was said, "On 6 month 29, 1781. The meeting was informed that a copy of the minute respecting the right membership of Charles Darragh has been delivered to him and he acquiesced therewith."[43] Two years later, on June 8, 1783, William would die, at age sixty-four. He was buried in the Friends Burial Ground on Fourth and Arch Streets. Only two months later, on August 29, 1783, Lydia would lose her membership in the Friends Meeting House as well. The minutes of the meeting read as follows: "Lydia Darragh having been frequently visited and tenderly treated with for neglecting to attend our religious meetings, which advice and care of Friends she appears to reject, we are therefore under the necessity of testifying our disunity with such misconduct, and that we do not esteem the said Lydia Darragh as continuing to hold a right of membership among us."[44]

A few years after William's death, on April 22, 1786, Lydia purchased property on the west side of Second Street, between Market and Chestnut. Here she resided and kept a store until her death on December 28, 1789, at sixty-one years of age. She left five children, one of whom would narrate and transcribe her mother's story in 1827. Ann was twenty-one years old in 1777, the year her mother did her espionage work. For a time, Lydia's story was taught to schoolchildren, but then it became "relegated to the realm of romance."[45] Ann died on August 17, 1840.

In 1877, Thompson Westcott was the first to cast doubt upon Lydia's narrative. And in 1909 the *Evening Bulletin* ran an article echoing his disbelief. Lydia's story was first published as an article in the *American Quarterly Review* in 1827, by Robert Welsh, given to him through statements of Ann Darragh and a Mrs. Hannah Haines, an old friend of Lydia. Though the account stated that the information got to Washington, it was not corroborated until 1909, when Boudinot's memoir was published, in it the story of the woman at the tavern on December 4 and his subsequent delivery of her message to Washington.

Not until 1877, when Thompson Westcott "first cast doubts upon the Darragh narrative,"[46] did anyone assume it might not be true. It had been taught in school to children and was considered trustworthy from the sources through which it came. In 1909 the *Evening Bulletin* echoed the doubt, with a list of questions pertaining to the story that they found irreconcilable with Lydia's narrative. Those doubts were answered in a publication by the City History Society of Philadelphia, written by Henry Darrach (no relation) in 1915. Without certain proof that Lydia's intelligence found its way to Washington, her story will remain debatable for some.

After surviving the attack at Whitemarsh, however, Washington and his troops faced a famously dreadful winter at Valley Forge, after which they regrouped and pressed onto face what lay ahead. Little did they know at the time that a much greater battle loomed in their future, one that would put them to the test as no other had. It was in this battle, the Battle of Monmouth, that another woman would make her way into history, a woman whose story would stir more protest than even Lydia's. While the idea of Lydia's work as a spy was resisted by some, spying was universally acknowledged by all as a profession that women did engage in quite frequently during the Revolution. The woman who entered history on the battlefield with George Washington's troops six months after they were attacked at Whitemarsh was of a different species than Lydia Darragh. She was rough and dirty, poor and crass, unfeminine and bold; but when Washington's troops faltered, and soldier after soldier collapsed in the desperate heat, it was this woman who would come to their rescue to help save the day.

MOLLY PITCHER

Caption TK

A Sister in Arms

MOLLY PITCHER

*Not a woman belonging to the army is to be seen
with the troops on their march thro' the city.*

—GEORGE WASHINGTON

Battle of Bemis Heights, New York, October 7, 1777

SHE HELD HER BREATH instinctively as she moved toward the
body—she had been through this before and was amazed to realize she had not yet grown used to the stench. Bodies lay all around her, but one in particular stood out, as his clothes looked less blood-soaked than the others. The clothes were important—their condition could make the difference, and too much blood meant extra work. She inched her way forward and reached the body she had set out for, then lowered herself to the ground. Sitting beside it, she felt moved. This soldier had been a young boy, still a teenager, she thought; he looked as innocent in death as he must have looked in life. Slowly she slid his haversack over his head, hearing its contents jingle. She opened it, scanning for anything inside that might be of use. She reached in and pulled out a small book, a Bible. His eyes remained open, a sight she had grown to hate. Carefully she closed the lids.

Then, without letting herself dwell on the terrible task before her, she bent over the man and began removing his clothes.

The dreadful work of stripping dead bodies on the battlefield was just one of many tasks performed by women camp followers of the army, a group long unacknowledged and barely remembered. "Camp followers" was the name given, years after the Revolution, to describe the thousands of women who traveled with the army, tending to the needs of the men: washing, cleaning, nursing the wounded and sick (almost all the British nurses were female by 1750). They were family members, servants, friends, and companions; they were young and predominantly poor. And though many were there following the men in their lives, there were a myriad reasons to explain their presence on the battlefield.

To truly understand why women in such large numbers suffered the hardships of army life, it is imperative to understand the context of the war, to realize what their alternatives were. By the time the Continental Army was formally declared in 1776, British ransacking of homes and destruction of property was just beginning. This side effect of war would increase, however, rendering many families, women, and children homeless. With a husband or father or son away fighting the war, women and children were particularly vulnerable. Faced with the choice of remaining home near the British army, or seeking cover with the men in their lives on the field, many women chose the latter. The British troops were not known for their genteel treatment of women. Women were constantly raped, and rumors of vile treatment by the redcoats had spread quickly. Also, many of the women who followed the army wanted to remain with their husbands as of the real fear that they might, otherwise never see them again. By bringing domestic comforts of home, like cleanliness and cooking, to a terrible and dangerous situation, the women might actually have been able to help. There were those who were single, patriotic, seeking adventure, but they were most likely the exception. And there were those who worked, or tried to work, as prostitutes in the American army, but they were in the minority.

Most likely because of their poverty, filth, and lack of manners, women camp followers were viewed with an unusual amount of disgust and disregard, not only historically but during their own time. Not to be confused with officer's wives, who would never see a battlefield though they visited camp quite often, these women and children not only saw the battlefield, they lived on it, sometimes with no shelter but an empty sky. Many died with their children, although records have not been kept of the numbers who perished. The social composition was well marked from the beginning; these women's lives were filled with such hardship, it is impossible to imagine their sufferings. Besides enduring the physical forces of nature—excessive heat, cold, downpours, snow—they plodded on carrying babies in their arms and household goods on their backs, trudging after the men and the army that gave them food and water, a half ration for the women, a quarter ration for the children. Camp followers traveled in the back with the baggage, as they were ordered to stay out of sight. Although they were an essential part of eighteenth-century military life, as their services helped bring hygiene and comfort to the men, far from being appreciated, they were an embarrassment to the army. Most of the army personnel, even the soldiers themselves, were prejudiced against the female gender.

Male ideas of femininity in eighteenth-century culture were laced with specific notions of what it meant to be a lady. It wasn't ladylike to be dirty, smelly, and coarse; it wasn't desirable to be rough, rugged, and tough. Yet all these were qualities a woman would need to have, or acquire, to survive life at camp. Those who did not perish along the way were treated with ridicule, ostracism, and scorn.

Though their presence was epidemic during the Revolution, the concept and reality of women traveling with the army was not new: camp followers existed in Roman times, in early European armies, in Italian armies during the Renaissance, and in Spanish armies in the sixteenth and seventeenth centuries, "where those among them working as prostitutes were acknowledged for their value."[1] Americans first became exposed to the concept during the French and Indian War, where the British army kept an estimated ratio of one women to every eight men, thereby earning the distinction of maintaining the highest number of camp followers. In contrast, when America adopted the practice, the number of women actually traveling with the army was much less. Of the twenty-five orders George Washington would eventually give relating to women, one was that they should not exceed one to every thirteen men.[2] Washington despised the idea of women camp followers burdening his army, initially forbidding them as hangers-on and prostitutes and complaining that pregnant women and mothers were "a clog upon the movement."[3] But as the war progressed, he began to realize their value.

One of the values in having women accompany men onto the battlefield was that less men deserted for home. In 1775, Washington acknowledged that his hands were tied, lest he risk losing valuable husbands, fathers, and sons. Further, with most loss suffered by the army due to sickness and disease, having women clean, launder, and nurse could only be good. Indeed, in the early days of war, more men died of lack of hygiene and disease than from battle wounds. Malnutrition, lack of supplies, and unhealthy camp and hospital conditions all combined to make camp life deadly. In this light, the services provided by the women were essential in helping preserve order. One fellow observed that as men were not used to doing things for themselves, they would rather "let the linen rot on their backs before troubling themselves over cleaning it."[4] Washington eventually put women to work, not only assigning chores such as emptying slop pails, laundering, scrubbing floors, washing dishes, foraging for horses, and changing bed straw, but also in a more traditional military role.

There are many reports of women making cartridges, loading cannons, and bringing water to the guns. A cannon would require three to five men to man it: one person to swab—clean it with water after each blow to prevent explosion; one person to load; one to ram the barrel and gunpowder down it; one to aim; and one to fire. Women would regularly provide water for the cannons.

Along these lines, another horrible task given to women was the scavenging of dead bodies on the field. For an army in desperate need of clothes, boots, and military gear, the loot retrieved by these women proved most valuable. Many times, after stealing the enemy's clothes, the women would bury the bodies themselves. On that sweltering hot day when the woman at the Battle of Bemis Heights performed this task, she was one of many women on the battlefield, one of many transformed by war. When she had finished picking through the remains of the dead soldier, she found herself covered in dirt, blood, and sweat. She had grown used to the smell of her own odor, but not to the smell of death. The air, thick with dust and gunpowder, offered no relief. She gathered the soldier's clothes in her arms, quietly saying a prayer. Then she left the naked body on the ground where she had found it, sadly turned, and made her way back to camp. She was doing this for the men who were still alive, she told herself. She was doing this for her husband. And last but not least, she was doing this for her army.

Molly Pitcher is a name that has come to symbolize a legend, a female figure powerful enough to fight on a battlefield with men. In reality, it was the nickname given to a woman whose existence, to this day, is bitterly debated, with her legendary status and all it represents at stake. We do know from an eyewitness report, and many other pieces of circumstantial evidence, that a woman manned her husband's cannon and fought at the Battle of Monmouth in 1778. Most of the research seems to indicate she was a woman named Mary Hays McCauley. There are those, however, who argue Molly Pitcher was really a woman named Margaret Corbin, who manned a cannon at the battle of Fort Washington in 1776. Still others hold that Molly Pitcher never existed at all.

Many stories have emerged of different women fighting with the army on the battlefield during the Revolutionary War, some there as camp followers, some disguised as men in uniform. To speak of one woman's bravery is, in a true sense, to speak of all those who suffered and fought in the same way, the many souls whom history has left behind. In the case of Molly Pitcher, we do know that her legend obscured the real story behind the thousands of women whose service was invaluable to the winning of the Revolution. The story of one young woman's bravery has become a symbol of female strength and ability, but beneath the legend existed real women whose lives were defined by that war and that time.

The main contender for the title of Molly Pitcher is Mary Hays McCauley, the details of whose life are still bitterly contested. Everything from her date of birth (October 13, 1744 or 1754) to her place of birth (Carlisle, Pennsylvania, or Allentown, Pennsylvania), her nationality (German or Irish), and even her maiden name (Ludwig or Ludwick), is debated. There has been speculation she was hired out as a servant to a Dr. William Irvine of Carlisle at the age of fifteen, where she lived and worked until 1769, when she met and married her husband. All court records show she married a William Hays, although it has also been claimed she married a John Casper Hays. William Hays lived in Carlisle, Pennsylvania, and his family came from Ireland. He worked as a gunner in the Pennsylvania State Regiment of Artillery, which became the Fourth Regiment on September 3, 1778. This would place both him and Mary at Monmouth, lending credence to the claim that it was she who manned his cannon during the battle. He served under Colonel Thomas Proctor from May 1777 until January 1781.

The only descriptions we have of Mary Hays McCauley come from neighbors and friends in Carlisle, Pennsylvania, who remembered her as "homely in appearance, not refined in manners or language," a "very busy talker," "buxom," a "tobacco chewer," and "strong."[5] It has been said that she "swore like a trooper," and was illiterate. An eyewitness described her as a "very masculine person, alike rough in appearance and character; small and heavy with bristles in her nose, who could both drink whiskey and swear."[6] She was "prone to indulge in passions and profanity,"[7] and as her granddaughter remembered, "she drank grog and used language, not the most polite."[8] A neighbor, Harriet Foulk, recalled that "she was a vulgar, profane, drunken old woman. . . . I was afraid of her; she was uncouth, really vulgar, very profane, was homely, yes, ugly and gray."[9] Yet, she has also been described by many who knew her as "kind hearted and a good woman,"[10] ready to help anyone in need.

The second contender for the title, Margaret Corbin, did not fare much better in the femininity department. Though alternately called Captain Molly and Molly Pitcher, she was usually known as "dirty Kate."[11] Margaret Cochran was born November 12, 1751, in Franklin County, Pennsylvania, the daughter of Robert Cochran. When she was five years old, Indians invaded her home, killing her father and capturing her mother. She and her brother, away from the home at the time, would be raised by a relative until 1772, when she met and married John Corbin, a member of Captain Francis Proctor's company of artillery. Following him into battle in 1776, she fought alongside him dressed in a soldier's uniform, making no attempt to hide her sex. (She has been called a transvestite by some for this reason.) Manning her husband's cannon after he was shot dead, she fought during the Battle of Fort Washington on November 16 of that year, suffering a terrible injury when a musket tore out her arm and part of her shoulder, permanently crippling her.

The similarities between the two women's stories are striking, and in no small measure add to the quagmire of doubt surrounding the authenticity of any definitive claim regarding Molly Pitcher. Corbin, like Mary, took her husband's place at a cannon in battle; both women answered to the name Mary; both of their husband's names were thought of as being John for many years; both men served in the Pennsylvania regiment under Colonel Thomas Proctor; both women were from an area which in 1776 was Cumberland County, Pennsylvania; both were pensioned by the Congress for "services during the revolutionary war"; and both were buried with military honors.

~

The Battle of Monmouth, as it would come to be called, has been described as one of the most decisive battles in the history of the American Revolution, not because of its victory (which is contested), but for what it represented: the bedraggled, undisciplined group of colonial soldiers formerly fighting a makeshift, haphazard fight had now encountered and stared down the British Royal Army, at the time the world's best. After the Valley Forge winter of death, starvation, and suffering, the militia men had emerged stronger, in no small part due to military lessons received all winter from Lafayette. They would stand against the British in this battle, who had with them some of their best and mightiest regulars, the Queen's Rangers, plus a number of Loyalist militia numbering in total almost 17,000 splendidly trained, physically fit men.

The battle, which took place on June 28, 1778, was the last important engagement in the North and the longest action of the war. It was fought on what has been called one "of the most scorching, hot days America has ever known," one of the hottest days on record—103 in midday—under an unforgiving sun, from dawn to twilight. American soldiers, combined with different infantry and artillery regiments, banded together as one. The fighting would claim the lives of approximately 500 British and 394 Americans, many of those dying from the heat. The British alone lost thirty-seven to sunstroke.

The story of the Battle of Monmouth began two months earlier in the spring of 1778, when after a long and protracted occupation in Philadelphia, beginning that autumn of 1777, Clinton, the British general in command, was given orders to evacuate and head for New York. Giving up Philadelphia, the capital at the time, was a crushing blow, but British troops were needed in New York, where they would join forces with the Royal Navy in harassing Patriot coastal towns. Evacuation meant Clinton needed to move thirteen thousand men across the Delaware, through the state of New Jersey, on into New York. As Clinton prepared, Washington remained holed up in Valley Forge, trying to gather intelligence on Clinton's next move. It was clear the British were packing up and heading out of town, but it was not clear where they were going or what route they planned to take. Scattered reports proved indefinite, so Washington had been forced to watch and wait.

Throughout late May and early June, Clinton "loaded ships and ferried baggage and advance units"[12] until June 18, when the army seemed to disappear into thin air one night. As one eyewitness described it: "Last night it was said there were 9,000 of the British troops left in town and 11,000 in New Jersey. This morning when we awoke there was not one redcoat to be seen in town. The encampment in New Jersey also vanished."[13] Washington held a council of war on June 17. He was forced to decide whether to pursue the British through New Jersey and attack, or to let them leave the city peacefully and regroup his own troops. He understood both sides of the argument well. No one, British or American, was ready to suggest that the Continental Army could at this point hold their own against the "cream of the British army," which these men were. After much consideration, he put Benedict Arnold in charge of a reoccupied Philadelphia and ordered approximately 3,600 men to march in pursuit of the enemy. Although this was a sizable number of men, Charles Lee, second in command at the time, denied the assignment. He was adamantly opposed to Washington's plan of attack. Lafayette eagerly took responsibility for the troops, however, and they set out on June 21 in pursuit. (Washington would later and regrettably replace Lafayette with Lee, after Lee changed his mind and decided he wanted to control the force). Sensing the urgency of the situation, New Jersey militiamen had turned out impressively, and the march was on.

After a week traveling by foot through swampy, rain-soaked, broken terrain in New Jersey, both the British and American forces were exhausted. The British had not made good time, largely due to the Patriots, who burned every bridge and felled every tree in the redcoats' path. The heat was unbearable, as were the mosquitos, and they suffered torrential downpours. Furthermore, the length of both the British and American columns was unbelievable. Upon leaving Philadelphia, Clinton had put his sick, wounded, and weak aboard some boats to sail down the Delaware, lessening his burden; but between his own force, a huge number of Loyalists who left Philadelphia with him, and his extensive groups of camp followers, wagon trains, and vital supplies, his train was twelve miles long. He had specifically ordered that "the women of the army are constantly to march upon the flanks of the baggage of their respective corps and the Provost Martial has received positive orders to drum out any woman who shall dare to disobey this order."[14] Those who had climbed upon wagons in desperation had indeed been drummed out, forced to march away alone.

The American train was just as long. Behind the infantry and artillery regiments up front, and the officers with their horses and gear, marched miles of wagons, baggage, women, and children, trailing the army through its dreary and exhausting trek. It was here that the woman at Monmouth later named Molly carried herself, over rutted roads marked with potholes; across creeks swollen from rain and infested with mosquitos. She had been given a load of pots and pans to carry on her back, and as she did so, with each step she wondered where her husband was and how he was faring, she wondered how much longer until they could rest, and she prayed for the nightmare to end. She had met two women when she joined the troops who were new to the army as well. They had treated her shamefully, each one mocking her when a groan of pain and sorrow escaped her lips. She had thought they might be comrades, maybe even friends, but realized soon enough that that would not be so. She was tough enough, she told herself; she didn't need a friend. But as the days went on and the weariness set in, she would have liked to have had someone to speak with. By the end of the fourth day, she noticed that the women weren't laughing anymore. One had been left behind, and the other now straggled in the back, alone, bitter, and quiet.

The backside of the battlefield had its own agony, its own suffering, and the women and children were steeped in it. They marched fourteen hours a day, through all weather, with very little stops. They were on a mission to catch Clinton's troops, the pace kept high. At night when they camped, she would see William, but it somehow only made her feel worse. He looked so worn and pained that she honestly wondered whether he would survive. Her short white gown and striped linsey skirt were black from mud and dirt; her bare feet, filthy, cut, and bleeding. Her broad white cap with its large flared ruffles helped keep the glare out of her eyes only slightly; she found it more helpful to keep her head down. Indeed, an eyewitness to the camp followers wrote of their appearance as they entered Boston in 1777. Hannah Winthrop, writing to her friend Mercy Otis Warren, had this to say: "I never had the least idea that the Creation produced such a sordid set of creatures in human figure—poor, dirty, emaciated men, great numbers of women who appeared to be the beasts of burden, having a bushel basket on their back by which they were bent double; the contents seemed to be pots and kettles, various sorts of furniture, children peeping through grid irons and other utensils, some very young infants who were born on the road, the women barefoot, clothed in dirty rags, such effluvia filled the air while they were passing, had they not been smoking all the time I should have been apprehensive of being contaminated by them."[15] Yet each night, when William made his way back to the wagons and followers hidden behind the baggage, he tenderly embraced Molly, genuinely grateful to see she had survived another day.

By the afternoon of June 27, Washington's main body now lay in Cranbury, only six miles away. Everything seemed under control, but Lee would falter. Orders became confused, and men lost ground, so when Cornwallis headed toward him, Lee decided to withdraw. At this moment, Lee met Washington. (There is mixed opinion about the circumstances under which Lee retreated. Although he would subsequently be court-martialed and found guilty on three offenses, one being an unauthorized withdrawal, he denied guilt to the end of his days and had many supporters on his side.)

George Washington's beautiful white stallion beat the ground at a furious pitch; as Washington pulled to a stop, the horse reared with the full might of his body. Washington had heard of the retreat, but had held the soldier who gave him such news in contempt. Now there was no mistaking it. There, before his very own eyes, he could see for himself: a swarm of defeated-looking, confused, worn soldiers making their way toward him a beaten, desolate look in their eyes. There, on "the yellow road in front of him, a merciless furnace in 100 degree heat, was crowded with armed men. They were moving toward him, not in wild disorder, but manifestly in retreat, staggering, exhausted." Washington felt a lump in his throat as his heart twisted and sank. Where was Lee?

Washington remained mounted on his horse, now aware of General Knox to his left and Lieutenant Colonel Alexander Hamilton on his right. The men stood on a ridge, looking down upon the swamp of the West Ravine, but could not determine whether Lee, the general in charge of these troops, was even present. Suddenly Washington spotted him. Breaking into a wild gallop, he rode about four hundred yards east of the bridge across West Ravine, reaching Lee in moments. Unceremoniously, he demanded an explanation— "What is this? What is all this confusion for?"

"Sir? Sir?" Lee is reported to have asked, apparently not understanding the question. Manifestly embarrassed and confused himself, he began babbling about unclear intelligence reports and fear of a British attack.

"What do you mean to say, man?"

"Well, sir," Lee responded, "I did not want to attack in the first place anyway, as you well knew."

"Whatever your opinion," Washington replied, "I expect my orders to be obeyed. If you did not believe in the operation, you should not have taken it." With not another minute to waste, Washington rode off. (There is mixed evidence of what was really said between Washington and Lee. Lafayette reported that Washington called Lee a "dammed poltroon" and ordered him to retreat, although he was not a witness. General Scott related that "Washington swore that day till the leaves shook on the trees. Charming!

Delightful! Never have I heard such swearing before or since." Scott was also not a witness.

The meeting between the two men, some would later say, was a pivotal point in the battle, for as Washington took command again, he suffused the troops with new invigoration, determination, and will. Molly and the other women lay in back with the baggage, far from the men's sight. Once they heard orders to halt, they fell down with weariness, where they still remained. Molly and a small group of women lay hidden behind a wagon, unable to move or whisper or talk. The sun baked Molly like an oven, her lips parched, her throat, feet, and arms weak to the bone. The silence descending on the back of the trail as they stopped was like that of death, she thought, as she pictured all those dead bodies she had knelt down beside, their ghastly expressions not too different from those in front of her. This was a living death, she thought to herself, wondering who of these women would be the next to die. She watched as one mother tried desperately to console a wailing child, whose cries of pain and agony were the only sound now for miles. Molly had seen this woman before, had noticed her painful effort on the march to remain with the camp and not fall behind. She had even offered her a hand at one time during the week, an offer that had been quickly rebuffed. There was an unspoken rule among the women: those with children stayed together, as did those without. The woman's friend lay pregnant beside her, and did not offer help, herself too far gone in pain. Molly felt relief that it was not she responsible for the little creature crying its eyes out; but at the same time she felt a sadness too, for herself, the woman, and the child. Somehow, though different, they were all in this together. Molly ached with an unbearable burden of pain, drenched in her own sweat, fatigued, swollen, beaten by weather and marches—she didn't feel as if she could ever rise again.

The torturous sounds of the child and mother soon became too much to bear. Molly stood, trying desperately to see if she could find a well or a creek from which to retrieve water. Artillery and gunfire began exploding all around her, and the shrieks of the women and children started to grow. Grabbing a cannoneer's bucket under a wagon, she leaped away from her small group and ran back in the direction from which they had come, remembering they had crossed a creek. She ran until she found it and, filling the bucket with water, ran back to quench the thirst of the young child who lay dying. After drenching his body with cool water, she ran back a second time, then a third, until this became her routine. As the sun climbed high into the sky, it pressed its rays upon her with an oppressive, ghastly heat. There was no shade to be found. Rays from the sun shot into her eyes as she squinted and tried hard to keep moving. She began to hear calls and cries for water, as she kept rushing to and fro, filling her bucket.

As a group, the militiamen and Continentals were not middle-class farmers but the very poor, as were their wives. Many would have been in prison had it not been for the army; the war had given them a chance to attain personal freedom and respect for themselves and their families. The women who lived and died with these men were badly undernourished and underdressed. Three thousand men had died at Valley Forge, but so had many women and children, whose numbers are still unknown. These women had spent their winter mending uniforms, making shirts, dispensing food, nursing the sick and the wounded, keeping their families together. At Monmouth, the death rate would only climb as the day became hotter and hotter.

The Battle of Monmouth was fought from dawn to dusk. Not until a deadly exchange later in the day would the woman at Monmouth earn her reputation for bravery. After fetching water for heat-soaked men, women, and children for what felt like hours amid gunfire in the sweltering heat, the woman known as Molly finally rested near her husband, as he and his men waited in an area of high ground left of the causeway. It is unclear whether she and her husband remained with General Stirling and his troops in this location, a spot elevated and south of the highway, or if they fought with General Wayne's troops as they recrossed the West Morass Causeway. (Molly's position in battle has never been determined.) Wayne had sent for three Pennsylvania brigades, but only three regiments had shown up. The troops prepared their cannons for firing, as the explosions around them grew louder and closer, but the dirt and smoke filling the sky made it difficult to see. Moments earlier the gallant Aaron Burr had led a charge against the British, and his horse had been knocked out from under him. Molly's effort to bring water to the cannon had brought her close to the battle, closer than she would have been otherwise. "During the eighteenth century artillery was, for all practical purposes, stationary once it was deployed. Normally, it was removed from the direct force of the battle as a result of its placement on the flanks or at the rear of the field. . . . it was rarely the object of attack. Because it was immobile and removed from direct fire, access to it was relatively easy for the women camp followers."[17] Also, its position made it easier for women who were helping bring water to the cannons to reach it.

Immediately upon crossing the highway, Wayne and his troops met with the first grenadiers and were hit hard. Molly watched as her husband and his group struggled to fire the cannon. She continued to bring them water to swab the cannon, as artillery and cannon blasts sounded all around her. It was late afternoon already; the heat was barely tolerable, and her strength was gone. Suddenly, without warning, there was a deafening explosion. She dove for cover under open sky, choking back soot in her mouth, her eyes stinging and burning, her mouth dry and parched, the weight of her own body too heavy to bear. She tried to stand and fell back down again, hearing wails and groans and cries from men all around her. She immediately thought of her husband. Standing now, she inched forward a little but did not have far to go: there on the ground he lay, unconscious from the heat or a wound, she could not tell. There was no time to go to him, as she heard the screams of an officer ordering the cannons to be pulled back.

With her husband and one other man down, there were not enough people to help swab, load, aim, fire, and shoot. They were going to have to pull the cannon back. They needed help. She could do it, she thought. If only she could see far enough to get to the cannon, she could help them so they wouldn't have to pull back. They couldn't lose their cannon; she had heard stories of how the British frequently stole those left behind on the battlefield. As there were no foundries in the country then capable of producing cannons, such a loss was disastrous.

"I can help you," she shrieked, in a voice filled with defiance and rage at the enemy who dared attack them, in agony for the suffering of all those who had come here.

They had been pushed back almost three hundred yards, and were soon to be outnumbered. They were losing men fast. With a precision spoken of years later, with a bravery lauded even then, the woman known as Molly Pitcher took her husband's place at the cannon and manned it with the other soldiers on the field, fighting to win the war as desperately as any of the men, helping them save their cannon.

There was one eyewitness to the event, a Private Joseph Martin who recorded the incident at Monmouth in his diary without naming the woman he saw. He wrote,

One little incident happened during the heat of the cannonade, which I was eyewitness to, and which I think would be unpardonable not to mention. A woman whose husband belonged to the artillery and who was then attached to a piece in the engagement, attended with her husband at the piece the whole time. While in the act of reaching a cartridge and having one of her feet as far before the other as she could step, a cannon shot from the enemy passed directly between her legs without doing any other damage than carrying away all the lower part of her petticoat. Looking at it with apparent unconcern, she observed that it was lucky it did not pass a little higher, for in that case it might have carried away something else, and continued her occupation.[18]

From this sole eyewitness observation in Private Martin's journal sprouted the notion that a woman was most definitively on the field at Monmouth, whoever she may have been. It is interesting to note Martin's lack of surprise at seeing a woman on the battlefield; rather, his focus is on the incident and what occurred. One more account has been used to corroborate a woman's presence on the battlefield, and that is from a surgeon in the field, a Dr. Albigence Waldo. He noted the following in his journal, dated July 3, 1778: "One of the camp women I must give a little praise to. Her gallant, whom she attended in battle, being shot down, she immediately took up his gun and cartridges and like a Spartan heroine fought with astonishing bravery, discharging the piece with as much regularity as any soldier present. This, a wounded officer, whom I dressed, told me he did see himself, she being in his platoon, and assured me I might depend upon its truth."[19]

When the battle ended that evening, at approximately 6:00 P.M., Clinton and his troops had been pushed back, and both sides rested and took stock. Retreating to a parsonage from a hedgerow, Wayne spoke of the "unparalleled bravery of these few troops,"[20] though what few troops he refers to remains sketchy: the three regiments were never formally identified. We do know a Private John Casper Hays fought in Colonel William Irvine's Seventh Regiment, placing him with General Wayne at the proper time and giving credence to the claim of those who believe it was John, not William, to whom the woman at the cannon was married. Though William's whereabouts on the battlefield are less clear, what has lived on in the general population's mind two hundred years after the battle is the memory of a woman, whomever she may be, who fought with a bravery and commitment to freedom equal to the of any of the men surrounding her. Hence, the legend of Molly Pitcher.

Postscript

After the war, in 1783, Mary and William Hays moved back to Carlisle, Pennsylvania, with their three-year-old son, John. They purchased property on South Street, and he resumed work as a barber. By all accounts they lived comfortably, but on his death during the summer of 1786, Mary was left in debt with a five-year-old child. She would sell one-half of her lot on South Street to pay off this debt.

Mary Hays worked hard during her years in Carlisle. Records show she did "hard manual work" where she was paid $15 for "washing and scrubbing the courthouse," and $22.36 for "cleaning and washing and whitewashing the public buildings."[21] She also worked as a domestic in people's homes. In 1793 she met and married John McCauley, as the 1793 tax records show. They lived in her house on South Street. He was probably a laborer, as records show he was paid for hauling stone for the local prison, but sometime between 1807 and 1810 he disappeared. No record of his death has been found.

Her son would marry, and by 1830 she was a member of his household until her death on January 22, 1832, in Carlisle, Pennsylvania. In 1822, she would apply for a pension from the state of Pennsylvania. On February 11, when the bill was read for the first time, it would say "for the relief of Molly Mkolly, widow of a soldier of the revolutionary war."[22] But the House would amend the bill, so that it would read: "for services rendered in the war."[23] She received $40 annually for the rest of her life, an amount equal to a widow's pension. No one knows why the words were changed or upon what proof the House and Senate agreed to it.

Newspaper accounts of Mary's life were published after her death in 1832, reporting her heroism but failing to mention where her specific acts of bravery took place. The articles mention her name and reputation for having fought in the war, and the pension she received.

Although accounts of Mary Hays McCauley existed in newspapers before 1848, as did reports of a woman at the Battle of Monmouth, it wasn't until then that the name Molly Pitcher appeared, accompanying the earliest known image of her. Nathaniel Currier produced a print of a woman on the battlefield at Monmouth manning a cannon and called her Molly Pitcher. Until that time, any accounts of a woman manning a cannon, whether at Monmouth or at Fort Washington, called the woman Captain Molly. Why he changed the name is a mystery still, but it caught on.

The first reference at all to any woman manning a cannon was published in Joseph Martin's diary in 1830. Ten years later, Albigence Waldo's diary was printed, with its reference to a woman discharging a piece. In neither account is the woman's name mentioned, nor is it clear whether the battle Waldo refers to is Monmouth. The next published information found is in George Washington Parke Curtis's essays on the Revolution. Curtis was Martha Washington's grandson from her first marriage, and as a person who witnessed events from up close, he wrote a series of essays that were eventually turned into a book in 1859. Two of those essays speak of a woman at Monmouth who manned a cannon, embellishing and dramatizing the account heard by Martin and Waldo. In 1852 Benjamin Lossing would reiterate Curtis's story in his popular *Field Book of the American Revolution*, but Lossing would also make changes to the story as he saw fit. Still, both men referred to the woman as Captain Molly.

In 1876 some citizens in Carlisle, Pennsylvania marked the grave of Molly McCauley as that of Molly Pitcher, claiming she had been the unacknowledged heroine of the Battle of Monmouth; by 1916, a large monument was erected claiming as much. No one bothered to ask whether records before 1840 supported this "fact."

Simultaneously, information about a woman who fought at the battle of Fort Washington was coming to light, a woman named Margaret Corbin, also called Captain Molly. What little is known of Margaret Corbin's last years tells us they were filled with hardship. After suffering a crippling injury, she was captured by the enemy. On her release, she was taken to a hospital in Philadelphia. Though treated, she would never fully regain the use of her arm. Where she spent the following years has not been traced, but it seems she was not an easy patient to care for. In the order books of West Point for 1787 and 1788, General Henry Knox, who was then secretary of war, refers to her as a "disagreeable object to take care of."[24] In July 1779, Congress resolved that "Margaret Corbin, who was wounded and disabled in the attack on Fort Washington, whilst she heroically filled the post of her husband who was killed by her side serving a piece of artillery, do receive, during her natural life, or the continuance of her disability, the one half of the monthly pay drawn by a soldier in the service of these states; and that she now receive out of the public stores, one complete suit of cloaths or the value thereof in money."[25]

By 1783 Margaret Corbin's name appeared on the roll of the invalid regiment commanded by Colonel Lewis Nicola when the regiment discharged in April. She died on January 16, 1800, at age forty-eight in Westmoreland, County, some say as a result of her war injuries and some from syphilis, hence the nickname "dirty Kate." In 1926, after efforts by the Daughters of the American Revolution to acknowledge her bravery and heroism were successful, her remains were disinterred from a cemetery in New York, and she was transferred to West Point, where she is buried under a beautiful monument whose inscription reads in part:

In Memory of Margaret Corbin,
A heroine of the Revolution,
known as Captain Molly.

She has the distinct honor of being the first woman ever pensioned by Congress.

The distinction between the making of a legend and the historical account of a person's bravery is fine; historical sources can be documented, but sometimes they cannot, and it is then that the student of history decides to make the leap of faith—or not. In the case of Molly Pitcher, she reached legendary status through a series of comments, recollections, surmises, and contrary circumstantial proof. No unquestioned eyewitness accounts solve the mystery. No letters prove definitively that the name Molly Pitcher refers to a woman at the Battle of Monmouth, and if so, whether that woman's name is Mary Hays, or whether Margaret Corbin is the real heroine represented by that name. Then again, some have suggested that the symbol of Molly Pitcher represents a "mythic creature constructed by artists and writers years after the war." The Molly Pitcher legend that developed in the nineteenth century transformed an unknown camp follower from a rugged, brazen member of the lower classes into a pretty young woman who elicits sympathy, not disapproval, making the story easier to relate to for all.

As legend, the character Molly Pitcher has seeped into our national heart, and as legends reveal something about the country that embodies them, it is important to ask, Why do we need a female legend in the first place? Are instances of female bravery so hard to come by, or are they just not spoken of enough? In either case, there were many instances of female bravery during the Revolutionary War, mostly by women defending their homes, children, or neighbors. It is less common to hear of a woman who fought as a soldier, who fought continually with the men on the battlefield as a compatriot and sister in arms. And still, after Molly, there was one.

DEBORAH SAMPSON

Caption TK

Soldier with a Secret

DEBORAH SAMPSON

ᵛ

*I became an actor in that important drama with an inflexible resolution
to persevere through the last scene; when we might be permitted to
acknowledge and enjoy what we had so nobly declared we would possess,
or lose with our lives—Freedom and Independence.*

—DEBORAH SAMPSON

New York, 1782

THEY HAD BEEN MARCHING over eight hours, south toward Eastchester, the woods growing darker with their every step. It had been a brutally hot day for June, and their uniforms and equipment made it worse. They plodded on, through dense, unforgiving brush, groping their way forward as their path became darker with the setting sun. They had set out this morning at dawn; it was now so dark they could hardly see in front of them.

"Halt!" Captain Webb bellowed.

Immediately, as though her body understood the command, she stopped.

"Set up camp!"

Deborah breathed, relieved. She let her knapsack and gear slide off her and fall to the ground. She sat down, feeling the heaviness in her legs. She began unloading her gear.

Suddenly the captain's voice boomed out again. "Quiet!" he commanded. Deborah froze, and all fell silent.

"On your feet!" the captain commanded in a tight whisper.

Gripping her musket, Deborah rose and clenched her finger around its trigger. She heard muffled voices and movement, but could not see anyone in the darkness. The cracking sound of branches echoed between the trees and grew closer. There was nowhere for them to go. They dared not move, for fear of being spotted.

Deborah crouched, her heart beating so loudly she was sure all those around her could hear. The dead silence suddenly surrounding them no longer felt reassuring; she and her Patriot brothers waited and listened.

A furious blast of anger suddenly lit the trees in front of her as she struggled to grasp what was happening. Men's screams wailed through the air, as did the sounds of musket balls flying, horses hooves clattering, and men struggling violently with one another on the ground, near the trees. She was knocked to the ground before she even knew what had happened, but hauled herself up and dove for cover behind a giant tree. She checked her position and strained her eyes to find an attacker. But the blackness of night obliterated all distinction between Continental soldier and wild, violent Tory: all she could see were large figures before her, fighting to their deaths.

The year was June 1782, and the American Revolutionary War had entered its sixth year. Though Cornwallis had surrendered in Yorktown on October 19, ravaging bands of Tories still roamed the land, terrorizing Patriot homes and families. These men were desperate and determined Loyalists, vehemently opposed to the idea of America's winning the war. They fought to their deaths to forestall American victory.

Gathered in certain pockets of the country, Tories were concentrated mostly in New York, where half the state's population, estimated at the time to be 182,000, were considered loyal to the crown.¹ "Many were descendants of the British Duke of York, who had brashly marched into New Amsterdam one day in 1664, seized it from the Dutch without firing a shot, and renamed it in his honor."² Aggressively pursuing Patriots and their cause, Tories posed a grave danger in the area, as they traveled through the backwoods, looting Patriot homes and destroying families in a form of guerrilla warfare that had become a serious threat to the countrymen. These bands of warriors—made up not only of Tories but also of disgruntled workers, criminals, and cowboys—fought to the death to deaden the new spirit of independence that was infecting the land; but the colonists, nearing the end of a bitterly fought and hard-won struggle for independence, were not about to relinquish the victory they were so near to achieving.

Deborah remained hidden, or so she thought, when a figure came violently at her on a horse, knife in hand. Clenching her musket with all her might, she shot at him but missed. The sounds of screams and groans and death filled her ears as she strained to follow the figure, who had ridden out of sight. Suddenly a force pounded down upon her head as she was propelled forward into a tree and knocked to the ground. The earth below her shook. More screams penetrated the air, as she lay there, dirt in her mouth, a throbbing pain ringing through her ears. She still held her musket. Rolling onto her side, she attached her bayonet.

Holding her bayonet, Deborah became angry, feeling the strength in her body. She stood and, following the screams, ran headfirst into a fight, bayonet outstretched, a surge of noise coming from her own throat. Tackled to the ground in an instant, she felt a heavy weight upon her, crushing her. Face to face, she could now see that the man on top of her was a Tory, a wild look in his eyes; she felt his iron grip on her throat and felt herself gasping. Hands shaking, Deborah struggled to grasp the musket. She did, and slid her hand along its body, losing air, until she reached the bayonet. She detached it, grasped it, leaned back, and with the last of her strength swung it out from under her body and plunged it into him. He groaned, a deep, dark noise, and then slowly fell.

Deborah knew she was covered in blood; she could taste it in her mouth. But she still did not realize the blood was her own. She tried to stand but was knocked back down to the ground. It was then she felt a terrible, burning pain run through her thigh. Clutching her leg with her hands, she immediately passed out.

Deborah awoke minutes later to the sound of voices; she felt herself hoisted onto the back of a horse. Too weak to speak or resist, she found herself galloping through the woods to she knew not where.

Deborah was brought by two soldiers in her detachment to a French army hospital, set up at Crompond, six miles away. She had suffered a saber slash to her forehead and a musket wound to her leg. Her knife wound bled so profusely it occupied the sole attention of the French doctor treating her, who somehow neglected to tend to her upper leg. Left alone on a stretcher, she lay still, slowly realizing that through this whole ordeal, no one had suspected she was a woman; the soldier's uniform she had worn as a male disguise had remained on her large, muscular body, hiding what lay beneath. She would have to act fast, or she would soon be discovered.

Born on December 17, 1760, Deborah Sampson was the fifth of eight children who lived in a small, shingled house in the town of Plympton, Massachusetts. Her grandfather, Jonathan Sampson, "had cleared the wilderness to build the house in which Deborah was born."[3] It was a dark, unpainted pine house, with a large chimney, a low-pitched roof, and a well in the front. It had two bedrooms, one on each end. Sadly, the firstborn son would die at age eight, a little boy whose name, Robert Shurtliff, would later make Deborah famous.

Her family's poverty made life on their small farm difficult. When her father was disappointed in his hopes for an expected family inheritance, life at her house only became harder. Though her mother was a good, hardworking woman who reportedly did all she could to keep her children fed and sheltered, her father's spirit had been crushed by disappointment and regret. When Deborah was five years old, her father informed his family that he was leaving on a trip to England, to seek new fortune. Saying good-bye to his wife, who was pregnant with their eighth and last child, and kissing the little ones once, he walked out of the house, never to return.

Years later, Deborah would say that she never forgot that day as long as she lived. The image of him walking away would stay with her the rest of her life. (Some historians have stated that he died at sea off the coast of England in 1766; others claim he simply moved to Maine, where he continued to live in poverty, and then died in 1811.) This was a sad and bitter end to a family whose illustrious relatives had descended all the way back to the *Mayflower*.

As Deborah lay now on the stretcher, the oppressive heat of the night mingling with the pain of what would be two of the worst wounds she would receive during her service, she thought of her family and "was gripped with the sickening terror at the probability of her sex being revealed."[4] She had been a soldier only five months. As she lay there, bleeding, she knew that, if discovered, she could face severe punishment and disgrace. "I considered this as a death wound," she would write later, "or as being the equivalent of it, as it must, I thought lead to the discovery of my sex."[5] A French surgeon approached.

"How did you lose so much blood at this early hour?" he asked.

Her head having been bandaged and a change of clothes being ready, she did not answer right away.

"Do you have other wounds?" she was asked now.

"No," she answered.

"Sit you down, my lad, your boot says you tell a fib."

He took off her boot and stocking and, with great tenderness, washed her leg to the knee. But having come to her senses, she realized the dangerous position she was in. If she was forced to remove her pants, her secret would be discovered.

"I will retire and change now, and if other wounds should appear, I will let you know," she reasoned, uncertain if he could tell she was hiding something.

Her leg throbbed with pain. She needed to get out of there before he made her sit down again. She was trying to stand but almost fell back down, reeling with the pain. It was then, when she thought all was lost, that she thought of the Sampson coat of arms, which Deborah's father had prided himself on and shown her when she was very young: "a cross between two escallops, a very ancient insignia, with the motto 'Disgrace is worse than death.' The cross denoted that the first bearer of the arms took part in the early religious wars and the escallops indicated a pilgrimage which in all likelihood was the Crusades."[6] This was her heritage, she thought to herself; these were the people she had descended from.

Infused with new energy and will, she pulled herself up, quickly limping out of the hospital, away from the surgeon, whose back was turned. Before he had the chance to turn again, she was gone. After two unsuccessful attempts, she would manage to extract the musket ball from her thigh with a silver probe, lint, and bandages, in an act of sheer desperation.

Deborah's family's colonial ancestry dated back to the *Mayflower* on both her mother and father's side. Her paternal great-grandfather, Isaac Sampson, was among the first settlers in Plymouth, Massachusetts. His uncle, Henry, had sailed over on the *Mayflower* with Miles Standish and John Alden, two distinguished men who shared ancestry with the Sampsons. Her mother's side of the family included Deborah's maternal great-grandfather, William Bradford, also aboard the *Mayflower*, who would become the second governor and the first historian of Plymouth Colony. Deborah's maternal grandmother, Bathsheba, an eccentric, cultured woman, came to the colonies from Paris. She visited her grandchildren often and adored Deborah, regaling her with stories about Joan of Arc and strong women from the Bible, including the ancient biblical figure Deborah.

Alone with eight children, Deborah's mother struggled until she could no longer provide for everyone. Rather than offer her children to strangers, she found relatives willing to take them in. In a heartbreaking decision, she gave away her oldest five children, Deborah among them. At five and a half, her big hazel blue eyes perpetually downcast and scared, Deborah went to live with Ruth Fuller, her mother's cousin, a woman who had never married. The new house was in Middleborough, four miles southwest of Plympton. Ruth proved to be a kind woman, providing Deborah with her own room and pretty dresses, reading books to her, and not demanding she do heavy chores. Deborah lived with her happily for three years until one day, unexpectedly, Ruth Fuller became ill. Three days later, she died.

Deborah wished to return to her mother and two siblings, but she was unable to, so a new family was found, a Reverend and Mrs. Peter Thacher. Mrs. Thacher was nothing like Ruth: she was eighty years old, bitter, and ailing. Deborah would survive in this house for two years, until one day, when her mother finally saw the amount of heavy lifting and chores Deborah was required to do for the Thachers, she decided it was time to find Deborah a new home. After consulting with a local reverend, she quickly found another family.

The Thomas family lived in a large white oak house on a farm, two miles outside Middleborough. The home was situated in a quiet part of town, surrounded by fields and pastures. The large kitchen had a great open hearth, a Dutch oven, and a long red-oak table where the family would gather along long benches for meals. Jeremiah Thomas, his wife, and their eight sons were a large, happy, kind family and had been looking for a helper when the reverend contacted them about Deborah. She was ten years old at the time and was placed with them as an indentured servant until eighteen years of age, at which time she would be free to leave. In return for room and board, she would help with the children and the home. Deborah knew Mr. Thomas, as he had offered her rides over the years in his farmer's cart when she traveled to visit her mother and siblings. He remembered her too, the lively, talkative little girl who had inundated him with questions about the moon and the stars and the universe on their trips from Middleborough to Plymouth together.[7]

Deborah would spend the next ten years of her life living with the Thomas family, the only true family she would ever know. She was treated kindly and fairly by them from the first day she arrived, given her own room over the kitchen, her own wooden desk, made by Mr. Thomas himself, her own dresser, and a candle, birch paper, a goose quill, and homemade ink. The boys in the house, who eventually numbered ten, became like brothers to her over the years, and though she was the servant in the house, she was also the only girl in the house, and because of that held a special place.

Her days were filled with spinning and weaving, baking and cooking, helping care for the farm animals, helping tend to the babies—all the work expected of a woman and a girl at that time. But with plenty of food and sleep and hard work, Deborah grew quite quickly and quite tall, reaching five feet, nine inches at a time when the average height for a woman was four foot seven. Adopted by the Thomas boys as an eager and worthwhile companion, she was treated as one of them in her time off, accompanying them on fishing and hunting expeditions and learning to use a musket, with which she would become expert at shooting game. The boys also let her listen in on their tutelage with a local clergyman, a graduate of Harvard, whenever she wished, which was always.

She would spend much of her free time listening in on her "brother's" school lessons and reading, both to herself and to them. Mr. Thomas had a well-stocked library, and Deborah would devour the likes of Shakespeare, Dryden, Voltaire, Swift, and Locke. Though Mr. Thomas was impressed by her intelligence and love of learning, even commenting once, "Deborah, you are always either buried in some book or scrabbling over paper,"[8] his feelings against a girl's educating herself were clearly understood: it simply wasted time when she could be doing important things like spinning and weaving. Deborah was not deterred, however; his attitude only made her want to learn more. She felt strongly about the value of education for girls, and bristled at the suggestion that girls were somehow inferior. She saw for herself how capable she was in the field and with a gun, and she knew how well she read and how much she enjoyed it. She felt in no small measure that, during certain moments, she was just as capable as one of the boys; and that felt good.

Deborah's sense that there was so much more to learn and know than life on a farm was exacerbated by events of the day, events that would prove decisive for her as well as for the others. The ten years Deborah spent in the Thomas home, from 1770 to 1780, shaped her growing sense of awareness through a crucial prism: an ardent, feverish patriotism was raging through the land, a patriotism that was infectious. News of outside events, specifically in Boston and Philadelphia, filtered into the smaller towns quickly: the large tower bell of the First Congregational Church in Middleborough would toll with important news, and when that happened, the Thomas family would gather with their neighbors to listen. Deborah listened, too. She heard when a band of Patriots dumped tea into Boston Harbor in December 1773. She paid attention one year later when England declared the port of Boston closed. And the news of April 18, 1775, when Paul Revere warned of what would become the battle of Lexington and Concord, filtered down to her ears as well. On that day she was only fifteen years old.

Deborah would remember, years later, the deep indignity she felt every time she heard another story about England's attempts to control the colonists, and her pride when she heard of men like Paul Revere, who gallantly risked their lives in the name of freedom. The fight belonged to all of them, and the war had now come directly home, as she longingly watched Captain William Shaw of Middleborough turn young men like her "brothers" into militiamen.

She ached to be able to go out on the field and train with them. Not that she wasn't participating in the war effort: each day she and Mrs. Thomas would sit home, tirelessly spinning and weaving cloth for uniforms, knitting socks for the soldier's long march ahead, even sending money when they could. But Deborah still felt a stir of envy as she watched the men in action. Freedom and independence had become fiercely important to her: having worked for a living from the time she was ten, she viscerally recoiled from the idea of paying taxes to a king miles away in another country, and of being deprived the choice of how to live her life. The king's behavior toward the colonists felt deeply unfair to her, and she burned with anger and pride.

Her eighteenth birthday had arrived four years earlier, on December 17, 1778. Though free to leave the Thomas home, she had chosen to stay on briefly, rejecting the suitor her mother arranged for her to marry. She would later say, "I did not . . . escape the addresses of a young man, of whom my mother, I believe, was passionately fond, and seemed struck with wonder that I was not. . . . I had not the eyes to see such perfection in this lump of a man."⁹ Instead, in May 1779, she began work as a summer-school teacher, a long-coveted goal. Teaching gave her a new kind of satisfaction and pleasure, yet she yearned for something more. She often thought of the Thomas boys, three of whom were away serving as soldiers in the Continental Army. A restlessness brewed inside of her. She ached for the chance to travel as they did, to see the places she had heard so much about, to fight these enemies who had landed on her soil with their mandates and their guns, killing innocent families and brashly denying her people their rights.

At that time in history, however, a woman's sphere was clearly circumscribed as domestic: colonists fought for freedom and independence for all Americans, but denied it to women and slaves: "Even as late as the Revolutionary era, women could still engage in patriotic acts, such as boycotts or fund raising for the war effort. But by the end of the century, the virtue of any woman who completely abandoned the domestic sphere for a public venture was suspect, and one who left home to travel with a company of soldiers of course would be anathema."¹⁰ Keenly aware of her limitation as a woman, Deborah did not know what to do. Until one day, she had an idea.

❧

The night was cold and brisk and crystal clear; the stars shone so brightly through her bedroom window that she imagined them companions. She rose from her bed and opened the chest, flinching as it squealed. She waited in the darkness, then removed her clothes. There, waiting, were the fake uniform and soldier's boots she had hidden for over a month. She reached in and took them out. She stared at herself in the mirror. The brown fustian fabric was coarse, hard to the touch, in direct contrast to the ruffles of the white man's shirt underneath. Her breeches fit perfectly, and the waistcoat with handkerchief finished the look. An outer coat, brown hat, and farm boots rested on the bed near the window, the last remaining elements of a perfect disguise. She had taped her breasts to her chest with a piece of linen cloth in a painful way, but the ruse worked. Her chest appeared uncannily flat.

She was not beautiful, she knew that, but she had never really cared about her looks the way a lot of girls did. She had always towered over most other girls, at five feet nine inches. Her arms were strong and muscular, most likely from the physical work of her farm life, as was her body. Her eyes were hazel blue, and her nose was rather large and regal looking. Her hair had always been her favorite thing about herself a dark golden blond; she had always kept it long and messy, and had always felt secure when curling her hands around it as she read, or feeling it wet on the back of her neck after a bath on a hot summer night.

But she was not like other girls. She had never really had a girlfriend, never enjoyed the intimacy of femininity, never dreamed of a husband the way a lot of girls did. Instead, she had grown into a fiercely independent soul, taking pleasure in the outdoors and in the feeling of being on her own. While described as having "very prepossessing features, with an intelligent, animated expression, a fine, tall form, and such an air of modest courage and freshness as inspired confidence and respect in all who knew her,"[11] she had always seemed unconcerned with her appearance. But as she stood now, facing herself in the mirror in this soldier's uniform, the only sign left of her womanhood was her hair. It cascaded down over her shoulders. She felt a twinge of sadness that surprised her, for she had lived with the idea of cutting it off for so long now, it was almost as if it had already been done. But as she lifted her hair between her fingers, feeling its soft, reassuring presence, the memory of getting caught resurfaced, and she knew she had no choice but to proceed as planned.

It had been an embarrassing ordeal. The idea to disguise herself had come to her one day as she snooped around in an attic chest in one of the homes she boarded in, and found an old soldier's uniform. As she tried it on for fun, the image she had seen in the mirror surprised even herself. She looked like a man. For a moment, she imagined the freedom that would entail. Testing the disguise out on others had proven trickier, however.

She had walked out of the house and down the road one mile to the home of Israel Wood, a local recruiting officer. Sauntering over to a table where men were enlisting, she was told she could collect a bounty by signing her name. Shocked that no one recognized her, she continued the ruse, signing the name Timothy Thayer and collecting the bounty. When she didn't show up the next morning for service, a neighbor who had watched Deborah sign her name told local authorities she had questioned Timothy Thayer's identity after noticing that the "gentleman holds his quill in the same funny way as the girl Deborah Sampson."[12] The neighbor led them to the house where she knew Deborah boarded, and it was soon discovered that young Timothy Thayer had really been young Deborah Sampson. The townsfolk, especially Deborah's mother, were none too happy about it. She was forced to return the money and warned not to engage in such behavior again, amid gossip and laughter.

Even her church would eventually weigh in, expelling her from its ranks on September 3, 1782:

> Considered the case of Deborah Sampson, a member of this Church, who last Spring was accused of Dressing in men's Clothes, and inlisting as a soldier in the army and altho she was not convicted, yet was strongly suspected of being guilty and for sometime before behaved very loose and unchristian like, and at last left our parts in a secret manner and it is not known among us where she is gone; and after considerable discourse it appeared that as several brethren had labored with her before she went away without obtaining satisfaction, con-

cluded it is the Church's duty to withdraw fellowship until she returns and makes Christian satisfaction.[13]

The criticism only hardened Deborah's resolve. Though she was slightly ashamed by the scandal, the feeling of being treated like a Patriot stayed with her. She had seen the look of pride in the other men's eyes as she had stood among them, dressed like them, part of something bigger than themselves. She knew well the risks: she remembered painfully the day Mr. Thomas had come home weeping over the loss of two of his sons, killed in battle in Virginia fighting under the Marquis de Lafayette; and she knew that as a woman, should she be discovered, disgrace would only be the start of her punishment. Once she had made the decision to disguise herself as a man and join the army, there was no turning back. It was the only way she wanted to fight for her country: out on the battlefield, defending liberty, defending freedom, defending all that she and her family and friends stood for. She held the shears up to her long, thick golden blond hair, and cut.

❧

A sliver of light fought its way through a crack in the tiny, blackened windowpane, the sole reminder of life outside. Deborah struggled to straighten herself, but the weight of the soldier's body on her own kept her down. His head, buried in her lap, faced the only window in the room. His hands still tightly gripped his musket. She gently nudged him, whispering his name, "Snow," but all was silent. No response. She spoke his name again, this time making a gigantic effort to move her body out from under his. She succeeded, and his body fell back down against the filthy attic floorboards with a thud. She now saw his face, those eyes—which had only last night looked agonizingly into her own—now fixed and open, a look of sheer terror still frozen about them.

She hung her head low over the body of her fellow soldier and friend. She had lost track of how many days they had been locked up in this tiny, hot, airless place. (She would later learn it was seven.) She had realized almost at once that the homeowner who had offered her and her sick compatriot shelter in his beautiful home in Collerbarack, New York, was really a Tory; and, as the days and nights had passed with hardly any food or water for either of them, as Snow lay in a semi-coma, his high fever raging, the damning realization that they had been put there to starve to death had come upon her. She had remained with her friend in the field and had thought she was carrying him to safety. Instead, they had walked willingly into the doorways of hell.

Alone, she felt a new and sudden panic: if she didn't get out of there, she too would share this soldier's fate. She shed no tears over his body but instead licked her parched lips and tried to stand. She fell down, her head and body throbbing with pain; her leg wound, received months earlier, reopened, leaking blood. There was nothing more she could do for this man, and dying alongside him would not bring him back. With what little strength she had left, she crawled for the window, her muscles aching, the sores on her feet stinging. She inhaled the rotten smell of death and decay that had filled the air since she had been put in there. She lifted herself and wiped the dirty pane with her sleeve, noticing for the first time how the entire sleeve of her once white uniform was now red, covered in dried blood. She peered outside. A dog barked, but other than that there was no sign of life.

She fell back down, unable to move, and as she lay there, she reflected on the past eight months of her life: how she had wanted so desperately to be here, to be part of her country's army, to be part of the fight for independence. She wistfully remembered the young girl she was only eight months earlier, the girl who had set out bravely on that beautiful spring night with courage and daring in her blood, filled with the notion that nothing was worth fighting for as much as freedom.

🙢

She thought back to her journey from Middleborough to Taunton, the first of many long walks she had endured, alone, dressed as a man. Deborah had learned that the nearest enlistment post was over seventy miles away in Boston. She had saved whatever money she could, a total of twelve dollars, and placed it in a whale-skin wallet, hoping it would last until she made it to the post. She would walk the distance and, hopefully, find places to stop and sleep along the route. It had taken her the entire night to reach town, but she hadn't stopped, for fear of being recognized. She remembered the fear she felt upon seeing her first familiar face, and the relief at realizing he hadn't recognized her. She almost laughed now at how nervous she had been, nervous enough to send her in a different direction. Switching course, she had followed a road heading southeast toward New Bedford, where she had walked another twenty-five miles, alone. She had found an obscure path off a main road and slept fitfully under a big old elm. After breakfast in a nearby tavern, she had headed north toward Boston, knowing it was seventy miles away.

Boston had been everything she had imagined. The streets and shops, the people and carts, the buzzing life of activity and purpose to which she was not accustomed, had affected her greatly: she had loved the stimulation of activity before her eyes, the clatter of horses hooves on the cobblestone, the architecture. She had loved seeing daily life in so many forms right before her; it had been a feast for her eyes and soul.

After a few days in Boston, sleeping in cheap taverns and traveling through town, unnoticed, she had walked southeast to the towns of Roxbury, Dedham, and Madfield. When she had reached Bellingham on the border, just north of Rhode Island, she was forty miles directly west of Middleborough, but the journey had been "150 miles as she had walked it."[14] Exhausted and starving, she entered a tavern, spending the last of her twelve dollars on food: corn cakes, molasses, and a cup of tea. Sinking down into a low chair in the corner, she slept.

Deborah was startled to awake to a voice addressing itself to her. Her heart beat furiously in her chest as she lifted her head to see a stranger speaking to her. A speculator named Noah Taft, he was trying to convince her to join the army. It was a few minutes until Deborah appreciated exactly what the man was saying, but as she listened to him speak about free food and travel, a new uniform, and a sixty-pound bounty to be earned, she had laughed inside at the irony of being approached at this time and in this way. Momentarily forgetting her new identity, she rose to speak, but was taken aback when she heard his words, "a fine young man such as yourself." This had reminded her of her image to those who looked upon her.

She would be part of the quota for Uxbridge, he had told her, a nearby town not too far from where they sat, and he offered to drive her to Worcester, twenty miles west, where she could enlist. Understanding her luck, and reading the situation as a good omen, she had pretended to think it over for about half an hour. When the man returned, she told him she agreed to go. This was the moment she had dreamed of for quite some time now; it looked as though her dream was happening. She followed him to his cart, and they rode off.

The ride to Worcester had not been long, her mind racing with so many things that she barely noticed the approach. What would she say if they questioned her too closely? What if they wanted a physical exam? What if she were detected? Was this a mistake? For the first time since she left Middleborough, she was seized with real apprehension. Approaching the moment she had longed for, she now suddenly questioned her wisdom and her strength. But circumstances were not conducive to her turning around and running; they had reached Worcester and had been ushered into a room to meet Captain Eliphalet Thorp, chairman of class 22 for Uxbridge, the man in charge of enlistments.

Captain Thorp studied her and questioned her, and she remained as calm and poised as she could. She had told him she was seventeen and that she knew how to hunt. She lowered her voice as best she could, standing tall, acting serious as she knew a man would, avoiding the captain's direct gaze as much as possible. The entire process had lasted only fifteen minutes, much shorter than expected. And when the captain slid a piece of paper across his desk with the date and place written clearly on top—May 20, 1782, Uxbridge—she immediately recognized it to be her enlistment paper: the moment had come for her to sign. Reaching down to take the pen that was offered, she stared in disbelief. Then, slowly, with meaning and with pride, she signed the name Robert Shurtliff, the name of her deceased older brother, and with that, she instantly became a soldier in the Fourth Massachusetts Regiment of the Continental Army.

Deborah most likely did not know at the time, but enlistments in the army had dropped sharply. In 1781 Congress had requested 37,000 men, but instead only received 8,000 responses. George Washington, understanding this very real danger, issued a request for 20,000 more volunteers in the winter of 1782, as army enlistments continued to dwindle. It had become increasingly difficult to find men: many soldiers were dismayed and disillusioned with the lack of pay, the meager food, the spread of smallpox and malignant fever sweeping through the bases, and the long separation from their families. The dangers and risks inherent in service had become painfully clear, as many opted out of service and could not be required to fight. For Deborah, however, this only made her chances of being accepted better. The army, desperate for new recruits, scrutinized the men who showed up to volunteer much less than they had six years earlier, at the start of the war.

Deborah must have understood the hardship army life promised, though the degree to which she realized this is unknown. In any case, her patriotism triumphed over fear, and during this new wave of recruitment in May 1782, the twenty-two-year-old woman successfully outwitted the recruitment officers in Worcester, Massachusetts, and enlisted in the Continental Army as Private Robert Shurtliff. (Historians disagree as to the exact date of her enlistment. Although her enlistment papers state May 20, 1782, as the formal date, years later when she petitioned for relief from Congress, she would state she was injured at the Battle of Yorktown in 1781.)

Deborah had become one of fifty new recruits to join this regiment, led by Sergeant William Gambel from West Point. She would march two hundred miles through the Berkshire Hills of western Massachusetts, then on to Connecticut and New York, their destination being West Point. Along the way, their small group of fifty would turn into a sizable one of three hundred. They had slept on the ground, under the stars, not stopping to bathe except to wash their hands and face in the rivers.

As they marched toward New York, she and her fellow soldiers had learned that the British still held New York and that George Washington, the commander in chief of the Continental Army, worried that the British might try to recapture points along the Hudson, even attempt a recapture of West Point. Washington and his main core of troops, numbering almost nine thousand, had stationed themselves along the Hudson, he in his new residence in Newburgh and the troops in nearby New Windsor. After passing a bitterly cold winter in Philadelphia, they had arrived on the Hudson in March 1782 and now awaited the arrival of a wave of new recruits to help protect West Point, of which she was now one. This very spot, where the Hudson met the Highlands, was one of the most strategic points in the war.

Deborah was shocked at the sight of West Point; she would never forget how it looked to her the first time she lay eyes on it. It stretched a mile long and a mile wide, perched on a cliff six hundred feet above the river.[15] As tattered flags bearing the insignia of thirteen colonies waved from ramparts and flagpoles, she felt a pride unlike any she had known, an emotion she had been unprepared for. Nothing up to that point in her life had affected her like the sight of that mighty fortress and those flags, and for a brief second she felt the peace that comes with knowing something is right. This was where she belonged.

Her introduction to life as a soldier at West Point was swift. She and her new "brothers" were shown their living quarters—tents that housed five to eight men, each with wooden bunks, crocus-sack mattresses, and plenty of pine branches and leaves for warmth. The officers were luckier: huts made from surrounding trees had been erected for them to sleep in, two at a time. She was handed a French musket the first day she reached West Point, along with thirty cartridges and a cartouche cartridge box with a sling, which she carried continuously on her left shoulder. She was issued a wooden canteen and a haversack, a coarse white linen pack for extra rations, clothing, toothbrush, mirror, handkerchief, writing material, and a Bible. She received a blanket.

What had really impressed her, however, was the new uniforms: beautiful, regal uniforms with a deep blue regimental or outer linen coat. The coat was lined with white on its cuffs, lapels, and collar, with a white lining and blue heart for reinforcement on each of the regimental coattails. She had been given a waistcoat and overalls, made of white linen, a pair of wool stockings, and black leather stout boots. She managed to get the uniform on without anyone noticing her body, keeping herself as private as she possibly could. Thankfully, the soldiers slept in their uniforms and did not bathe regularly.

Their daily drill began the very morning after they arrived, an exercise whereby each soldier learned to handle and use a musket and how to swing a bayonet. Her years with the Thomas boys now paid off, as she proved herself capable, steady, and fast. In no time she was promoted to a special group in the Light Infantry Division called the Rangers a core, elite section of the Continental Army sent out on special missions separate and apart from the main body of the army. This promotion came as a shock to her, as well as to some of the other soldiers around her, who had seen her as a young, inexperienced boy with no military background.

She eagerly and immediately accepted the honor, marveling at her good fortune. When the need arose, the Rangers detached from their parent regiments for special missions, such as spying on the enemy's movements, bringing back intelligence information, and capturing Tories. Her division, led by Captain George Webb of the First Brigade, was commanded by General John Patterson. All of the brigades were under the command of Major General Henry Knox, commander of West Point, who had been a bookseller in Boston before the war.

When the first order had come from George Washington to set out for Harlem, a place eight miles from New York City, she had been thrilled. It was a trek that would cover the neutral territory between American fortifications at Peekskill and British headquarters in Manhattan, for the purpose of ridding the territory of British spies, Loyalists, and Tories. The British control at that time extended just outside New York City to Kings Bridge and West Farms on the Bronx River. This area was riddled with violence and danger. If any American soldier was captured within British lines, he could be hung as a spy.

Patterson had sent Deborah's regiment to regain territory recently lost to British general Oliver DeLancey in a bloody battle. A particularly vicious group of Tories, known as the Westchester Light Horse, under the command of Colonel James DeLancey, were "raiding homes, raping women, looting possessions and burning down houses."[16] It was on this mission that Snow had become ill.

Deborah had volunteered to stay behind with him, thinking she might be of help; here she now lay, close to her own death.

Deborah thought of her mother, of her brothers and sisters, whom she had never really had a chance to know. She thought of the Thomas family, remembering the day in 1780 when Mr. Thomas had come from town crying, with news of his two sons' deaths. She thought of how she had disappeared into the night, of how all who had loved her probably believed her to be already dead. And she thought of her father, the memory of him walking away from her house, never once looking back.

Deborah felt a wetness on her cheek and realized, with shock, that she was crying. She hadn't cried in years. But it meant something: she was still alive. She was not dead yet, and she had not come this far to die in a filthy attic in some Tory's house. Anger seized her, infusing her with a new determination. She lifted the weight of her body up with one arm, leaned forward, and took Snow's cartridge box and musket. His musket was full, as was hers. With both weapons in her hands, she raised herself and decided to leave the room and meet her fate, whatever it would be. It couldn't be worse than where she now lay.

She slowly opened the door and descended the stairs. To her amazement, the house was quiet and still, as though she were the only one in it. She reached the first floor, an agonizing trip, but her anger overcame the pain, her new determination winning. She crept silently toward a side door she could now see. All was still quiet in the house. She held the two muskets firmly in one hand as she opened the door with the other. Then she limped as quickly as she could into the woods before her, astonished at the ease with which she had just left.

Deborah plodded on, the fresh air revitalizing her, at a fast limp, mindful of the danger she was still in should they discover she was gone. But the farther away she got from the house, the safer she began to feel. She remembered the direction from which she had approached with Snow: from the west. She followed a course she felt was right, her body succumbing to her will. She was free now, she realized. Free.

Two days later Deborah would reach an army barge, where she was given food and water and medical care by army personnel. She would be brought back to West Point, lauded for her bravery and loyalty. She offered information to her superiors about the circumstances under which she and Snow had suffered, and helped arrange a group to return to the house, an obvious Tory destination. They would ambush the house a few nights later when it was filled with drunken Tories, taking prisoners and horses, as well as reclaiming Snow's body. It was a successful raid, and her reputation for bravery only grew when it was over.

On April 1, 1783, as Deborah was working on the construction of Fort Edward, a new fort being erected near West Point, a soldier approached and told her General Patterson requested her presence. It was a moment of shock and fear, a moment years later she would poignantly remember as she recounted her tales to others. Her heart pounding, she walked slowly to his bunker, straining to understand when and how her secret had been discovered.

General Patterson, as it turned out, had requested her presence for quite a different reason: he wanted her as his exclusive aide-de-camp, now that his prior orderly, Major Elnathon Haskell, had fallen ill. The appointment had meant she would be moving into his quarters and be responsible for menial tasks, such as polishing his shoes, cleaning his boots, doing his errands. She would be given her own horse to carry messages and would be the general's right-hand man. Patterson, a man of great integrity and honor, was a graduate of Yale

(1762), a schoolteacher, and a lawyer. He had fought in many battles until promoted to major general.

The appointment was a huge honor, one she could not and did not turn down. It signified a real trust in her ability and trustworthiness as a soldier; that the general would choose her of all the soldiers at his disposal spoke volumes. As it happened, two weeks later, on April 19, a preliminary peace treaty was signed by England, France, and Spain, making operative the November pact between England and America. George Washington could finally announce the cessation of hostilities. The war was over.

No sooner had this announcement come than an uprising took place among the ranks of the Continental Army. Many officers and soldiers had staged a revolt in Philadelphia, going so far as to attack the State House with artillery seized from local barracks. The uproar occurred over matters such as pay and conditions, but Congress had been forced to flee to Princeton. General Washington immediately ordered 1,500 troops under General Robert Howe to quell the uprising.

Deborah and four other soldiers were given leave to join Howe's force, but by the time she reached Philadelphia, the mutiny was over. Unfortunately for her, a malignant fever was raging in the city, one that would attack her as no other enemy had, bringing her to the brink of death.

Taken to a hospital in a state of delirium, she was left on a stretcher for hours, assumed to be dead. A Dr. Barnabus Binney, working at the hospital that day, discovered her lying there and, upon examining her, felt a slight pulse. Slipping his hand inside her shirt, looking most probably for a heart beat, he opened her tunic and, upon cutting the linen cloth, discovered what no one else knew: the soldier lying there half dead was a woman. Shocked and sympathetic, he removed her to his home, telling those who asked that she needed constant care; within a few weeks, she recovered.

With the signing of the Treaty of Paris, in September 1783, Deborah was ordered back to West Point, where her regiment was to be disbanded. Saying good-bye to the Binneys in Philadelphia was emotional for her; she felt a closer bond with this doctor than with anyone she had ever met: Not only had he saved her life, but he had also kept her secret. As she said good-bye, she noticed a letter in his hand and looked up at him questioningly. He caught the meaning in her eyes, but simply and gently instructed her to pass the letter on to General Patterson. She took the envelope from him, bewildered; why would Dr. Binney write a letter to the general? Might he reveal her secret after all? She searched his face for a sign of what this meant, looking down at the envelope, then back to him, waiting for some explanation to come from his lips; but all she received was a gesture of reassurance: a pat on the arm, and a smile.

"You are a special woman, my dear. My God bless you and care for you. I hope we meet again soon."

That was all he said, and as he turned to leave, walking away, Deborah felt a sadness well up inside of her; she thought of her father. This time she too turned to go, letter in hand, unsure whether her fate and her future rested inside the envelope she now held. Hours later, as she waited on the dock for her boat to New York, she found herself obsessed with the thought of what his letter might say. She looked down at the letter and considered opening it, the temptation to do so almost unbearable. She wanted to throw it away, to let it slip out of her hands and be carried away with the wind. She peered out over the restless water, noticing gathering storm clouds above. The sky was growing darker, and gusts of wind were beginning to blow; she leaned over the tired, splintered wooden rail, an image of strength on the outside, a distraught, worried young woman underneath. She knew this letter was about her; she felt sure of it. Dr. Binney was the only one who knew her secret; he was the only one who could tell.

But he had trusted her, this man and friend who had saved her life and hidden her identity had asked her to do something for him after he had done so much for her. The thought of betraying him was almost worse than the fear of being discovered. Deborah knew, in the end, she could not and would not lie. She would give the letter to the general, as she had been asked to do. She would suffer whatever consequences of that decision came her way. She had never betrayed a friend, and she wasn't about to start now.

She folded the letter and pushed it down deep into her pocket. Her haversack filled, she checked one last time that she had her diary, the one she kept faithfully for almost a year. The weather had turned terribly damp and cloudy, with reports of a storm brewing, but the passengers, Deborah included, had been anxious to board. So they did.

Two hours into the trip, the weather became brutally severe, with a harsh rain pounding down upon them and gale-force winds tossing their small boat. Another boat in the water could be seen struggling, and it was not long before her captain's voice could be heard, shrieking unintelligible orders. She held on to the side of the boat with all her might, still not feeling the strength she possessed before her illness.

Moments later, with land in sight, people aboard began jumping overboard, their screams lost in the wind. It had become clear the boat would not last much longer, the current and water tossing it wildly from one side to the other. She gripped the side but was thrown back violently when a wave hit the boat, sending her crashing backward onto the floor. She slid on the wet deck and was forced to watch as her haversack flew from her shoulder out of her reach. She struggled to stand, to reach for the bag, but before she knew it, another wave hit with such force, she was knocked back down to the ground. That was the last time she would recall seeing her bag, her diary lost forever. Deborah managed to stand and, grabbing hold of the side of the boat, leaped off the deck into the dark freezing water churning below.

When the nightmarish ordeal was over, Deborah found herself onshore with a few of the other passengers from their boat. She wouldn't remember many details, but her bag would be lost, and her diary along with it. It was hours before they were rescued, cold, fatigued, worn. By the time she would reach General Patterson's quarters, her anguish at what her future held only compounded by the storm at sea. Ironically, the only possession that survived the boat's capsize would be Dr. Binney's letter, stuffed into a pocket away from her other belongings. It was still wet when she discovered it, and a bit shredded, but otherwise intact.

She entered the general's room, bedraggled and weary, the events of the last month finally taking their toll. The warmth in Patterson's greeting made what was sure to follow only that much worse. After a brief explanation of her whereabouts, she sheepishly pulled the letter out of her outer front right pocket, handed it to the general without looking him in the eye, and stood before him, staring solemnly at the ground. Her new diary would record that this moment "was worse than facing a cannonade."[17]

With a bemused look on his face, he took the letter from her and read it. She waited. A few more seconds went by, but still all was silent. She didn't dare raise her head for fear of the expression she would encounter. But as she continued to stare at the ground, as if frozen in time, the silence only became louder. What was he doing? Wasn't he reading the letter? Finally, she couldn't take it one moment more. She raised her head slowly, and found herself face to face with an expression of such complete shock that, for the first time since she had joined the army, she became truly aware of the level of deception she had engaged in.

At that moment all became clear. It was the end of the line. Her farce had gone too far, she had betrayed everyone who knew her, and she would now suffer the consequences.

Patterson spoke first. After what felt to her like an unbearably long silence, he put the letter down on the table and quietly asked, "Is it true?"

"Sir," she began, but was suddenly stopped by his hand, high in the air.

"Is it true?" he asked again, staring straight into her eyes with a wonder and astonishment she could now also hear in his voice.

"Yes," she said, praying she was answering the correct question, still not completely sure what Dr. Binney's letter said.

"Take off your hat, please," he instructed her, waiting, watching, greedy for confirmation.

She did as she was asked. Still no dent in his perception.

"Who are you?" he questioned.

For the first time in a year and a half, she uttered her name, her real name, a name that sounded strange after all this time, even to her.

"Deborah Sampson, sir. My name is Deborah Sampson."

It would be many days until her whole story would become clear, but when it did, Deborah was spared the punishment and agony she had been sure she would have to endure. While Dr. Binney's letter had revealed Deborah's secret, it had also commended her patriotism with the utmost pride and admiration. Rather than be ostracized, embarrassed, or persecuted for her transgression, she was instead, oddly, escorted by Patterson and Colonel Jackson through the tented encampment, dressed as a woman, and introduced to the troops. She saw soldiers "with whom I had been as familiar as inmates of a family only hours before, but none of them recognized me."[18]

The following day, October 25, 1783, she received an honorable discharge signed by General Henry Knox, commander of West Point, based on impressive testimonials of her faithful performance, by head of the First Brigade, General Shepard, originally head of the Fourth Massachusetts Regiment, and his successor, Colonel Jackson. Through the entire ordeal, Patterson treated her with unusual respect; twenty years later, when they saw each other again under very different circumstances, he would still consider her a friend. With her discharge papers now in hand, she felt sad to be leaving the men and the "family" she had grown so accustomed to, but proud and thankful to have served in the army—she had accomplished what she had set out to do, and she had excelled. She had fought for her country as she had wanted to; she had done her part to help preserve freedom and independence for years to come. Years later it would be said that "she went into the service because men were few and her heart was in the cause." She was headed for a sloop of war to New York, where she would board Captain Allen's packet for Providence, her trip paid for by the army. She was going home.

Postscript

A definitive treaty of peace was ratified on September 23, and by November 3 Congress had issued a proclamation disbanding the army. Upon arriving in Boston on November 1, 1783, Deborah traveled to Stoughton, where she went directly to the home of her aunt and uncle, a Mr. Zebulon and Alice Waters. Tellingly, she would not go to her mother, possibly feeling she would not be welcome after all this time. They would eventually reunite, but her instinct would prove to be right. Deborah's mother remained ashamed of her daughter for years afterward, not only because of her joining the army, but also because of her expulsion from church.

Two years after returning home, Deborah met a man named Benjamin Gannett, the son of a local farmer, a man six years her senior, and they would marry on April 7, 1785, at his father's farm in Sharon, Massachusetts. She would move in with her in-laws and in 1786 give birth to a son, Earl. She and her husband would buy their own home on March 18, 1786, in Sharon, a few blocks away from the Gannett farm, at the cost of thirty-four pounds, seven shillings. Over the next few years Deborah gave birth to two girls, Mary in 1790 and Patience in 1791. She and her husband would also adopt another daughter, Susan Shepard, who had been orphaned at only five days old.

Soon after Deborah's discharge from the army, a New York newspaper published a story about her, taken from facts reportedly obtained through officers at West Point. The story, which originally appeared in a Massachusetts paper, told of the female soldier who had disguised herself as a man and served in the army. It was then that Herman Mann, printer, publisher, and sometime editorial writer for the *Village Register* in Dedham, Massachusetts, became interested in writing the story of her life. He interviewed her, and after much persuasion she agreed to let him write her story, with his promise that she would have the final say. *The Female Review; or, Memoirs of an American Young Lady* was printed in 1797 in Dedham, but there is reason to believe Deborah never did get final review. Mann arranged for a list of subscribers to pay the costs and promised Deborah a share of the profits, but it seems she did not receive much of these. He commissioned Joseph Stone of Framingham, Massachusetts, to paint Deborah's picture for a front is piece for the book, and this picture, oil paint on paper, about fifteen inches by ten, pasted on wood, is in the John Brown Museum in Providence, Rhode Island today. (Subsequent printings of Mann's book would serve to correct some of the misconstrued "facts" in the first edition and lessen Mann's embellishments to Deborah's story. Though he claimed to be her official biographer, many historians believed the wording of the story to have come from his mouth, not hers. He was also not an unbiased reporter of events, having fiercely strong opinions about the Revolutionary War and about women's role in society at the time. Further, he himself noted in the introduction to the book that he was adding his own moral reflections and words.)

In 1802, five years after her story was published by Mann, Deborah and Benjamin still struggled financially, trying to manage their meager farm. It was then that she was again approached by Mann, who suggested Deborah might earn money by traveling through various states, speaking publicly about her time in the military. Mann offered to write the speeches, and Deborah, desperate to earn some money for her family, agreed. At forty-two years of age, Deborah would leave home again, alone, and begin a lecture tour that would bring her to Providence, New York, and various cities in Massachusetts. She was billed as "The American Heroine," with newspapers advertising her performances and audiences lining up to see and hear the woman who had served as a soldier. Traveling alone from March 1802 through the spring of 1803, she kept an itemized list of all her expenses and would arrange her own performance after she arrived in each town. Deborah returned to Boston, going back to the city she remembered from almost twenty years earlier, but now she returned as a billed performer, the first woman ever to go on the professional lecture circuit. Audiences waited outside the Federal Street Theatre, where, on March 20, 1802, she would give her first public performance.

Though each performance would reveal Deborah standing onstage in complete military regalia, armed with a musket and demonstrating the twenty-seven arms maneuvers at the command of an officer, Deborah would explain why she had gone to war, saying,

Know then that my juvenile mind early became inquisitive to understand why man should march out tranquilly, or in a paroxysm of rage against fellow man, to butcher or be butchered. But most of all, my mind became agitated with the inquiry—why a nation, separated from us by an ocean more than three thousand miles in extent, should endeavor to enforce on us plans of subjugation, the most unnatural in themselves, unjust, inhuman, in their operations, and unpracticed even by the uncivilized savages of the wilderness? We indeed originated from her, as from a parent, and had, perhaps, continued to this period in subjection to her mandates, had we not discovered that this, her romantic, avaricious and cruel disposition extended to murder, after having bound the slave. I only seemed to want the license to become one of the severest avengers of the wrong.[19]

She continued:

Wrought upon at length, you may say, by an enthusiasm and frenzy that could break no control—I burst the tyrant bonds, which held my sex in awe, and clandestinely, or by stealth, grasped an opportunity, which custom and the world seemed to deny, as a natural privilege. And whilst poverty, hunger, nakedness, cold and disease had dwindled the American Armies to a handful—whilst universal terror and dismay ran through the camps . . . did I throw off the soft bailments of my sex, and assume those of the warrior, already prepared for battle. Thus I became an actor in that important drama with an inflexible resolution to persevere through the last scene; when we might be permitted to acknowledge and enjoy what we had so nobly declared we would possess, or lose with our lives—FREEDOM and INDEPENDENCE![20]

Deborah's diary entries reveal that, far from feeling apologetic, she not only enjoyed her life in the military but was also, to some degree, enjoying her stint as a speaker. For instance, an entry for May 2, 1802, refers to her talking at Amidon's Hall in Providence: "When I entered the Hall I must say I was much pleased with the appearance of the audience. It appeared from almost every countenance that they were full of unbelief . . . I mean in regard to my being the person that served in the Revolutionary army. Some of them which I happened to overhear swore I was a lad of not more than eighteen years of age. I sat for some time in my chair before I rose to deliver my address. When I did I think I may with all candor, applaud the people for their serious attention and peculiar respect, especially the ladies."[21]

Deborah's journey on the road after twenty years at home was singularly different than her first, for this time she was traveling as a mother. Her diary entries show the strain of being away from her children and, fascinatingly, paint a portrait of the modern-day struggle between independence and motherhood that existed, at least in this woman's heart, over two hundred years ago. Her entry on June 28, 1802, talks of "a heart filled with pain when I realized parting with my three dear children and other friends; I may say four dear children—my dear little Susan Shepherd."[22] In September she reveals more signs of strain, using the word *gloomy* to describe her route. By October, she writes, "The homesickness continues. . . . Nothing in the least inviting to the weary traveler."[23] Though she did spend one month as a guest in the home of General Patterson, in Lisle, New York, during his tenure as judge and member of the New York State Legislature, she wrote on November 11, "To think of myself so far from my dear children, no opportunity of hearing from them, and God only knows when I shall be so happy as to see them."[24] (The following year Patterson was elected to the U.S. Congress and would be instrumental in securing a much-needed pension for Deborah, from the federal government, of four dollars a month for services rendered during the war.) Sadly, money from her lectures was scarcely enough to help her husband run the farm. Like so many other farmers at the time, they were deeply affected by postwar inflation, as prices for food and clothing rose dramatically. As a result, she formally petitioned the Commonwealth of Massachusetts for money in January 1792. The petition read in part, "The memorial of Deborah Gannett Humbly Sheweth that your Memorialist from zeal for the good of her country was induc'd, and by the name Robert Shurtliff did, on May 20, 1782, Inlist as a Soldier in the Continental Service . . . and was constant and faithful in doing Duty with other soldiers and was engaged with the enemy at Tarry town, New York, and was wounded there by the enemy, and continued in service until discharged, by General Henry Knox at West Point October 25, 1783." It continues, "Being a female and not knowing the proper steps to take to get pay for her services, has hitherto not received one farthing for her services." [25]

The petition was presented to the Massachusetts House of Representatives, and a resolve was printed granting her a pension for life. The resolve read in part, "Whereas it further appears that the said Deborah exhibited an extraordinary instance of female heroism by discharging the duties of a faithful, gallant soldier, and at the same time preserving the virtue and charity of her sex unsuspected and unblemished." [26] Included with the petition were letters from Colonel Jackson and Private Thorp, both of whom attested to her military service and described her as a good soldier, and she was granted the sum of thirty-four pounds bearing interest from October 23, 1783, "which amounted to little over one hundred dollars for her eighteen months of service." [27]

In 1804, she was visited and befriended by Paul Revere, who, after seeing the dire financial straits she had come to, wrote a letter on her behalf to William Eustis, the Massachusetts representative in Congress. Speaking of her frail physical condition, Revere wrote in part, "I have conversed about her, and it is not a few, speak of her as a woman of handsome talents, good morals, a dutiful wife, and an affectionate parent. She is now much out of health. She has several children, her husband is a good sort of man, 'tho of small force in business; they have a few acres of poor land which they cultivate, but they are really poor. . . . She told me that no doubt her ill health is a consequence of her being exposed when she did a soldier's duty, and that while in the army she was wounded . . . I think her case much more deserving than hundreds to whom Congress has been generous."[28]

As a result of this letter, in 1805 Deborah was placed on the Massachusetts invalid pension roll, entitling her to four dollars a month, retroactive to the January 1, 1803.

Even with this pension, she and Benjamin were painfully poor. Her son Earl, a captain in the War of 1812, would earn money in his military career and build his parents a nice house at 300 East Street in Sharon, the place in which she would spend the last years of her life, watching her twelve grandchildren grow (a home that still stands today). She would live only nine years more; in 1827, at sixty-eight years of age, she died in that very same home.

Only five years before her death, another woman, Nancy Ward, whom Deborah would never have the chance to know, quietly died an unknown warrior to all but those who knew her best. Just like Deborah, this woman knew war; just like Deborah, she had killed and been threatened with death many times. Just like Deborah, she had fought for a cause she believed in with all her heart, one she was willing to risk her life for. Had the two women met, they would have discovered they were fighting a common enemy in the same land, not with a band of sisters at their sides, but as women, alone. They would have also discovered a very great difference, however—this woman, Nancy Ward, whom Deborah would not meet, had never been forced to hide. Rather than chop off her hair and hide it under a hat, she had let it flow long and untamed, in full view as the great female warrior she was. They lived in the same time, on the same land, two strikingly brave women willing to risk their lives for the one thing they believed in above all else: freedom.

NANCY WARD

Caption TK

A Woman Warrior
NANCY WARD

*The white men are our brothers; the same house holds us,
the same sky covers us all.*

—NANCY WARD

Taliwa, South Carolina, 1755

S HE PEERED OUT from behind the log to see where her husband, Kingfisher, had gone. She spotted a musket and feathers
behind a tree, lowered her body, and crawled in the dirt, inching her
way forward. Her sunburned, golden brown skin blended with the
forest floor, her beauty camouflaged by the earth; her long, black
hair, pulled back in a braid, fell over her shoulder as she crawled. Her
teeth were sore from chewing bullets, and the taste of lead remained
in her mouth. But the bullets were sharper now, ready to fire. All she
needed was to find her man.

Dawn was breaking, spreading an amber light over the forest.
She rounded a tree and found the musket and firearms. They were
his. She lifted her head and searched in vain for a sign of Kingfisher.
All was eerily silent. No sign or signals from her brother Long Fellow
or her uncle Attakullaculla; nor did she see Oconostota, their chief,

where he had been moments earlier. She strained her neck forward and, sensing danger, tightened her moccasins and sprang up, sprinting through the dense forest. Running through dark thickets, as quick as a fawn, over rugged paths, along narrow passes in the dismal wilderness, she could hardly see three feet in front of her. She finally pressed her body against a great oak and rested for a moment, crouching low to the earth. It was then that she saw him.

Kingfisher lay on his back, facing the morning sky, arms spread to his side, motionless. She crept over to his body and, looking into his eyes, saw instantly he was dead. A musket wound was still bleeding in his side. In his hand remained the bow he had made just last week. She lifted the bow and stroked its flat, broad surface, the honey locust he had used a tarnished brown. She felt a sorrow unlike any she had ever known, a welling up of grief and sadness for herself and the two beloved children she had shared with him. She had met him five years earlier, when he was a young brave of the Deer clan. She had traveled with him not only as a wife but as a warrior; she was as committed to her people as any of the men in the tribe, if not more so. A fierce anger now began to take hold. She suddenly felt an overwhelming urge to kill. She would go after whoever had done this and avenge her husband's death. She would fight like the Cherokee warrior she was.

Nancy bent down, putting her arms under her husband's; using all her might, she pulled him out of the open and dragged him to a darker, hidden spot. After gathering his belongings and placing them together with hers, she marked for herself the spot where he lay, vowing to come back for him. She was on her own warpath now, and she would not back down until she killed as many of the enemy as she could find. Nancy rose slowly, spear and musket in hand, as she directed her gaze to the morning sun.

She crept silently along the narrow path as she ventured to keep herself hidden. Crouched low to the ground, her back arched like an animal on the prowl as she slithered through the thicket, unaware of danger or risk to herself. She made her way to a spot where she thought she might find the others, and it wasn't long until she arrived there and saw the sight she had prayed for: her brother, Long Fellow, leaning by a tree, his head hung low. The men next to him seemed frozen as they stood, unmoving, in a circle of apparent defeat. Panting, she approached her brother, instantly noticing the look on his face. Slowly she approached the circle, where she saw a body on the ground, that of a beloved member of their clan, his limbs ripped off, his heart pulled out, only the tortured expression on his face remaining.

She heard a crackling sound and turned immediately, only to see Kingfisher's horse by a tree. Long Fellow looked at the horse, then at his sister, and he understood instantly what hadn't been said. Though heartbroken for his sister and himself, Long Fellow felt that this last blow, Kingfisher's loss, would have to be the last. They were outnumbered and the losses had become too much to bear; all agreed and they now turned to go home. But the sight of his horse, Kingfisher's favorite animal, appeared as a sign to Nancy, an omen; if he were alive, he would be on the animal, charging forward to battle the Creeks, their native enemy; it was her choice now whether to take his place or leave with her brother and the men. Without thinking, she walked over to the horse, hoisted herself up on its strong, muscular back, and let out a war cry, as she had seen and heard her husband do many times before. Yelling to the men to join her, she paced back and forth on the agitated horse, energy, excitement, and fear running through her veins. If the men would not lead her, she would lead them. With a swift kick, the horse spun on its hind legs and raced headfirst in the direction of their enemy. She heard the men's cries of protest behind her but did not turn around as she flew through the forest, a force of one. The men jumped on their horses and followed.

The Battle of Taliwa in 1755 was one of the fiercest ever fought between the two ancient southeastern tribes, the Cherokees and the Creeks, bitter enemies for ages. It was a fight for land, with five hundred Cherokee braves eventually pushing back one thousand Creeks, to regain northern Georgia and part of present-day Alabama. The losses on both sides had been bloody and raw, but this battle was only the climax to a long and costly struggle beginning in 1715, when the Cherokees had pushed into northern Georgia, then Creek territory. That was also the year when the Creeks, fighting with the Yamasee in their war against the English, faced opposition from the Cherokees, who fought on behalf of the crown. The following thirty to forty years brought continuous fighting between the two tribes, only to end at this very battle, one in which the seventeen-year-old Nancy's bravery and determination had rallied her people to conquer their enemy and taste victory.

Because of her bravery in battle and the way she had taken Kingfisher's place, leading her people to victory, she would now be considered a Ghigau, a "Beloved Woman" or, alternately, Agiyagustu, meaning "Honored Woman."[1] (As history would reveal, she would become the last honored woman of the tribe.) Riding back to Chota alongside her uncle, the great civil chief Attakullaculla (or Little Carpenter, as he was also called), Nancy looked regal in her war assemblage. In contrast to her uncle, who was small of stature and slender, with a delicate frame, her tall, erect form balanced on her horse looked large and imposing. Her deep-set, piercing black eyes stared out at her people; her long, silken black hair sat on top of her head, pulled up with a silver brooch, in a wreathed topknot. She saw her people stare at the Negro slave following close behind, a gift to her from her grateful Cherokee brothers, left behind by retreating Creeks. She would be the first slave owner among the

Cherokees, a circumstance that contributed to the personal wealth she would accumulate in life as the first cattle owner of the tribe. She strode back onto her land with a kind but imperious gait. She was not the same woman she had been days earlier. She had left her home as a young, helpful wife; she now returned as a widowed mother of two. But to all who looked upon her, the young woman was the essence of power: a female warrior and chief.

Born in 1738 to Tame Doe, sister to the great chief Attakullaculla, civil chief of the great nation, Nancy is rumored to have come into the world with both Indian and white blood flowing through her veins, though the identity of her father is unknown. Some have claimed he was a British officer, while others think he may have been from Delaware and joined the Wolf clan by marriage. At least one prominent historian claims she was a full-breed Cherokee. Nancy's tribal name was Nanye'hi, a derivative of a tribal myth name meaning "spirit people," and this was how she was known to her tribe. Legend has it that because of the texture of her skin, so like that of a rose petal, she was given the nickname Tsistu-na-gis-ka (Cherokee for "wild rose," a flower which people loved; the Cherokee rose, *Rosa sinica,* the official flower of Georgia, is closely associated with her name today.)[2] James Robertson, one of the white leaders of the Wataugan settlement who had visited her during this time, described her as "queenly and commanding in appearance and manner."[3]

Ghigaus held a holy place in the hearts of the Cherokee tribe: "It was the only title ever bestowed upon a woman."[4] It was selectively offered to a woman who had proven her bravery in battle, and it represented a sacred place among the Cherokee. If an Indian woman took her husband's place in battle after he had died, as Nancy did, and that man had been a chief, the woman would automatically assume his title upon death. As a Ghigau, she would become a member of the Cherokee War Council and would be revered, looked to for wisdom and bravery in matters of war. It was believed that the Great Spirit used the voice of the Beloved Woman to speak to the Cherokees, and consequently her words were always heard, if not heeded. In the matter of prisoners, a Ghigau had absolute power to decide their fate. Nancy Ward would also be the head of the influential Woman's Council, made up of a representative from each clan, which did not hesitate to override the authority of the chiefs if they thought best.

Life in a Cherokee tribe was supremely matriarchal, with Cherokee women having more rights and power than either their American or European sisters. A Cherokee woman decided whom she would marry, and the man would build a house for her—which was considered her property—or else live on her mother's property with her. The house and children were hers. She and her brothers raised them if need be. To obtain a divorce, she packed her husband's clothes in a bag and set it outside the door. Any reason for a decision to divorce would suffice: adultery, laziness, or boredom. She would be free to marry someone else, and so would her ex-spouse. Many divorces and remarriages occurred, and laws against adultery were generally not enforced. James Adair, one of the first white settlers in the area, observed that "the Cherokee women divorce bedfellows at their pleasure."[5]

Never idle, most Indian women spent their time planting, caring for hogs and poultry, smoking venison or other meat procured on the hunt, tanning hides, manufacturing clothing, cooking, and rearing children. The men would make bows, tomahawks, war clubs, canoes, and earthenware. The Cherokees' specialty craft was stone pipes.

But the Cherokee men's respect for women did not translate into gentleness with others: the Cherokee were one of the most feared and ferocious tribes living in the southeastern section of North America. They were also the largest tribe in the South, with an estimated population of 22,000 in 1650. They called themselves

Yunwiya, which means "Principal People," probably due to the size of their tribe. By 1771, forty-three Cherokee towns existed in the Southeast, with towns varying in size from a dozen to 200 dwellings, the average being about 100.[6] In the center of town was an open square for dances and ceremonies. On the west side of the square stood the council house or temple, and around the square were groups of dwellings and gardens. The houses resembled one another, with a small, scooped-out fireplace in the center, and beside it a large "flat hearthstone for baking cornbread." The Cherokee women were described as "excellent cooks," whose "bread bakes to as great perfection as in any European oven."[7] Besides bread and meat, as farmers the Cherokee made use of all the resources available to them in the wilderness. Corn was their main crop, but they also grew pumpkins, beans, gourds, and sunflowers. The Cherokee ate nuts, wild fruits, roots, mushrooms, fish, crayfish, frogs, and even birds' eggs.

Beds were made of saplings and woven splints. Each family also had a smaller, hidden winter house, where the members slept during cold weather. These homes were furnished with beds and had a fireplace burning all day to provide warmth. The white traders, who called these hot houses, borrowed the idea and built similar ones for their own comfort. Hot houses were also used by medicine men for giving sweat baths to treat certain diseases. Myth Keepers, priests who "recited and discussed the lore of the tribe and instructed chosen young men in the secret knowledge of myth keeping," held secret meetings in these as well.[8]

The Cherokee were comprised of seven clans, each a familial community, and members of a clan were barred from marrying within the clan because it was so strongly viewed as family. Nancy was a member of the Wolf clan, the most revered of the tribe. Each had its own customs and rituals, war dances and beliefs, sharing some similarities and also some differences. There were three dialects spoken. The other tribes in the region—the Iroquis, Creeks, Choctaws, Chickasaws, and Shawnees—eventually all vied for the Mississippi Valley. Living in what would later be considered the heart of the Mississippi Valley, the Cherokee were surrounded on all sides by enemies, both Indian and white.

Unbeknownst to Nancy, her elevation to Ghigau came at a time when relations between the Cherokees, the English, the French, and the white South Carolina and Virginia settlers were about to explode. In only a few short years, the entire balance of power in the region would shift from her people's happy alliance with South Carolina against the French, to an all-out war between the Indians and their newly discovered white American brothers. It was during this time that Nancy Ward would begin risking her life to save those of the white settlers in the region, while simultaneously leading her own people in their struggle to preserve their land and culture.

&

The year was 1758. In the backcountry and wild terrain of the southeastern colonies, an insidious trouble was brewing, trouble that would eventually lead to the relocation of an entire people and way of life. As she sat deep in thought, weaving a basket, Nancy thought about what she had been told by Oconostota earlier that day. French agents had whispered warnings in Oconostota's ears about their new English friends, citing instances of murder and betrayal against the Indians in the lower Cherokee towns, with a threat that Chota would be next. In Nancy's view, the French were clearly vying for control of the Overhill Cherokees, those living in towns farther west, lining the Tennessee River. Both Oconostota and Attakullaculla had been unnerved by the warning and had seemed preoccupied that whole day. Nancy could sense danger brewing, but dared not speak to them of it yet until she had more information.

What Nancy had come to feel sure of was the precarious position her people were in, approached daily by one or another opposing faction for their own alleged good. The English were sending ammunition to the Cherokees in the hope of enlisting them to fight against the French; the colonists also wooed the Cherokees to fight against the French; and the French, meanwhile, warned the Cherokees not to trust either the English or the colonists. Meanwhile, South Carolina's Governor Lyttleton had heard stories about hostile Indians who refused to hand over a zealot named Piper. He decided, in response, that South Carolina needed to build a fort to protect its interest against the Indians and, in another twist, to protect South Carolina's relations with the Indians against the French. A new fort was designed and constructed as the amazed Cherokees watched with both awe and trepidation; Fort Loudin would tragically, in a few short years, be home to a horrible war, with casualties on a scale that few could ever have contemplated at the time.

The Cherokees did not protest the construction of the new fort on their land, as they saw the opportunity for more ammunition. The site eventually chosen for the fort put it directly across the river from Chota, Nancy's home, and, as the South Carolina men worked day and night to construct it, French rumors and agitation continued to fill the air. Fortunately for Demere, the fort's building supervisor, the Cherokees resisted the entreaties of the French, and by the time the fort was completed in 1757, despite French agents sneaking into Chota and making flattering proposals to the Cherokees, the Cherokees agreed to go on raids against the French, and to work with the Americans in exchange for ammunition and friendship.

From 1757 to 1759, real peace between the South Carolinians and the Cherokees seemed to exist. The two cultures integrated their people and customs in a way they never had before. Cherokee women moved freely in and out of the fort, and many white men took Cherokee brides with the permission and blessing of the tribe.

Several traders set up homes in Chota, a practice that led to many marriages between white tradesmen and Indian women. In fact, tribal law dictated that no white man could remain permanently in Cherokee country and have the protection of the Cherokee chiefs unless he married into the tribe and made his home in the tribal domain. It was in this way that Nancy met her second husband, a white tradesman named Bryant Ward.

A swarthy, strong man with jet-black hair and a muscular build, Brian Ward had traveled to Chote from South Carolina in an effort to build up his finances. He had heard stories of the beautiful, woman Indian chief; had heard of her bravery in battle, and that she was the niece of the Great Chief. But when he saw her for the first time, his heart stopped. No words were adequate to describe her. She had suffered the loss of her husband a short time ago, he was told, and was completely free to do as she wanted. When Nancy saw him, she too fell in love. Soon after Kingfisher's death, she married for a second time, taking his name and becoming Nancy Ward.

This marriage was prescient for Nancy; it would cement the affinity she had for the white man and deepen her understanding of their way of life, their thoughts, and their point of view. She would learn how to speak English and would grow to understand, more than most in her tribe, that the white man was here to stay, and that the only way to ensure her people's survival would be to coexist as best they could.

While Attakullaculla and Oconostota agreed with Nancy that harmony with the white man was the ultimate goal for their people, their willingness to ignore increasing insults was not as strong as hers. Attakullaculla particularly had always been a good friend of the English, traveling with Sir Alexander Cummings in 1730 as one of six great chiefs to visit the king. In fact, it was he who was responsible for encouraging trade between the Cherokees and the eastern coastal towns. But lately his feelings toward the white man were changing. He still wandered freely in and out of Fort Loudin, and the white men were on the friendliest terms they had ever been with the Cherokees—marrying their women, planting corn together, smoking tobacco with them, even sitting in on council meetings with their chiefs. Attakullaculla himself was seen saunter-ing around in gifts from his new friends, the white men, "clad in a new shirt, frilled and fine, the lobes of his ears, distended by silver bangles, drooped to his shoulders, and his scalp lock bobbing."[9] But beneath the cordiality, all was not so great. Attakullaculla was slowly becoming disillusioned with white men, as their manners, morals, and habits came into stark contrast with those of the Indians. Ulti-mately, the Indians would come to see that those white men were not traders at all but backcountry settlers of Virginia, settlers who were fierce in their belief that they had a right to be where they were, and who looked upon the Indians as unruly, uncivilized dirty savages to be tamed or killed, whichever came first. This last fact, combined with the Indian warriors' strong sense of military code and the enemy's need to avenge the dead, would eventually end peaceful relations between the two nations. Sadly, many on both sides would die.

1758

The cold of winter was upon them, and Nancy's hearth was nearly empty. Elizabeth, her youngest child, born to Brian Ward, lay sleep-ing on a deerskin mat inside. Brian had returned to South Carolina to be with his white wife, and Nancy had understood. In fact, throughout her life she would visit Brian and his white wife, consid-ering herself a friend. Many marriages between white men and Cherokee women took place during the years between 1757 and 1760, when the two cultures lived peacefully together. But as history would show, this coexistence was short-lived: by 1760 the white men and the Cherokees would be bitter enemies, fighting ferociously with one another. Nancy would raise their daughter with the help of her mother, her brother, Long Fellow, and her clan.

Nancy had dropped an armful of fresh wood beside the hearth. Her home was a tan rawhide tepee she had built with the help of her brother. It was exquisitely appointed for a tepee, described by one who saw it as "furnished in accord with her high dignity; it was barbaric splendor."[10] She was building the fire when suddenly her mother burst through the door.

Nancy saw the look of terror in her mother's eyes. "What news?"

Tame Doe spoke very quickly and quietly. "Attakullaculla was taken prisoner last night by the white man. They arrested him and have taken his weapons. You are needed in the council now. Oconostota is still at the peace talk. He took thirty-two of our men with him. I have not heard whether he knows of the arrest."

Nancy understood the danger immediately. "It will be okay, mother," Nancy said, touching her mother's arm lightly. She bent over little Elizabeth, still asleep, wrapped the cloth around her, and kissed her on the cheeks. Tame Doe nodded to Nancy—a nod that meant "go"—and without another word, Nancy was gone.

The council house was buzzing with activity when Nancy reached the entrance, and immediately she saw that the war poles had been raised. Walking through the winding hallway, built to prevent the interior from being seen by the outside, she entered the amphitheater, a large, round room with three tiers of benches around its walls. The room was large enough to hold up to five hundred people, but at this moment she stood staring at it, alone. She looked on at the seven sections built to represent the seven clans of her tribe, then let her eyes wander over to the west side of the building, the sacred area, determined by the sacred seventh pillar—where all the main officials were seated. Three of the seats had high, carved backs and were whitened with clay, white being symbolic for purity and sacredness. Three additional seats had been installed, painted red to symbolize war. In the center was an altar where a perpetual fire burned.

Nancy looked over to her seat in the sacred section, where the head of the clan would occupy the middle white chair and on either side would be his two assistants—his right-hand man and his speaker. Five other advisers would make up his council of seven. The military part of the equation was separate, consisting of a chief warrior, three main officers, and seven counselors. Nancy's seat stood in the center of the council, where for the past three years she had held a vote in deciding whether or not formal war would be declared. With Nancy voting, no formal war had been declared.

The council house combined a temple for religious rites and a public hall for civil and military councils, sacred and secular, sacred predominating. Councils were set up in the tribe as a means of governing decisions relating to war. When these war councils met, those in positions of power would discuss, consider, negotiate, and decide crucial matters, such as the decision to and time of attack, strategy, the fate of captured prisoners, and other weighty matters relating to war. Custom dictated that an assemblage of war women (or Pretty Women), be present at every war council. And since war women themselves had won honors in previous wars and were the mothers of warriors, they played an important role. Seated in the "holy area," these women sagely counseled the war chief. A place on a war council was an honor, and carried with it a respect and power akin to the white man's place in Congress. Some would say it was even more powerful, because of the intimacy and personal nature of those lives whom the decisions were being made for. James Adait, a white man who lived among the Cherokees for forty years, accused the Cherokee men of "living under a petticoat government."[11] About Nancy Ward he said, "She must have possessed remarkable traits of character to have retained almost autocratic control over the fierce and untamable Cherokees, when she was known to sympathize with their enemies, the white settlers."[12]

Making her way through the crowd, Nancy searched in vain for her brother and son but could see neither of them. Her daughter Catharine was sitting on a bench diagonally across from Nancy's seat, and at the sight of her, Nancy felt a sudden urge to cry. Instead, she walked swiftly and resolutely to her place and took her seat near the altar.

Attakullaculla's headstrong son, Dragging Canoe, began the meeting, as both Attakullaculla and Oconostota were absent. He recounted the news that had come to them from a white trader and a group of Indians who had made their way back from the mountains where the incident occurred. Nancy and the assembly listened intently to the story. A group of their brothers, making their way home from an expedition against Fort Duquesne, where they had gone to help General Forbes, came upon some horses roaming the land. Mistaking them as belonging to traders, they took them. Apparently, these horses belonged to some white settlers in the backcountry, who, upon realizing their horses had been taken, set out to find the thieves. The settlers caught up with the Indians and attacked them, scalping and killing many of them. (At that time, Virginia and South Carolina unwisely offered a bounty for scalps, encouraging the sickening practice to continue on both sides of the war.) General Forbes had Attakullaculla arrested as a deserter, deprived him of his weapons, and sent him under guard to the Virginia front.

Wails and moans rose up from the many women in attendance, who were now hearing confirmation of their fears, that indeed their male relatives were dead. There was a brief pause in Dragging Canoe's speech, but the look on his face was not one of sympathy; a murderous rage seethed from his eyes, his mouth curled in a snarl.

In Nancy's eyes, one could find a different look; a far-off, sad real-ization of events about to take place. She canvassed the wailing women with her eyes, remembering the day in battle when she found Kingfisher dead. She knew their sorrow; she understood their pain. But as she looked at Dragging Canoe's visible wrath, and the men around him who shared his lust for revenge, she could see that her people's loss was about to grow even larger. As a mother of a warrior, she recoiled inwardly at the idea of losing her son, Fivekiller. She knew action must and would be taken, but as she sat there listening to the events unravel before her, she struggled with conflicting ideas about what the best move should be for her people.

There was a sudden uproar in the far right corner; a clamor of injustice venting itself through the mouths and hearts of its owners.

The Raven of Chota, an old, revered chief, was standing now, his full majesty visible to all. He was dyed blood-red, with a raven's skin and eagle's feather tied to his scalp lock, his collar of wampum beads fastened securely around his neck. Baubles, beads, and feath-ers hung down from his ponytail as he asked this question of the war council, of which Nancy was a part: "It is beyond insult that they should dare to take Attakullaculla. Is there no more respect for our leaders? Who shall be next?"

In arresting Attakullaculla, their beloved and revered leader, the last of the great chiefs who had traveled to London in 1730 and vis-ited the king, the white men had indeed made clear their absolute lack of understanding of and respect for the Cherokee culture. Attakullaculla had been a good friend of the English since his visit in 1730, and had continued to help them in their fight against the colonists in numerous ways. But if the Cherokee revolted blindly against their enemy, giving up all hope of peace or mutual under-standing, would that not lead to more war, more death, more grief? Were the Cherokee really in a position to ignore the changing land-scape? Nancy stood to address Raven's question in the language of her people, smoothing the folds of her knee-length skirt, wary of the factions in the council who stood ready to pounce. The room fell silent.

"We have indeed been wronged very badly. We have suffered a great loss. We have suffered a great insult. We shall get Attakullac-ulla back, we can negotiate his release. We cannot ever get our men back. But we must be very careful of our next move, not to risk our warriors' lives until we know exactly what has happened and who specifically must pay. If we attack indiscriminately, the white man will only come down harder."

Nancy's face revealed her pain and sorrow, but it also displayed a strength of purpose and a confidence in her words. She spoke with the insight and understanding of a warrior, tempered by the wisdom of a mother and a woman. Though the council alternately attacked and sided with her view, in the end it was decided that the first and best plan of action was to retrieve Attakullaculla and to reach Oconostota, who was at that very moment in South Carolina for the purpose of negotiating peace.

As history would show, the Cherokee were successful in freeing Attakullaculla, and the chief did allow himself to be appeased by Governor Lyttleton's gestures of apology. But he was rankled nonetheless, as were his people. To compound matters, Oconostota had suffered humiliation and contempt during his time in Charlestown when, after he had attempted to work out the details of a truce, Governor Lyttleton rudely cut him off in midspeech, not allowing him to continue, and took Oconostota and his thirty-two warrior prisoners. Locking them in a hut built to hold six people, the governor would not release them until Attakullaculla agreed to a treaty whereby the Cherokee would hand over warriors responsible for murdering a white settler family. At the time of the war council, Oconostota's circumstances in Charlestown were not yet known to the clan; but they would learn of them soon enough.

After this, there was no way for Nancy to control the murderous elements of her clan, for two chiefs had been gravely insulted and many of their warriors unjustly threatened and killed.

Tensions between the white men and the Cherokees continued to escalate in 1759, until no voice in all the world could contain the primitive lust for revenge and war growing daily in the hearts and minds of the Cherokee warriors. Two Cherokee women were raped and assaulted by English men when their husbands were away. Around the same time, the English stopped sending ammunition and goods to the Cherokee. The French continued to whisper in their ears. Then smallpox broke out.

Fearing the deadly, contagious disease, the white men packed their bags and headed home, the new treaty signed by Attakulaculla all but forgotten. The lower Cherokee towns were in tumult, while the Overhill towns remained stable for a while. (When the smallpox hit, half of the Cherokee population were wiped out, with almost ten thousand lives lost. Some historians would later claim the smallpox virus was intentionally let loose among the Indian population, becoming one of the first known instances of biological warfare.) But the damaged trust from recent events could not be erased or forgotten. The attack, the insults, the injustice, and the maltreatment would prove more than they could bear.

Upon his return home, Oconostota and Attakulaculla held a war council meeting immediately, and though Nancy tried desperately to soothe the wounds and make them see the larger picture, no words could assuage the collective grief and anger of her tribe. Consequences were cast aside; the only issue at hand was revenge. As war cries rang through the air, and the warriors prepared themselves for battle, Nancy found her son and pulled him aside, begging him to listen to her reasons for waiting. He would not. He had been asked by Oconostota personally to be part of the planned attack, and it was an honor he would never think of turning down. Of all people, she should understand. And as a Cherokee warrior herself, she did. As a woman who had borne a child of a white man, and was mothering her half-breed daughter, Nancy also saw the larger danger. But at twenty-two years old, with only limited experience as a Ghigau, the young, fiery girl would have to wait. She knew her people's bloodthirsty appetite for revenge, their love of war. But this was a different enemy now. There were many of them, strongly armed. In the end, there was nothing she could do.

Attakullaculla and Oconostota turned their backs on Nancy's pleas and staged an attack on Fort Prince George to free the Cherokee prisoners held there. They would trap the white men inside the fort, as smallpox raged within, until they agreed to free the Indians. And this is what they did. But all did not go as planned. In desperation, the white men did not free the Cherokee prisoners, but attacked and killed every single one of them. This last act of murder and brutality would give rise to first all-but war between the Cherokee and the English. In the negotiations that followed, Attakullaculla spoke, and peace settled upon the two nations—a peace that remained unbroken until 1776.

July 1776

The westward movement of the white colonists had indeed begun to seriously threaten the Cherokees. Despite the Royal Proclamation of 1763, "which forbade further movement west, ever-increasing pioneers crossed over into Indian Territory."[13] Nancy loved her clan and her tribe as she loved her children; the land she had been raised on held memories for her in every tree, river, and valley. She would fight willingly as she always had to defend a Cherokee life, and she would die for one happily as well. Still, she fought for peace, for a rational, measured counterattack of words and goodwill, not for senseless violence. She had spoken her mind at the war council and pleaded for a different approach, but the ferocity and anger of the many Cherokee men toward the white intruders was, in the end, too strong for her to overcome. As more and more white settlers encroached on Cherokee land, it became increasingly difficult for her to temper the indignation.

Compounding the problem was her cousin, Dragging Canoe. Although Dragging Canoe was son to the great and peace-loving Attakullaculla, he shared nothing of his father or his cousin's desire for peace. Filled with blinding fury over the white settlers' invasion of Indian land, and gripped with an unquenchable appetite for murder and torture, Dragging Canoe and Raven were two of the fiercest, most vicious warriors among the Cherokees. They scalped men, women, and children for fun. It was common for them to rip the flesh off their prisoners while they were alive, laughing at each victim as the poor and dying wretch was forced to dance, naked and bleeding to death. In fact, six years later in 1782, a committee of the North Carolina Legislature would meet and report that "there is little or no probability of peace during the ensuing summer. The Indians under Dragging Canoe and other Chiefs averse to peace are pushing the war and almost daily perpetrating acts of cruelty and murder."[14]

Now they would take their violence to a new level. Nancy learned that Dragging Canoe and Raven had enticed another old war chief, Abram of Chilhowee, to take part in a plan using seven hundred warriors to attack Virginia, the Carolinas, and Georgia in one highly orchestrated attack. As a member of the war council who unwillingly went along with the decision to attack, she was familiar with all the details of the plan. Dragging Canoe would strike the white settlements near the Great Island of Holston and those in nearby Virginia. On the same day, Abraham would strike on the Nolichucky and Wataugan Rivers, and Raven would attack settlements in Carter's Valley. If word did not reach the settlers in time,

Watauga and Holston would be ravaged, including women and children, and retribution would surely follow.

Now, as they prepared for battle, the warrior Indians looked to Nancy. As Beloved Woman, it was her job to prepare the sacred Black Drink, an emetic of holly tea, one which all warriors drank in preparation for going on the warpath.[15] Nancy sat in the quiet blackness of night, under a vast, moonless sky, slowly stirring the drink. Over and over she repeated her prayer to the spirit god, in a low, soft chant, an age-old hymn bequeathed to the Cherokees from the Stone Man, a mythic magician and supernatural wonderworker. She reached into her deerskin bag and took a handful of salt, flinging some at Dragging Canoe's feet and the rest into the fire. She then took a swan's wing and held it over the kettle as she continued her prayer. Moments later she reached into her bag again and pulled out an ancient yaupon shrub, which she threw into the kettle to simmer. Then she returned to her seat next to the warriors and headmen.

But while her prayer should have been for her people's victory, for the complete slaughter of the white man who had of late stolen the Indian's land and killed Indian children, instead it was her own private prayer—for the peace and well-being of them all. She went through the motions of a war woman, as expected, but secretly she had other plans, and the time had come to put them into action. The ceremony over, Nancy rose from her seat and watched her young, brave Cherokee men prepare for battle. Two Cherokee mothers sat a few feet away, hunched over their work, helping the sons ready themselves for war. When the time was right Nancy crept past the guard post and down the path.

Nancy had not been able to dissuade her men from war this time. Dragging Canoe was bloodthirsty in his desire for revenge, completely unable to listen to reason. None of the other war chiefs feared the consequences of war either; her voice alone had been raised in protest, advocating restraint, but the men in the tribe would not hear her. Distraught, she had contemplated various ways to get word to the white settlement in time for an evacuation, mercifully preventing bloodshed for them all. To do this, she had decided to use her prisoners.

Nancy lifted the hanging cloth and slipped into the tepee where two of her white prisoners lay curled up, asleep in the corner. Isaac Thomas, a trader and one of three who had escaped Fort Loudin, had taken refuge in Chota. He shared a hut with William Faulin, a horse thief. Nancy didn't know much about Faulin, but of all the prisoners at Chota she had spoken with, she had been most impressed with Thomas and his seeming understanding of Cherokee life: she decided to risk trusting him. She tapped Thomas with a stick, and he woke with a sudden start, jumping up and back, a look of fear and confusion on his face. It was too dark for Nancy to look into his eyes, and she realized suddenly he might not know it was her.

"It is Nancy," she quickly said. He attempted to stand, but she motioned for him not to move, instead circling him so that their faces were very close. "My men are planning an attack on Watauga and the Holston settlements. You must go and warn your men. I will help you leave tonight. Take this man with you," she said, motioning to Faulin. "Meet me in fifteen minutes behind the oak by the horses. You will hear me call for you." He stared back, his eyes widening. Nancy could see his thoughts racing. This meant freedom for him, but it could also mean death.

According to Cherokee law, once a prisoner escaped, he could be hunted down and killed. And Chota was not easy to leave, even for natives: "It was surrounded within five miles of its center by a low valley covered so thickly with brush that within its walls, even in broad daylight, it was dark as night. Muddy rivers ran through this wilderness, on whose sides were steep, clay banks."[16] Across the river lay the remains of what had once been Fort Loudin. He started to speak, but Nancy turned and disappeared into the darkness and was gone.

As Thomas and Faulin approached the great oak, they saw an old woman sitting under the tree, immersed in her work. As they neared, she quickly and without a word pointed to a spot in the deep shrub. She went back to her work, and the men understood she had passed a message. As they walked in that direction, Thomas looked back and suddenly recognized the woman as Nancy's mother, Tame Doe, one of the revered older woman in the Wolf clan.

Nancy saw the men approaching and made noise in the brush. Darkness enveloped them all, but as they neared, she called Thomas's name, and they found one another. She whispered to them to follow, leading them through thick brush, thorns, branches, and underbrush. After a while they stepped out into a clearing of sorts, where Nancy handed them each a musket and urged them to head towards Wolf Hills (Abingdon, Virginia), westward, on a journey that would cover 120 miles "Do not stop until you reach Watauga and Holston. Go. Be quick."

The two men fled without looking back, terror mixed with determination in their eyes.

Nancy ran back to the village, back to her brew of tea, stirring the drink over and over, reciting the prayer to the gods as a war woman should. She sat awake that entire night, staring into the mixture, painfully aware of the deceit she was now engaged in.

As Nancy waited, she reflected on the wisdom of what she had done. Would freeing the prisoners help or harm to the people she loved most? Her clan looked to her as a main source of wisdom, and she prayed that wisdom had indeed come to her that night. She knew only time would tell.

⁄ₒ

Many historians have speculated on Nancy Ward's motivations for warning the settlers of the Cherokee attack. Some have seen an "ultra-patriotism" in her actions, postulating that she envisioned what would one day be the great United States of America. Others have argued that she understood the wisdom of befriending white men in power, such as John Sevier, leader of the Wataugans, and was able to use those friendships to her advantage later when needed. Still others have seen a practical wisdom in her choice, a recognition that the Indians were simply outnumbered and outsupplied by the white man, and that it was clearly in their best interest not to provoke more bloodshed. Her willingness to risk her own life and those of the prisoners shows us the extent of her opposition against this attack, a position she must have made well known at the war council meeting in Chota.

Sadly, as history would show, bloodshed was suffered on both sides. Though John Sevier was reached in time to warn his people to flee their cabins and move into Wythe County, Virginia, many of the men stayed behind to ambush the Indians. In fact, instead of remaining out in the open (as they had always fought), the white men employed the Indians' own war tactic of bush fighting, and hid in the forests behind gigantic trees, almost completely unseen. Dragging Canoe and his men entered the valley, unaware the settlers had been warned, and were quickly attacked, losing thirteen warriors, with Dragging Canoe himself suffering musket wounds in both thighs.

An outraged Cherokee war council had gathered upon their return home from the Wataugan and Holston defeat to discuss strategy. It was not clear to Nancy whether suspicions had arisen as to her involvement, though she was prepared to speak her mind and accept the consequences should she need to. She walked through the town square, feeling the many eyes upon her as she entered the council house from the east, only entrance, past one of seven large pillars that surrounded the outside of the house.

Nancy stepped up past the altar and took her seat. There she waited patiently for the others to arrive, slowly and solemnly filling the benches and seats until almost every chair in the house was full. Oconostota sat across from her, his silver breastplate reflecting rays of light from the fire, the bracelets on his arms and wrists shimmering. Attakullaculla sat to her left, flanked by his two assistants. She was deeply aware of her presence among these great chiefs, both as a woman and as a woman with power. She watched Dragging Canoe and Raven enter together and caught the look Dragging Canoe shot her as he passed. She knew well his look of disapproval, but had learned over the years to shrug it off. Her son and brother were there as well, the two men in her life who had always supported her unwaveringly. Elizabeth sat next to Catharine, both girls watching her, as always, taking in her every move. She saw the look of pride in both her daughter's eyes, a look she had grown accustomed to at these meetings; she could only pray nothing would happen tonight to change that.

When Oconostota walked in, the meeting officially began. Oconostota stood tall and spoke of the great losses they had suffered at Watauga and the Holston Valley. He recounted the new tactics the white men had used, and spoke of Dragging Canoe's courage in the face of such treachery. He exalted Dragging Canoe for his bravery, loyalty, and foresight, and spoke of the scalps and prisoners that he and his party had returned with. Nancy sat quietly through all of this without uttering a word. She knew they had returned with prisoners, but she was sure that, because of her warning, the damage to the white settlers had been far less. She waited until the moment came, and when asked her opinion, she stood, facing the council, gazing at Oconostota.

"My Chief, you have asked for my feelings, and I will speak my mind. We have had peace between ourselves and the white man for almost fifteen years now. We have learned from them and they from us. There are some among them who are evil and do not wish to see peace anymore. But there are many more of them who do not feel that way. As I was a wife of a white trader, and am a mother to his daughter"—and when she said this, she looked over to Elizabeth with love—"as a widow of our own brave one and a mother to his two children, I know and understand that peace and patience between us is the only way to guarantee our survival, to keep a stake in our land. We must preserve our land at all costs, and if the white men intrude upon it we must fight and defend. But I am against these unprovoked attacks, such as Dragging Canoe and Raven have carried out. They are angering the whites against us and putting us all in more danger."

"We are defending our lives," an outraged Raven cried. "We may not have killed all the ugly white men this time, but we did not leave empty-handed. Many prisoners lie on the hill, and we shall burn them alive as an example. We cannot back down and allow them to take over our land and our homes. What would you have us do, roll over and die?" Raven mocked her in his tone and face, rolling over onto the floor, playing dead. Dragging Canoe and his band of men laughed, and a snicker was heard in the assembly. Attakullaculla banged his fist down on the table and barked out a cry of anger at the disrespectful behavior.

"You will remember who you speak to, men. Do not embarrass yourselves anymore than you already have," he said, offering in his eyes an apology to Nancy.

"You go too far," Dragging Canoe cried suddenly. "Your love of the white men is known to us all, and your constant refrains have led us into danger. We have an enemy we need to destroy, who continues to pursue, and you would have us talk. Talking has done no good. We will kill our new prisoners one by one and send their charred remains back to their families to play with. Watch me burn our new prisoners, especially the new woman."

At this remark, she lifted her head and stared into her cousin's death-filled eyes. He was challenging her in front of the council, mocking her place and position in the tribe, belittling her power and wisdom and very reason for being there. From somewhere inside of her, she let out a cry of anger and, as records indicate, shouted with all her force: "No woman shall be burned at the stake when I am Beloved Woman!"[17]

One of the Cherokee captives was a Mrs. William Bean, wife of the first permanent white settler in Tennessee, who had the misfortune of riding back into town just as the raid took place. As Ghigau, Nancy held total control and power over the fates of any and all prisoners in Chota. Condemned to death by fire without Nancy's knowledge, Lydia Bean had been taken to Toquo and tied to a stake at the top of a large mound.[18]

"It is too late." Dragging Canoe laughed. Attakullaculla pounded his fist down even harder and began to speak, but Nancy did not wait. She left her seat and strode out of the council house to the top of the hill, where she knew the woman was being kept.

There she saw the young white woman tied to the stake, her dress torn, her arms bound tightly with rope, barefoot, dirty, petrified. Bands of warriors circled the lone woman, mocking and jeering, throwing dirt at her face. Enraged at the sight, at the challenge to her authority, Nancy quickly ran over to the woman and began scattering the burning brands. She then turned to her men and waved her swan's wing, her badge of authority. She ordered the chanting stopped and the woman to be freed. The fury in her eyes and the tone in her voice had its desired effect. Immediately the singing stopped; the men loosened the woman from the stake, threw her into Nancy's arms, and began to walk sullenly away.

Nancy brought Lydia Bean back to her home. There, Mrs. Bean remained for a while as Nancy's guest, where she taught the Beloved

Woman how to make butter and cheese. As a result of her time with Mrs. Bean, Nancy learned the value of the cow and bought her own cattle, being the first to introduce the cow into the Cherokee economy. When it became safe for Mrs. Bean to leave Chota and return home, Nancy sent her back to her family, escorted by Nancy's brother, Longfellow, and her son, Fivekiller.

Though Nancy saved Mrs. Bean's life, she was not able to temper or control Dragging Canoe, much as she tried. The humiliating Indian defeat at Watauga provoked Dragging Canoe and his party to even more vengeance. They continued to seek out white intruders and scalp them. In retaliation, from July until September 1776, the white settlers struck and destroyed many Cherokee towns. Then, in October, a Colonel William Christian led 1,800 Virginia troops on a devastating raid against the Cherokees, destroying most of their existing towns. Only out of respect for Nancy Ward would he spare Chota.[19]

Christmas Day, 1781

During the four years after Chota was spared, Nancy continued her desperate struggle to make her own clan see the white man as peaceful, eager to negotiate for land and peace. Realizing the white men were not leaving, she spoke continually of the need to coexist, to learn from one another, and to share and harvest the land together. Two years earlier, in 1778, Attakullaculla had died—a wrenching personal loss to Nancy, made more so by the responsibility he placed on her. Though Oconostota would replace him as chief, he reportedly left Nancy in charge of working toward harmony between the two races. Another band of Cherokee warriors were planning yet again to attack Watauga, and just as she had done earlier, Nancy again sent the same Thomas, who had returned to Chota after warning the Wataugan settlers the first time, with yet another message. But this time sending Thomas was not enough. The stakes were markedly higher: after four years of bloodshed and destruction between the two nations, even her chiefs recognized the escalated risk and danger in their every move. Nancy had been appointed by her chiefs as the one to go, herself, to the white men's camp where they were now based, just outside Chota. She did not hesitate. The very next day, she gathered her belongings and rode her horse into their camp.

Nancy entered the camp with two women flanking her side and cattle trailing her. She looked over the camp with a gaze filled with wonder.

It was Christmas Day, 1781. Nancy was led into the camp. She offered them some cattle from her private herd and told them of the plans of her people's attack. Most importantly, she brought a peace offering on behalf of her chiefs. She spoke from her heart to John Sevier and Colonel Arthur Campbell, two leaders of a group of whites advancing toward her town, imploring them to use restraint and wisdom in their affairs with the Indians. She spoke slowly and pointedly, having learned enough English over the years to communicate rather well, and left a lasting impression on all who heard her, men who were not accustomed to business dealings with women, especially of a military nature. She appealed to Sevier, a man she now considered a friend, one whose people she had helped save years earlier. Nancy left wondering whether her visit made any difference. She would find out three days later, when Chota was attacked and destroyed by Campbell, Sevier, and their bands of men. Nancy and her daughter Elizabeth were among those taken prisoner and forced to leave their home.

When Nancy followed behind the white men, with Elizabeth by her side, one of the first faces she saw as she entered the white man's camp was Sevier. Though his glance told her he had seen her, his eyes turned away from her fierce glare. Not too long after, she was informed that she and her daughter and the rest of her family were free to stay or go, that as a result of her good work in attempting peace, freedom would be theirs. She and her family chose, not surprisingly, to go back home to Chota and rebuild it.

Colonel Arthur Campbell wrote to Thomas Jefferson about the invasion and destruction of Chota, saying, "The famous Indian woman Nancy Ward came to camp, she gave us various intelligence, and made an overture on behalf of some of the Chiefs for Peace; to which I then evaded giving an explicit answer, as I wished first to visit the vindictive part of the nation, mostly settled at Hiwassee and Christowee. And to distress the whole, as much as possible, by destroying their habitations and Provisions." He continued, saying that notwithstanding Nancy Ward's kindnesses, they had destroyed Chota and all its provisions on December 28. After boasting of the many Indian prisoners he had taken, he went on to say that "besides these, we brought the family of Nancy Ward, who for their good offices we considered in another light."[20] Thomas Jefferson replied on February 17, 1781, "I am much pleased with the happy expedition against the Cherokees. Nancy Ward seems rather to have taken refuge with you. In that case, her inclination ought to be followed as to what is done with her."[21]

Jefferson had wrestled with the "Indian problem" many a night with his close friends John and Abigail Adams; the three had, in fact, spoken specifically of the Cherokees and what was to become of them and their nation. Ironically, as Abigail desperately tried to get her husband and Jefferson to see the wisdom of allowing women a degree of power, Nancy and her "backward" nation had seen that wisdom long before. Nancy held a power with her people equal to or greater than that of either Adams or Jefferson, a power she had used with restraint and wisdom in all her dealings with the white men.

Even Theodore Roosevelt in his *Winning of the West* wrote of the brutal assault against the Overhill Cherokees in 1781, stating how "twenty nine warriors were killed, a thousand cabins were burned and fifty thousand bushels of corn destroyed. Seventeen women and children were captured and they did not include the family of Nancy Ward, who were treated as friends, not prisoners." [22]

On July 20, 1781, after the vengeful destruction of their nation, the Cherokees were ordered to meet Sevier and his followers to conclude a peace treaty. When the time came, the white men were startled to find that the featured speaker was Nancy Ward. She stood to speak, and in doing so would be the first and only woman to participate actively in treaty negotiations with the white men when she told the commission, "You know that women are always looked upon as nothing; but we are your mothers; you are our sons. Our cry is all for peace; let it continue. This peace must last forever. Let your women's sons be ours. Let our sons be yours. Let your women hear our words." [23]

Colonel Christian, who had earlier spared Chota, made the reply, "Mother: we have listened well to your talk. No man can hear it without being moved by it. Our women shall hear your words. We are all descendants of the same woman. We will not quarrel with you because you are our mothers. We will not meddle with your people if they will be still and quiet at home and let us live in peace." [24] Nancy's words left such a deep impression on the white men that, after her talk, they revised their original demands. When the meeting was called, the commissioners had intended to take all the Indian land north of the Little Tennessee River. Instead, the Cherokees now had to cede only the land north of the Nolichucky River. The treaty divided the land from the mouth of the Duck River to the dividing ridge between the Cumberland and Tennessee Rivers.

President George Washington, after the frightful years of the Revolution, was determined to have peace, and he appointed a commission to meet in Hopewell, South Carolina, on the Keowee River. The Treaty of Hopewell, finalized on November 28, 1785, was the first treaty the Indians entered into with the United States. That day a group of commissioners met the Indians at the insistence of President Washington to create peace. The commission was composed of Joseph Martin (the same man who had married Nancy's daughter Elizabeth upon his appointment as agent of the Cherokees), Andrew Pickens, Benjamin Hawkins, and Lachlan McIntosh. Only citizens of the upper Cherokees were present. Old Tassel of Chota, chief after having succeeded Oconostota upon his death in 1782, was the principal speaker for the Indians as head chief; he brought with him thirty-six chiefs and 918 of his own people.

Before the treaty was signed, Old Tassel asked leave for the war woman of Chota to talk to the commissioners. He said, "I have no more to say, but one of our Beloved Women has, who has borne and raised up warriors."[25] After delivering two strings of wampum, a pipe, and some tobacco for the men, Nancy Ward stood solemnly and made a dramatic plea for peace: "I am fond of hearing that there is peace, and I hope you have now taken us by the hand in real friendship. I have a pipe and a little tobacco to give the commissioners to smoke in friendship. I look on you and the red people as my children. Your having determined on peace is most pleasant to me for I have seen much trouble during the late war. I am old, but I hope yet to bear children, who will grow up and people our nation, as we are now under the protection of Congress and shall have no more disturbance. The talk I have given is from the young warriors I have raised in my town, as well as myself. They rejoice that we have peace, and we hope the chain of friendship will never be broken."[26]

The Cherokee problem was to be referred to Congress for settlement, and this was supposed to guarantee the Cherokee territory against future invasion from white intruders. But while the settlers were ordered to leave Cherokee land or forfeit protection, the settlers on the Holston River would not leave. Not only did the frontiersmen and their families not leave Cherokee land, they dug in, challenging anyone to remove them. From the start, it was clear that Congress was not prepared to deal with this.

Then, in 1788, a horrifying event occurred that closed the door to any peaceful understanding between the two nations once and for all. Old Tassel, who had been a good friend to the whites, was invited to the headquarters of Major James Hubbert. He went with his son and two members of his tribe. As soon as they arrived, they were placed in a vacant house. A young white man with a tomahawk, whose parents had been killed, killed all the visiting Cherokees, including Old Tassel. The killing would mark a new level of atrocity as the first time a Cherokee chief had ever been murdered, and never again would the Cherokee and white man work together to build a peace mutually beneficial to both.

Postscript

In 1791 George Washington's determination to resolve the Cherokee conflict resulted in the Treaty of Holston, an agreement considered fair to both sides in its many dimensions, one which presaged a peaceful coexistence between the two nations for a while. The Cherokee made tremendous efforts to assimilate, allowing their children to be educated and dressed in white men's clothes, reconsidering ancient tribal laws in favor of a "civilized" form of republican government, and participating in trade with their new neighbors. But the years following the Treaty of Holston also brought with them disillusionment: between 1791 and 1819 the Cherokee nation found itself forced to make twenty-five land cessions in exchange for debt they owed white traders. In fact, during Jefferson's presidency, he actively wanted to keep them in debt as a way of acquiring more of their land, and he did so. Furthermore, the Georgia Compact of 1802—an agreement Jefferson made with Georgia, promising it all of the Cherokee lands then remaining unsold—hung in the air like the threat that it was, a constant reminder to the Cherokees of their precarious position. Desperately, the Cherokees tried to assimilate once again, believing this might afford them protection. The years between 1819 and 1827 saw a "phenomenal advancement" in Cherokee culture—more so, some have said, than the advancement of white settlers in Georgia at the time. Rather than ingratiate themselves with the men of Georgia, though, they received the opposite reaction: in 1820, jealous, bitter, and cruel, Georgia began a campaign to push all the Cherokees out of their state, sending them west of the Mississippi, in an attack that would last eighteen years. By 1835, when the infamous Treaty of New Echota was engineered by the federal government of the United States, the Cherokee were forced to cede all their eastern lands and move west of the Mississippi. In 1838 the Cherokee were forcibly removed, traveling west along what is now known as the Trail of Tears.

During the years between 1790 and 1800, Nancy visited Brian Ward and his wife in South Carolina often. Though Chota was no longer considered the capital, it was still a "city of refuge," and Nancy continued to live there during those years, "taking in orphans and homeless waifs, many of them half-breeds from all over the nation," where she earned the nickname "Granny Ward."[27] But by 1819 Chota had been sold, so she was forced to leave her ancient home and relocate. She moved to a place by the Ocoee River, where she would spend the rest of her days running an inn for travelers along the Federal Road.

In 1817, at seventy-nine years of age, Nancy was too weak to attend a council meeting, so she sent her walking cane instead with one last message for her people: "Your mothers and sisters ask and beg of you not to part with any more of our land. I have great many grand children which I wish them to do well on our land."[28] But by that time the Cherokee had abandoned their ancient tribal custom of giving women power, and adopted a more republican, patriarchal form of government, where there was "no place for a Beloved Woman."[29] This advocate for peace was no longer needed.

Nancy died in 1822 and was buried between Fivekiller and Long Fellow on a hill near her Tavern, mercifully spared the horror of watching her people suffer through that unbearable journey sixteen years later, the Trail of Tears.

Notes

✍

1. WITH THE WIND IN HER HAIR: SYBIL LUDINGTON

1. Vincent Dacquino, *A Call to Arms* (Fleischmanns, N.Y.: Purple Mountain Press, 2000), 23.

2. Ibid.

3. Ibid., 30.

4. Ibid., 37.

2. BREAKING THE CHAINS OF SILENCE: PHILLIS WHEATLEY

1. Russel J. Reising, *Loose Ends—Closure and Criticism in America* (Durham, N.C.: Duke University Press, 1996), 87.

2. Oloudah Equiano, *The Interesting Narrative of the Life of Oloudah Equiano; or, Gustavus Vassa, the African* (New York: Longmans, 1988).

3. Ibid.

4. Albertha Sistrunk, "The Influence of Alexander Pope on the Writing Style of Phillis Wheatley," in *Critical Essays on Phillis Wheatley*, ed. Williamth Morrison (Boston: G. K. Hall, 1982), 175.

5. Margaritta Matilda O'Dell, *Memoir and Poems of Phillis Wheatley: A Native African and Slave,* 2d ed. (Boston: Light and Horton, 1835), 17.

6. Ibid., 18.

7. William H. Robinson, *Phillis Wheatley in the Black American Beginnings* (Detroit: Broadside Press, 1975), 13.

8. Emily Foster Happer, *The First Negro Poet of America* (Greenwich, Conn.: The Literary Collector Press, 1904), 2.

9. Sistrunk, *Critical Essays,* 176.

10. Ibid.

11. Ibid.

12. O'Dell, *Memoir,* 13.

13. Reising, *Loose Ends,* 85.

14. William H. Robinson, *Black New England Letters* (Boston: Trustees of the Public Library of Boston, 1977), 51.

15. Ibid., 49.

16. Ibid., 50.

17. Ibid., 52.

18. John C. Shields, *The Collected Works of Phillis Wheatley* (New York: Oxford University Press, 1988), forward.

19. Robinson, *Letters,* 49.

20. Ibid., 30.

21. Shields, *Collected Works.*

22. Ibid., 273.

23. Robinson, *Letters,* 32.

24. O'Dell, *Memoir,* 21.

25. Robinson, *Letters,* 28.

26. Samuel Morrison, *Oxford History of the People* (New York: Oxford University Press, 1965), 289.

27. Robinson, *Letters.*

28. J. Saunders Redding, *To Make a Poet Black* (Durham, N.C.: Duke University Press, 1996), 10.

29. William H. Robinson, *Critical Essays on Phillis Wheatley* (Boston: G. K. Hall, 1982), 33.

30. Ibid., 36.

31. Ibid.

32. Ibid., 35.

33. Robinson, *Letters,* 42.

34. Robinson *Critical Essays,* 42.

35. Ibid., 6.

36. Shields, *Collected Works,* 273.

37. Ibid., 240.

38. Robinson, *Critical Essays,* 6.

39. Ibid.

40. Robinson, *Black American Beginnings,* 57.

41. fn1, p. 36 quoting *Lessing The Rev War of 1812,* 3 vols Ny, Ny, book concern, 1875 III 556–557

42. Robinson, *Letters.*

43. Ibid., 35.

44. Robinson, *Critical Essays,* 9.

45. Robinson, *Letters,* 35.

46. O'dell, *Memoir,* 23.

47. Robinson, *Critical Essays,* 20.

48. Robinson, *Letters,* 44.

3. FIRST ADVISER: ABIGAIL ADAMS

1. Phyllis Lee Levin, *Abigail Adams* (New York: St. Martins Press, 1987), 82.

2. Natalie S. Bober, *Witness to a Revolution* (New York: Aladdin, 1995), 179.

3. Paul C. Nagel, *The Adams Women: Abigail and Louisa Adams, Their Sisters and Daughters* (Cambridge, Mass.: Harvard University Press, 1987), 13.

4. Levin, *Abigail Adams,* 75.

5. Edmund S. Morgan, *The Birth of the Republic* (London: University of Chicago Press, 1992), 74.

6. Levin, *Abigail Adams,* 77.

7. Morgan, *Birth,* 75.

8. Levin, *Abigail Adams,* 77.

9. Levin, 82.

10. Levin, 83.

11. Levin, 84.

12. Levin 87

13. Bober, *Witness,* 91.

14. Levin, 148.

15. Levin, 152.

16. Levin, 173

17. Bober, 134.

18. Levin, 286, 287.

19. Bober, 180.

20. Thomas G. West, *Vindicating the Founders: Race, Sex, Class and Justice in the American Revolution* (Lanham, Md.: Rowman and Littlefield, 1997), 103.

21. TK. Levin, 414.

22. Levin, 413.

23. TJ to John Page, June 25, 1804, quoted in *Adams-Jefferson Letters,* 1:265.

24. TJ to AA, June 13, 1804, 1:270.

25. AA to TJ, July 1, 1804, 1:273–74.

26. TJ to AA, July 22, 1804, 1:275–76.

27. Ibid.

28. Ibid., August 18, 1804, 1:277–78.

29. Ibid, October 25, 1804, 1:282.

30. TK p217, Bober.

31. TK p217, Bober

32. AA to F. A. Van der Kemp, May 26, 1815, *JA Letterbook,* reel 423.

33. Alice Brown, *Mercy Warren* (New York: Charles Scribner's Sons, 1896), 240.

4. HER PEN AS SWORD: MERCY OTIS WARREN

1. Katharine Anthony, *First Lady of the Revolution: The Life of Mercy Otis Warren* (New York: Doubleday, 1958), 110.

2. Ibid.

3. Ibid.

4. Ibid.

5. Ibid.

6. Ibid.

7. Elaine Cravitz and Elizabeth Buford, *Courage Knows No Sex* (Hanover, Mass.: Christopher, 1978), 50.

8. Anthony, *First Lady,* 76.

9. Ibid.

10. Ibid., 15.

11. Ibid., 54.

12. Brown, *Mercy Otis Warren,* 41.

13. Anthony, *First Lady,* 55.

14. Ibid., 64.

15. Ibid., 82.

16. Rosemarie Zagarri, *A Woman's Dilemma: Mercy Otis Warren and the American Revolution* (Wheeling, Ill.: Harlan Davidson, 1995), 70.

17. Anthony, *First Lady,* 81.

18. Ibid., 82.

19. Ibid., 84.

20. Zagarri, *Dilemma,* 58.

21. Anthony, *First Lady,* 85.

22. Ibid., 83.

23. Ibid., 149.

24. Ibid., 107.

25. Ibid., 139.

26. Ibid., 141.

27. Ibid., 145.

28. Ibid., 146.

29. Ibid.

30. Ibid.

31. Ibid., 123.

32. Ibid., 123.

33. Ibid., 124.

34. Ibid., 126.

35. Ibid., 134.

36. Cravitz, *Courage,* 63.

37. Anthony, *First Lady,* 152.

38. Ibid., 153.

39. Ibid.

40. Ibid.

41. Ibid., 155

42. Ibid., 159.

43. Ibid., 163.

44. Ibid., 183.

45. Ibid., 206.

46. Ibid.

47. Ibid., 12.

48. Ibid.

5. SPY GAMES: LYDIA DARRAGH

1. Edward Tunis, *Colonial Living* (Baltimore: John Hopkins University Press, 1957), 126.

2. Henry Darrach, "Lydia Darrach, One of the Heroines of the Revolution," *Publications of the City History Society of Philadelphia 1* (1916):379.

3. Ibid.

4. Ibid., 389.

5. Ibid., 154.

6. Ibid., 385.

7. Ibid.

8. Sally Smith Booth, *The Women of 1776* (New York: Hastings House, 1973), 153.

9. Christopher Hibbert, *Redcoats and Rebels* (New York: Norton, 1990), 159.

10. Darrach, "Lydia Darrach," 388.

11. Ibid., 389.

12. Ibid., 380.

13. Ibid., 390.

14. John Bakeless, *Turncoats, Traitors and Heroes* (New York: J. B. Lippincott, 1959), 179.

15. Ibid., 182.

16. Ibid.

17. Ibid., 179.

18. Ibid., 214.

19. Ibid., 215.

20. Ibid., 209.

21. Ibid., 210.

22. Ibid.

23. Ibid.

24. Ibid.

25. Ibid., 218.

26. Ibid., 217.

27. Darrach, "Lydia Darrach," 403.

28. Ibid., 401.

29. Ibid.

30. Ibid., 383.

31. Ibid.

32. Bakeless, *Turncoats*, 217.

33. Darrach, "Lydia Darrach," 401.

34. Ibid., 391.

35. Bakeless, *Turncoats*, 220.

36. Ibid., 219.

37. Ibid., 220.

38. Ibid., 391.

39. Ibid., 220.

40. Ibid.

41. Darrach, "Lydia Darrach," 391.

42. Ibid., 393.

43. Ibid., 386.

44. Ibid., 387.

45. Ibid.

46. Ibid., 393.

6. A SISTER IN ARMS: MOLLY PITCHER

1. Holly Mayer, *Belonging to the Army: Camp Followers and Community during the American Revolution* (Columbia: University of South Carolina Press, 1996), 7.

2. Walter Blumenthal, *Women Camp Followers of the American Revolution* (New York: Arno Press, 1974), 72.

3. James Kirby Martin and Karen R. Stubaus, *The American Revolution: Whose Revolution?* (New York: Robert E. Kreiger, 1981), 103.

4. Blumenthal, *Camp Followers,* 62.

5. William Stryker, *The Battle of Monmouth* (Princeton, N.J.: Princeton University Press, 1927), in. 192.

6. Linda Grant DePauw, *Battlecries and Lullabies: Women in War from Pre to Present* (Norman: University of Oklahoma Press, 1988), 130.

7. Ibid.

8. Ibid., 131.

9. Ibid.

10. D. W. Thompson and Merri Lou Schaumann, *Goodbye Molly Pitcher,* collection in Cumberland County Historical Society, 17.

11. Martin, *American Revolution,* 101.

12. Mary R. Murrin, *Conflict at Monmouth Courthouse* (Trenton: N.J. Historical Commission, 1984), 11.

13. Ibid., 25.

14. Shirley Horner, *Ladies at the Crossroads: Eighteenth-Century Women of New Jersey* (Trenton, N.J.: American Association of University Women, 1978), 43.

15. Murrin, *Conflict,* 23.

16. Richard Ketchum, *The American Heritage Book of the Revolution* (New York: American Heritage, 1958), 223.

17. Martin, *American Revolution,* 104.

18. Ibid., 105.

19. Stryker, *Monmouth,* 189.

20. Samuel Steele Smith, *The Battle of Monmouth* (Monmouth Beach, N.J.: Philip Freneau Press, 1964), 22.

21. Thompson, *Goodbye,* 17.

22. Ibid., 18.

23. Ibid.

24. *Asbury Park Sunday Press,* March 1, 1931.

25. Emily J. Teipe, *"Will the Real Molly Pitcher Stand Up?" Prologue Quarterly of the NTL Archives and Records* 31, no. 2 (1999): 121.

7. SOLDIER WITH A SECRET: DEBORAH SAMPSON

1. Lucy Freeman and Alma Halbert Bond, *America's First Woman Warrior: The Courage of Deborah Sampson* (New York: Paragon House, 1992), 45.

2. Ibid.

3. Ibid., 67.

4. E. D. Ellis, ed, *Deborah Sampson: The Girl Soldier* (New York: Beadle and Adams, 1863), 21.

5. George Forty, *Women War Heroines* (London: Arms and Armor Press, 1997), 110.

6. Freeman, *Warrior,* 68.

7. Ibid., 75.

8. Ibid., 79.

9. Kathleen Doyle, " 'Pvt. Robert Shurtliff': An Unusual Revolutionary," *American History Illustrated* 23, no. 6 (1988): 30.

10. Hiltner, Judith, "She Bled in Secret," *Journal of Early American Literature* 34, no. 2 (1999): 5.

11. Ellis, *Sampson,* 20.

12. George Rogers, *"Woman's Liberation, c. 1784,"* *New England Galaxy* 16, no. 3 (1975): 4.

13. Freeman, *Warrior,* 183.

14. Ibid., 14.

15. Ibid., 26.

16. Ibid., 45.

17. Rogers, "Woman's Liberation," 7.

18. Ibid., 8.

19. Ibid., 8.

20. Freeman, *Warrior,* 191.

21. Ibid., 192.

22. Ibid., 193.

23. Ibid.

24. Ibid., 194.

25. Ibid., 195.

26. Ibid., 197.

27. Ibid.

28. Ibid., 198.

8. A WOMAN WARRIOR: NANCY WARD

1. Ben Harris McClary, "*Nancy Ward: The Last Beloved Woman of the Cherokee,*" *Tennessee Historical Quarterly* 21, no. 4 (1962), 353.

2. Ibid.

3. Samuel Cole Williams, *Tennessee during the Revolutionary War* (Nashville: Tennessee Historical Commission, 1944), 36.

4. Carolyn Thomas Foreman, *Indian Women Chiefs* (Washington, D.C.: Zenger, 1976), 76.

5. Grace Steele Woodward, *The Cherokees* (Norman: University of Oklahoma Press, 1963), 40.

6. Thomas N. Lewis, *Tribes That Slumber: Indian Times in the Tennessee Region* (Knoxville: University of Tennessee Press, 1958), 157.

7. Woodward, *Cherokees,* 36.

8. Lewis, *Tribes,* 158.

9. Donald Davidson, *The Tennessee* (New York: Rinehart, 1946), 112.

10. McClary, "Nancy Ward," 356.

11. Woodward, *Cherokees,* 40.

12. Annie Walker Burns, *Military and Geneological Records of the Famous Indian Woman, Nancy Ward* (Washington, D.C.: TK, 1957), 87.

13. McClary, "Nancy Ward," 355.

14. Williams, *Tennessee,* 205.

15. McClary, "Nancy Ward," 356.

16. Burns, *Records,* 87.

17. McClary, "Nancy Ward," 357.

18. Ibid.

19. Ibid., 358.

20. Ibid., 358.

21. Ibid., 359.

22. Ibid.

23. Williams, *Tennessee,* 201.

24. Ibid.

25. Foreman, *Chiefs,* 78.

26. Ibid., 79.

27. McClary, "Nancy Ward," 361.

28. Ibid., 360.

29. Ibid.

Bibliography

Anthony, Katharine. *First Lady of the Revolution: The Life of Mercy Otis Warren.* New York: Doubleday, 1958.

Ashby, Ruth, and Deborah Gore Ohrn. *Her Story: Women Who Changed the World.* Introduction by Gloria Steinem. New York: Viking, 1995.

Bakeless, John. *Turncoats, Traitors and Heroes.* New York: J. B. Lippincott, 1959.

Bergh, Albert E., ed. *The Writings of Thomas Jefferson.* 20 vols. (Washington, D.C: Thomas Jefferson Memorial Association, 1903), 2: 192–96.

Blumenthal, Walter Hart. *Women Camp Followers of the American Revolution.* New York: Arno Press, 1974.

Bober, Natalie S. *Witness to a Revolution.* New York: Aladdin, 1995.

Booth, Sally Smith. *The Women of 1776.* New York: Hastings House, 1973.

Browne, Alice. *Mercy Otis Warren.* Cambridge, Mass.: Charles Scribner and Sons, 1896.

Burns, Annie Walker. *Military and Geneological Records of the Famous Indian Woman, Nancy Ward.* Washington, D.C.: 1957.

Cravitz, Elaine, and Elizabeth Buford. *Courage Knows No Sex.* Hanover, Mass.: Christopher, 1978.

Dacquino, V. T. *Sybil Ludington: The Call to Arms.* Fleischmanns, N.Y.: Purple Mountain Press, 2000.

Darragh, Henry. "Lydia Darragh, One of the Heroines of the Revolution." *Publications of the City History Society of Philadelphia* 1 (1916): 379–403.

Davidson, Donald. *The Tennessee.* New York: Rinehart, 1946.

———. *Founding Mothers: Women of America in the Revolutionary Era.* Boston: Houghton Mifflin, 1975.

DePauw, Linda Grant. *Battle Cries and Lullabies: Women in War from Pre to Present.* Norman: University of Oklahoma Press, 1988.

Doyle, Kathleen. "Pvt. Robert Shuttliff': An Unusual Revolutionary." *American History Illustrated* 23, no. 6 (1988): 30–31.

Earle, Alice Morse. *Child Life in Colonial Days.* New York: Macmillan, 1904.

Ellis, E. D., ed. *Deborah Sampson: The Girl Soldier.* New York: Beadle and Adams, 1863.

Equiano, Oloudah. *The Interesting Narrative of the Life of Oloudah Equiano: or, Gustavus Vassa, the African.* New York: Longmans, 1988.

Foreman, Carolyn Thomas. *Indian Woman Chiefs.* Washington, D.C.: Zenger, 1976.

Forty, George. *Women War Heroines.* London: Arms and Armor Press, 1997.

Freeman, Lucy, and Alma Halbert Bond. *America's First Woman Warrior: The Courage of Deborah Sampson.* New York: Paragon House, 1992.

Happer, Emily Foster. *The First Negro Poet of America.* (Greenwich, Conn.: The Literary Collector Press, 1904).

Hibbert, Christopher. *Redcoats and Rebels.* New York: W.W. Norton, 1990.

Hiltner, Judith. "The Example of Our Heroine: Deborah Sampson and the Legacy of Herman Mann's Female Review." *Journal of American Studies* 41, no. 1 (2000).

———. "She Bled in Secret: Deborah Sampson, Herman Mann and the Female Review." *Early American Literature* 34, no. 2 (1999): 190.

Holliday, Carl. *Woman's Life in Colonial Days.* Williamstown, Mass.: Corner House, 1968.

Horner, Shirley. *Ladies at the Crossroads: Eighteenth-Century Women of New Jersey.* Trenton, N.J.: American Association of University Women, 1978.

Keller, Allan. "Private Deborah Sampson." *American History Illustrated* 11 no. 7 (1976): 30–33.

Kerber, Linda K. *Women of the Republic: Intellect and Ideology in Revolutionary America.* New York: Norton, 1980.

Ketchum, Richard, ed. *The American Heritage Book of the Revolution.* New York: American Heritage, 1958.

Landis, John. "Investigation into American Tradition of Woman Known as 'Molly Pitcher.'" *Journal of American History* 5, no. 1 (1911): 83–95.

Levin, Phyllis Lee. *Abigail Adams.* New York: St. Martins Press, 1987.

Lewis, Thomas N., and Madeline Kneberg. *Tribes That Slumber: Indian Times in the Tennessee Region.* Knoxville: University of Tennessee Press, 1958.

Martin, James Kirby, and Karen R. Stubaus, eds. *The American Revolution: Whose Revolution?* New York: Robert E. Kreiger, 1981.

Mayer, Holly. *Belonging to the Army: Camp Followers and Community during the American Revolution.* Columbia: University of South Carolina Press, 1996.

McClary, Ben Harris. "*Nancy Ward: The Last Beloved Woman of the Cherokees. Tennessee Historical Quarterly* 21, no. 4 (1962): 352–65.

McGeorge, Isabella Crater. "A New Jersey Heroine of the American Revolution." *American Monthly Magazine* 17, no. 5 (1900).

Mooney, James. *History, Myths, and Sacred Formulas of the Cherokees.* 262 Asheville, N.C.: Bright Mountain Books, 1992.

Morgan, Edmund S. *The Birth of the Republic.* London: University of Chicago Press, 1992.

Murrin, Mary R., and Richard Waldron. *Conflict at Monmouth Courthouse.* Proceedings of a Symposium Commemorating the 200th Anniversary of the Battle of Monmouth, April 18, 1978, 1984. Trenton: N.I. Historical Commission, 1984.

Nagel, Paul C. *The Adams Women: Abigail and Louisa Adams, Their Sisters and Daughters.* Cambridge, Mass.: Harvard University Press, 1987.

Nelson, William. *Documents Relating to the Colonial History of the State of New Jersey,* volume 22, *Marriage Records, 1665–1800.* Patterson, N.J.: Press Printing, 1906.

Norton, Mary Beth. *Liberty's Daughters: The Revolutionary Experience of American Women, 1750–1800.* Boston: Little, Brown, 1980.

O'dell, Margaritta Matilda. *Memoir and Poems of Phyllis Wheatley: A Native African and Slave.* 2d ed. Boston: Light and Horton, 1835.

Ogude, S. E. *Genius in Bondage: A Study of the Origins of African Literature in English.* Ile-Ife, Nigeria: University of Ife Press, 1983.

Perrine, William Davison. *Molly Pitcher of Monmouth County, New Jersey and Captain Molly of Fort Washington, N.Y.* Princeton Junction, N.J. New Jersey State Library. 1937.

Proceedings of the Historical Society of Pennsylvania, 1878. Notes and Queries, p. 109–111.

Raphael, Ray. *A People's History of the American Revolution: How Common People Shaped the Fight For Independence.* New York: New Press, 2001.

Reising, Russel J. *Loose Ends—Closure and Criticism in America.* Durham, N.C.: Duke University Press, 1996.

Redding, J. Saunders. *To Make a Poet Black.* Durham, N.C.: Duke University Press, 1996.

Robinson, William H. *Black New England Letters.* Boston: Trustees of the Public Library of Boston, 1977.

———, ed. *Critical Essays on Phillis Wheatley.* Boston: G. K. Hall, 1982.

———. *Phillis Wheatley in the Black American Beginnings.* Detroit: Broadside Press, 1975.

Rogers, George. "Woman's Liberation, c. 1784." *New England Galaxy* 16, no. 3 (1975): 3–12.

Shields, John C. *The Collected Works of Phillis Wheatley.* New York: Oxford University Press, 1988.

Smith, Samuel Steele. *The Battle of Monmouth.* Monmouth Beach, N.J.: Philip Freneau Press, 1964.

———. *The Search for Molly Pitcher. Daughters of the American Revolution Magazine.*

Somerville, Mollie. *Women and the American Revolution—The Two Molly's* Washington, D.C.: Daughters of the American Revolution, 1974.

Sparks, Jared, ed. *The Letters of George Washington.* Vol. 3. Boston: Hill and Gray, 1833.

Stryker, William. *The Battle of Monmouth*. Princeton, N.J.: Princeton University Press, 1927.

Teipe, Emily J. "Will the Real Molly Pitcher Stand Up?" *Prologue Quarterly of the NTL Archives and Records* 31, no. 2 (1999): 118–26.

Thompson, D. W., and Merri Lou Schaumann. *Goodbye Molly Pitcher*. Collection in Cumberland County Historical Society.

Tunis, Edwin. *Colonial Living*. Baltimore: John Hopkins University Press, 1957.

Voltaire. *Ouevres Complete*. Edited by Loius Moland. Vol. 48. Paris: Garnier, 1882–85.

Index TK